2000 DAYS OF RECIPES

BLACKSTONE OUTDOOR GAS GRIDDLE COOKBOOK

Discover the Grill Master in You with 2000 Days of Delicious American Recipes Perfect for Summer and Year-Round Feasts

EXTRA RECIPES EVERY MONTH!

2024

4 BONUS

FULL COLOR EDITION

© Copyright 2024 - All rights reserved.

The content contained within this book may not be reproduced, duplicated or transmitted without direct written permission from the author or the publisher.

Under no circumstances will any blame or legal responsibility be held against the publisher, or author, for any damages, reparation, or monetary loss due to the information contained within this book, either directly or indirectly.

Legal Notice:

This book is copyright protected. It is only for personal use. You cannot amend, distribute, sell, use, quote or paraphrase any part, or the content within this book, without the consent of the author or publisher.

Disclaimer Notice:

Please note the information contained within this document is for educational and entertainment purposes only. All effort has been executed to present accurate, up to date, reliable, complete information. No warranties of any kind are declared or implied. Readers acknowledge that the author is not engaged in the rendering of legal, financial, medical or professional advice. The content within this book has been derived from various sources. Please consult a licensed professional before attempting any techniques outlined in this book.

By reading this document, the reader agrees that under no circumstances is the author responsible for any losses, direct or indirect, that are incurred as a result of the use of the information contained within this document, including, but not limited to, errors, omissions, or inaccuracies.

TABLE OF CONTENTS

BLACKSTONE OUTDOOR GAS GRIDDLE 5
- Introduction 5
- Blackstone Griddle Presentation 6
- Features and Benefits 6
- Types of Blackstone Griddles 6
- Accessories Available 7

CHAPTER 2: MAINTAINING AND CLEANING YOUR BLACKSTONE GRIDDLE 8
- Daily Cleaning 8
- Deep Clean 8
- Seasonal Maintenance 9
- Conservation Tips 9
- Solving Common Problems 10

CHAPTER 3: BLACKSTONE GRILL COOKING TECHNIQUES 11
- Direct Cooking 11
- Indirect Cooking 11
- Temperature Control 12
- Cooking Times 12
- Tips for Cooking Meat, Fish, Vegetables, and Other Foods 13
- Smoking Techniques 13

CHAPTER 4: FOOD SAFETY 14
- Hygiene Rules 14
- Cooking at Safe Temperatures 15
- Food Preservation 15
- Contamination Prevention 15

CHAPTER 5: MEATS AND COOKING TIPS 16
- Types of Meat 16
- Beef Cuts 17
- Pork Cuts 20
- Chicken Cuts 22
- Meat Quality 24
- Meat Storage 24
- Meat Cooking 25
- Resting Meat After Cooking 28
- Temperature Control on the Blackstone Grill 29
- Cooking Times for Different Types of Meat on the Blackstone Grill 30

CHAPTER 6: RECIPES 30

› BEEF BURGERS RECIPES 31
1. Classic American Burger 31
2. Bacon Cheeseburger 31
3. BBQ Burger 32
4. Mushroom Swiss Burger 32
5. Spicy Jalapeño Burger 33

› PORK BURGERS RECIPES 33
6. Pork and Apple Burger 33
7. Hawaiian Pork Burger 34
8. BBQ Pulled Pork Burger 34
9. Italian Pork Burger 35
10. Spicy Chorizo Burger 35

› FISH BURGERS RECIPES 36
11. Salmon Burger 36
12. Tuna Burger 36
13. Cod Burger Recipe 37
14. Shrimp Burger Recipe 37

› VEGETARIAN BURGERS RECIPES 38
15. Black Bean Veggie Burger 38
16. Portobello Mushroom Burger 38
17. Chickpea Veggie Burger 39
18. Quinoa Veggie Burger 39
19. Lentil Veggie Burger 40

› HOT DOGS RECIPES 40
20. Chili and Crispy Onion Hot Dog 40
21. Guacamole, Pico de Gallo, and Cream Cheese Hot Dog 41
22. Chili Sauce, Pepper Jack Cheese, and Crispy Onion Hot Dog 41
23. French Fries and Melted Cheddar Cheese Hot Dog 42
24. Bourbon BBQ Sauce and Crispy Bacon Hot Dog 42

› STEAKS RECIPES 43
25. Steak with Sweet Potatoes and Caramelized Onions 43
26. Steak with Grilled Asparagus and Chimichurri Sauce 43
27. Steak with Porcini Mushrooms and Black Truffle 44
28. Steak with Macaroni and Cheese and Crispy Bacon 44
29. Steak with Tomato, Mozzarella, and Basil Salad 45

› RIBS RECIPES 45
30. Ribs with Bourbon BBQ Sauce 45
31. Ribs with Teriyaki Sauce and Grilled Pineapple 46
32. Ribs with Spicy Mango Sauce and Caramelized Onions 46
33. Ribs with Chimichurri Sauce and Sweet Potatoes 47
34. Ribs with Honey BBQ Sauce and Crispy Onions 47

› CHICKEN RECIPES 48
35. Lemon Chicken with Chives and Sweet Potatoes 48
36. Chicken Fajitas with Onions and Peppers 48
37. Chicken Thighs with Spicy BBQ Sauce and Potatoes 49
38. Italian Marinated Chicken Breast with Grilled Vegetables 49
39. Chicken Quesadillas with Green Sauce and Cheese 50
40. Chicken Burger with Guacamole and Bacon 50

› FISH RECIPES 51
41. Salmon with Chimichurri Sauce and Lime 51
42. Trout with Teriyaki Sauce and Grilled Vegetables 51
43. Shrimp with Spicy Mango Salsa and Caramelized Onions 52
44. Mixed Seafood Skewers with Aioli Sauce 52
45. Fish Burgers with Bacon and Tartar Sauce 53

› GRILLED VEGETABLES RECIPES 53
46. Grilled Zucchini and Bell Peppers with Olive Oil and Balsamic Vinegar 53
47. Grilled Onions and Mushrooms with Butter and Chives 54

48. Grilled Asparagus and Tomatoes with Pesto and Parmesan Cheese 54
49. Sweet Potatoes and Beets with Chimichurri Sauce 55
50. Grilled Eggplant and Bell Peppers with Spicy Mango Salsa 55

› **SAUCES FOR FISH DISHES** 56
51. Barbecue Sauce 56
52. Chimichurri Sauce 56
53. Teriyaki Sauce 57
54. Spicy Mango Salsa 57
55. Tartar Sauce 58
56. Tomato Sauce 58
57. Ponzu Sauce 59

› **RECIPES FOR FESTIVE OCCASIONS** 59
58. Salmon Burger with Avocado and Pancetta 59
59. Spicy Shrimp with Mango and Pineapple Sauce 60
60. Fish Nachos with Guacamole Sauce 60
61. Tuna Tartare with Avocado and Wasabi 61
62. Salmon Ceviche with Mango and Lime 61
63. Shrimp in Sweet and Sour Sauce with Pineapple and Peppers 62
64. Salmon Sashimi with Ponzu Sauce and Wasabi 62
65. Fried Fish Tacos with Mango and Avocado Sauce 63

› **LOW FAT OPTIONS** 63
66. Chicken and Marinated Vegetable Skewers(Low fat Recipe) 63
67. Turkey Burgers with Aioli Sauce 64
68. Sesame-Crusted Salmon Fillet 64
69. Herb-Marinated Chicken Breast 65
70. Grilled Mediterranean Vegetables 65

› **LOW CALORIE OPTIONS** 66
71. Asparagus Wrapped in Prosciutto 66
72. Grilled Shrimp with Green Sauce 66
73. Grilled Chicken Salad 67
74. Grilled Zucchini with Feta and Mint 67

75. Grilled Eggplant with Yogurt and Tahini Sauce(Low Calorie Recipe) 68

› **VEGETARIAN RECIPES** 68
76. Grilled Chickpea Burgers 68
77. Grilled Vegetarian Pizza 69
78. Grilled Marinated Tofu 69
79. Grilled Spring Rolls with Peanut Sauce 70
80. Grilled Polenta with Wild Mushrooms and Herb Sauce 70

› **VEGAN RECIPES** 71
81. Quinoa and Black Bean Burgers 71
82. Tofu and Pineapple Skewers 71
83. Grilled Sweet Potatoes with Guacamole ... 72
84. Grilled Chickpea Salad 72
85. Grilled Portobello Mushrooms with Arugula Pesto 73

› **MEXICAN RECIPES** 73
86. Grilled Tacos al Pastor 73
87. Chicken Quesadillas 74
88. Mexican Grilled Vegetable Platter with Guacamole 74

› **ASIAN RECIPES** 75
89. Teriyaki Shrimp Skewers 75
90. Korean Beef Steak (Bulgogi) 75
91. Asian Stir-Fried Vegetables on the Grill .. 76

› **ITALIAN RECIPES** 76
92. Grilled Pizza 76
93. Bruschetta with Tomato and Basil 77
94. Grilled Pesto Chicken 77

› **CARIBBEAN RECIPES** 78
95. Grilled Jerk Chicken 78
96. Grilled Shrimp with Mango Habanero Sauce 78
97. Grilled Bananas with Rum and Brown Sugar 79

⭐ **GET YOUR FREE BOOK BONUSES NOW!** .. 80

INDEX OF INGREDIENTS 81

BLACKSTONE OUTDOOR GAS GRIDDLE

"Turn your patio into a gourmet kitchen with fire and steel."

Introduction

Welcome to the transformative world of the Blackstone Griddle, where the robust flavors of outdoor cooking meet the finesse of gourmet cuisine. The Blackstone Griddle isn't merely a cooking appliance; it's a gateway to exploring culinary creativity under the open sky. In this chapter, we dive into how this revolutionary tool can not only simplify your cooking process but also amplify the flavor and healthfulness of your meals. Prepare to discover a new love for cooking as we unfold the magic of the Blackstone Griddle.

BLACKSTONE GRIDDLE PRESENTATION

The Blackstone Griddle epitomizes versatility and simplicity in outdoor cooking. Unlike traditional grills, the griddle's expansive, flat surface offers a stage where culinary arts play out in the most healthful and flavor-rich ways. **Designed with premium cold-rolled steel, the griddle surface presents an impeccable canvas for cooking everything from delicate crepes to hearty steaks.**

This outdoor griddle changes the dynamics of conventional grilling by allowing a broader range of cooking techniques such as sautéing, toasting, and even simmering — practices usually reserved for the confines of kitchen stoves. **Its sturdy construction ensures it withstands the rigor of outdoor elements, while its sleek design complements any outdoor setting.** Whether it's a family reunion or a quiet dinner for two under the stars, the Blackstone Griddle stands ready to make each meal memorable.

Features and Benefits

1. **Unmatched Cooking Versatility:** Whether you're searing fish, flipping pancakes, or grilling burgers, the griddle's uniform heat distribution ensures each dish is cooked to perfection. The adjustable heat settings provide precise control, allowing for diverse cooking techniques on one surface — from intense searing to gentle warming.

2. **Health-Conscious Design:** With its slightly sloped surface, the Blackstone Griddle naturally drains excess fat away from food, collecting it in a strategically placed grease trap. This feature not only makes for healthier meals but also simplifies cleaning, leaving behind less residue from cooked meals.

3. **Enhanced Flavor Profiles:** The seasoning of the griddle surface enhances over time, creating a natural, non-stick coating that imbues dishes with deeper, richer flavors — a characteristic cherished by culinary enthusiasts.

4. **Community and Convenience:** The expansive cooking surface accommodates multiple dishes at once, making it ideal for social gatherings. Engage in delightful cooking experiences with family and friends where everyone can partake in the cooking process, transforming meal preparation into an engaging event.

5. **Easy Maintenance and Durability:** Constructed with weather-resistant materials, the Blackstone Griddle promises longevity and ease of maintenance. Its solid steel base and powder-coated finish resist rust and corrosion, ensuring your griddle remains a centerpiece of your outdoor kitchen for years.

By embracing the Blackstone Griddle, you invite not only ease and efficiency into your cooking routines but also a healthier way of preparing meals that do not compromise on taste or quality. Let this chapter serve as your primer to mastering the art of outdoor griddle cooking, where every meal becomes a celebration of fresh air and great food.

Types of Blackstone Griddles

Exploring the diversity of the Blackstone Griddle lineup is akin to taking a masterclass in outdoor culinary versatility. **Each model is crafted with the outdoor cooking enthusiast in mind, providing unique features that cater to various lifestyles, from the bustling family cookouts to the serene couple's breakfasts on the deck.** Let's delve into the specific types of Blackstone Griddles available, highlighting their features and best uses to help you choose your perfect outdoor cooking companion.

1. **Blackstone 36-inch Flat Top Gas Griddle:** The Entertainer's Choice The flagship model of the Blackstone family, the 36-inch Griddle, boasts an expansive 720 square inches of cooking space, ideal for those who regularly host large gatherings. This model features four independently controlled burners, offering versatile cooking options— from searing high heat needed for steaks to low temperatures perfect for simmering sauces. Its durability is enhanced with a powder-coated black steel frame and stainless steel burners, making it a long-lasting investment for serious outdoor chefs.

2. **Blackstone 28-inch Outdoor Flat Top Gas Grill Griddle Station:** Compact Power Scaling down slightly, the 28-inch model offers most of the 36-inch's versatility but in a more compact form, making it suitable for smaller patios or for those who prioritize space-saving. With two independent burners and still a generous 470 square inches of cooking surface, it's perfect for family meals and small get-togethers, providing enough room to cook multiple dishes at once.

3. **Blackstone Adventure Ready 22-inch Griddle with Stand:** The Traveler's Dream The Adventure Ready 22-inch Griddle is built for on-the-go outdoor cooks. It features two H-style burners and a slightly smaller cooking surface, which is still ample for a portable unit. Its unique stand and compact design make

it ideal for camping, tailgating, or beach outings. Despite its size, it doesn't compromise on the quality and versatility Blackstone is known for.

4. **Blackstone Table Top Grill - 17 Inch Portable Gas Griddle:** The Personal Chef For those who prefer simplicity and portability, the 17-inch Table Top Grill is the answer. This model is designed for personal use or small gatherings. It's incredibly easy to transport and set up, making it perfect for intimate outdoor meals, road trips, or even balcony cooking in urban settings.

Each Blackstone Griddle model not only caters to different cooking needs and spaces but also encourages a healthier cooking style. **The flat top design allows for less oil usage than traditional grilling, and the even heat distribution ensures that food cooks thoroughly, locking in flavors while avoiding the charring associated with grilling.**

As we proceed, we'll explore the available accessories that can enhance your Blackstone experience, followed by insightful buying advice to ensure you make the most informed decision tailored to your outdoor cooking aspirations.

Accessories Available

To enhance your Blackstone Griddle experience and elevate your outdoor cooking, a variety of specialized accessories are available. **Each accessory is designed to optimize the functionality and versatility of your griddle, making every cooking session not only easier but also more enjoyable.** Whether you're looking to perfect your pancake flipping, streamline your burger grilling, or expand your culinary repertoire, there's an accessory tailored to meet your needs.

- **Griddle Tool Kit:** Essential for any griddle owner, this kit typically includes high-quality stainless steel spatulas, a chopper/scraper for dicing foods or cleaning the griddle surface, and often comes with a carrying case for convenient storage.

- **Basting Cover:** Perfect for melting cheese on burgers or steaming vegetables, a basting cover helps trap heat and moisture, speeding up cooking times and ensuring even heat distribution.

- **Hard Cover:** A hard cover is indispensable for protecting your griddle from the elements when not in use. It keeps the griddle clean and dry, extending its lifespan and maintaining its performance.

- **Breakfast Kit:** For the breakfast enthusiasts, this kit often includes pancake dispensers, bacon press, and egg rings, making it simple to serve up a perfect morning meal for a crowd.

- **Grill Top Adapter:** This accessory turns part of your griddle into a traditional grill, providing versatility when cooking items like steaks or veggies that benefit from direct flame exposure.

- **Grease Cup Liners:** Disposable liners that fit neatly into your griddle's grease cup make cleanup a breeze. They're great for keeping your cooking area tidy and grease-free.

- **Griddle Caddy:** Keep all your grilling essentials organized and within arm's reach with a griddle caddy that holds your sauces, tools, and seasonings.

- **Silicone Mats:** These non-stick mats are fantastic for cooking smaller items that might slip through a grill grate, ensuring nothing goes to waste.

From quick family dinners to elaborate meals, having the right tools at your disposal can transform your outdoor cooking experience.

CHAPTER 2:

Maintaining and Cleaning Your Blackstone Griddle

Proper care is a key ingredient in the recipe for long-lasting, high-performance outdoor cooking equipment. Keeping your Blackstone Griddle clean not only extends its life but also ensures that it continues to produce the most flavorful and healthy dishes. Below, we delve into the essential practices for both daily cleaning and the occasional deep clean.

Daily Cleaning

Regular daily cleaning of your Blackstone Griddle is crucial to its longevity and performance. Here are straightforward steps to ensure your griddle remains in pristine condition after each use, ready for your next cooking session.

- **Let It Cool:** Always allow your Blackstone Griddle to cool down somewhat before you start cleaning. It should be warm but not too hot to touch.

- **Scrape Off Food Particles:** Using a metal scraper or spatula, gently scrape off any food particles or residues stuck on the griddle surface. This step is essential as it prevents buildup and maintains the cooking surface's integrity.

- **Wipe Down the Surface:** After scraping, wipe the surface with a paper towel or a soft cloth. If the griddle is still warm, slightly dampen the cloth with water to capture any lingering bits. Avoid using too much water, which can cool down the hot griddle too quickly and potentially warp the metal.

- **Apply a Light Oil Coat:** Once the griddle is clean and dry, apply a thin layer of cooking oil to the surface. Use a high smoke point oil like canola or vegetable oil. Spread it evenly using a cloth or paper towel. This oiling acts as a seasoning agent and helps maintain the non-stick surface, preventing rust.

- **Inspect and Wipe the Exterior:** Don't forget the exterior and the catch tray. Wipe them down to remove dust, grease, or spills. Regularly empty and clean the grease catch tray to prevent overflow and potential fire hazards.

- **Cover the Griddle:** If your griddle is located outdoors, cover it with a weather-resistant cover after it has cooled down completely. This protection keeps it clean and safe from the elements, ensuring it stays in good condition.

By following these simple daily cleaning steps, you ensure that your Blackstone Griddle remains a reliable and efficient tool for your outdoor cooking adventures, always ready to perform at its best.

Deep Clean

While daily maintenance is crucial, periodically giving your Blackstone Griddle a deep clean is essential to maintain optimal performance and longevity. **This more thorough cleaning should be done every few months, especially after heavy use periods or before storing the griddle for a long time.** Here are the steps to effectively deep clean your Blackstone Griddle:

1. **Heat It Up:** Begin by heating your griddle to a high temperature. This heat will help loosen any stuck-on food particles and make it easier to scrape off residues.

2. **Scrape the Surface:** Once the griddle is hot, use a metal scraper to scrape the entire surface thoroughly. This step removes the top layer of seasoned oil and any tough debris. Be thorough but gentle to avoid scratching the surface.

3. **Apply Cleaning Solution:** Turn off the heat and allow the griddle to cool slightly. Mix a solution of warm water and mild dish soap. Using a non-abrasive pad or cloth, scrub the surface with soapy water to clean off any remaining food residue and grime. For extremely stubborn areas, you may use a small amount of cooking oil with kosher salt as a natural abrasive to help in the cleaning.

4. **Rinse and Dry:** After scrubbing, rinse the griddle surface with clean water using a cloth or paper towel. Ensure all soap and debris are completely removed. Then, thoroughly dry the surface with clean towels to prevent rust.

5. **Re-season the Griddle:** Once dry, it's crucial to re-season the surface to restore its non-stick properties. Lightly coat the entire griddle surface with a high-smoke-point cooking oil (like canola or flax oil). Heat the griddle until the oil begins to smoke, then turn off the heat and let it cool. Repeat this oiling and heating process 2-3 times to build up a good seasoning layer.

6. **Inspect and Clean Exterior:** Don't neglect the exterior and underside of the griddle. Wipe these areas down with soapy water and a sponge or cloth, rinse with clean water, and dry thoroughly.
7. **Cover and Store:** Once your griddle is clean and dry, cover it with a suitable grill cover to protect it from the elements and keep it clean, and ready for your next grilling session.

Performing this deep cleaning routine will ensure your Blackstone Griddle remains in excellent condition. It provides a reliable cooking surface that produces great results every time.

Seasonal Maintenance

Seasonal maintenance of your Blackstone Griddle is essential to ensure it continues to function optimally through changing weather conditions and after varied levels of use throughout the year. Here's a guide to performing thorough seasonal maintenance, ideally at the beginning and end of the grilling season or as needed based on your local climate and usage frequency.

1. **Inspect the Griddle Surface:** Start by thoroughly inspecting the griddle surface for any signs of rust or damage. This is critical after a season of use, especially if the griddle has been exposed to elements like moisture and sunlight.
2. **Deep Cleaning:** Perform a deep clean as detailed in previous instructions. This includes heating the griddle, scraping it down, applying a mild soapy solution, scrubbing with a non-abrasive pad, rinsing, and thoroughly drying the surface.
3. **Check for Gas Leaks:** For gas griddles, check all connections and hoses for signs of wear or gas leaks. You can apply a light soap solution to the hose and connections; bubbles will form if there's a leak. Replace any faulty parts immediately.
4. **Re-season the Cooking Surface:** Apply a fresh coat of cooking oil and heat the griddle to re-season the cooking surface. This process helps maintain a non-stick surface and prevents rust.
5. **Tighten All Fasteners:** Due to the thermal expansion and contraction, nuts and bolts may loosen over time. Check and tighten any loose fasteners on the griddle and stand.
6. **Lubricate Moving Parts:** If your griddle has any moving parts, such as wheels or adjustable legs, apply a suitable lubricant to ensure smooth operation.
7. **Cover and Store:** When not in use, always cover your Blackstone Griddle with a high-quality, weather-resistant cover. Store it in a dry, sheltered place to protect it from the elements and reduce the likelihood of rust and damage.
8. **Record Keeping:** Keep a record of all maintenance activities, including what was done, when, and any parts that were replaced. This record can be very helpful for future maintenance sessions or if troubleshooting is needed.

By adhering to these seasonal maintenance steps, you extend the life of your Blackstone Griddle and ensure it remains a reliable and high-performing tool for your outdoor cooking adventures.

Conservation Tips

Proper conservation of your Blackstone Griddle not only extends its lifespan but also ensures it remains in top condition for optimal performance. Here are essential tips to help you preserve your griddle, ensuring it continues to serve you well for many grilling seasons to come.

Regular Cleaning:

- **Daily Cleaning:** Wipe down the surface after each use with a paper towel and a light coat of oil to prevent rust.
- **Deep Cleaning:** Schedule a thorough cleaning every few months or after extensive use to remove built-up grime and maintain the griddle's integrity.

Proper Storage:

- **Use a Cover:** Always cover your Blackstone Griddle with a high-quality, weather-resistant cover when not in use. This protects it from the elements and keeps it clean.
- **Location Matters:** Store your griddle in a dry, sheltered area to prevent exposure to harsh weather conditions, which can lead to rust and deterioration.

Seasonal Maintenance:

- **Inspect and Repair:** Regularly check for any signs of wear or damage. Address issues such as rust spots or loose components immediately to prevent further deterioration.

- **Seal and Protect:** Apply a silicone sealant to any areas prone to moisture entry, especially around knobs and buttons, to prevent water damage and rust.

Preventative Measures:

- **Grease Management:** Regularly clean and empty the grease trap to prevent overflow and potential fire hazards.

- **Avoid Moisture Buildup:** After washing or heavy rain, ensure the griddle is completely dry before covering. Trapped moisture can accelerate rust formation.

Mind the Details:

- **Check Gas Connections:** For gas griddles, periodically check the gas connections and hoses for leaks or wear. Replace any damaged parts promptly to ensure safety and efficiency.

- **Non-Abrasive Tools:** Use only non-abrasive tools for cleaning to avoid scratching the surface, which could lead to rust and other damage.

By following these conservation tips, you can significantly enhance the durability and reliability of your Blackstone Griddle. Regular care not only preserves its function and appearance but also ensures it remains a dependable part of your cooking arsenal, ready to perform whenever you fire it up.

Solving Common Problems

- **Uneven Heating:** If you notice that your griddle is heating unevenly, it could be due to debris blocking the burners or uneven distribution of the griddle's seasoning oil. Start by checking and cleaning the burners and air intakes for any obstruction. Ensure that your griddle is on a flat surface during use. If the issue persists, it may be necessary to re-season the surface to ensure an even coating, which facilitates uniform heat distribution.

- **Difficulty in Ignition:** A griddle that won't ignite is often a result of issues with the propane tank, the regulator, or the ignition system itself. First, check to make sure the propane tank is not empty and is properly connected. Resetting the regulator by detaching it and then reattaching it after a minute can often resolve pressure imbalances. If problems continue, inspect the igniter for damage and consider replacing it if necessary.

- **Rust Formation:** Rust can be a common concern, especially if the griddle has been exposed to moisture. To tackle rust, first, scrub the affected area with a steel brush or sandpaper to remove as much rust as possible. Clean the area thoroughly, then re-season the griddle by heating it and applying a thin coat of high-smoke-point cooking oil, repeating the process several times to build a protective layer.

- **Sticking Food:** If food starts sticking to the griddle surface, it's likely a sign that the seasoning layer has worn off. To remedy this, clean the surface with a mild detergent and warm water, then dry it completely. Apply a fresh coat of cooking oil and heat the griddle until it smokes. Repeat this a few times to rebuild a non-stick seasoning layer.

By being proactive and addressing these common problems quickly, you ensure that your Blackstone Griddle remains in peak condition, ready to deliver excellent culinary results. This not only enhances your cooking experience but also prolongs the life of your griddle, making every outdoor meal a testament to your care and expertise.

CHAPTER 3:

Blackstone Grill Cooking Techniques

Mastering your Blackstone Griddle involves understanding and utilizing various cooking techniques that enhance the flavor and healthiness of your meals. Whether you're searing steak or gently cooking delicate fish, knowing when to use direct or indirect cooking methods can transform your dishes. This chapter explores these fundamental techniques, providing tips to maximize your culinary prowess with the Blackstone Griddle.

Direct Cooking

Direct cooking on the Blackstone Griddle refers to cooking food directly over the heat source. This method is ideal for foods that thrive under high heat and require a relatively short cooking time. Here's how to make the most of direct cooking on your griddle:

1. **Preheat the Griddle:** Always start with a preheated surface to ensure foods start cooking immediately upon contact, which helps to seal in flavors and juices.

2. **Oil the Surface:** Lightly oiling the griddle before cooking prevents sticking and contributes to the development of a desirable crust on the food.

3. **Control the Temperature:** Use the individual burners to create zones of different temperatures. This allows for greater control, enabling you to sear meats on high heat while gently cooking vegetables on a lower setting.

4. **Utilize High Heat for Searing:** Perfect for steaks, chops, and burgers, high heat searing locks in juices by forming a flavorful crust. Ensure the surface is hot enough to sizzle upon contact.

5. **Cooking Times Are Key:** Since direct cooking involves high heat, pay close attention to cooking times to avoid overcooking. Quick flips and rotations can help achieve an even cook.

Benefits of direct cooking include:

- Rapid cooking time, great for a quick meal.
- Ideal for creating rich, caramelized flavors and appealing grill marks.
- Effective for rendering fat from meats, making them crisper and leaner.

Indirect Cooking

Indirect cooking on the Blackstone Griddle utilizes the concept of creating heat zones, where the food is not placed directly over the heat source. **This technique is perfect for cooking larger or thicker cuts of meat that need to be cooked through without burning the exterior.** Here's how to effectively use indirect cooking:

- **Set Up Heat Zones:** Turn on one or more burners to high heat and leave others off or on low. Place food over the cooler part of the griddle to cook via ambient heat.

- **Preheat and Use a Cover:** Preheating and covering the griddle with a basting cover or aluminum foil helps maintain a consistent temperature, simulating an oven-like environment.

- **Use Low to Medium Heat:** Indirect cooking is all about slow and low heat, ideal for ensuring that your food cooks evenly and thoroughly without the exterior burning.

- **Rotate for Even Cooking:** Occasionally rotate your food between the direct and indirect heat zones to achieve an even cook and a delicious crust where desired.

Benefits of indirect cooking include:

- Excellent for cooking thicker cuts of meat or whole poultry without charring.
- Allows for slow cooking processes like smoking or braising, which can deepen flavors.
- Reduces flare-ups since fat and juices don't drip directly onto high flames.

Both direct and indirect cooking methods offer unique advantages and can be used in tandem to achieve perfect results on your Blackstone Griddle. By mastering these techniques, you'll elevate your outdoor cooking experience, making meals that are not only delicious but also tailored to optimize health and culinary satisfaction.

Temperature Control

Effective temperature control is essential for versatile cooking on your Blackstone Griddle. Here are some key tips:

1. **Understand the Zones:** The Blackstone Griddle allows for multiple heat zones. Use high heat for searing meats and lower heats for cooking items like eggs or delicate fish.

2. **Preheating:** Always preheat the griddle to the desired temperature before adding food. This helps in cooking food evenly and achieving a good sear.

3. **Use a Thermometer:** To ensure precision, use an infrared thermometer to check the surface temperature of the griddle. This will help you maintain the correct temperature throughout the cooking process.

4. **Adjust as Needed:** Be flexible and adjust the burner settings based on the cooking response of your food. If items are cooking too quickly or burning, reduce the heat.

Benefits of mastering temperature control:

- Prevents overcooking and undercooking, ensuring optimal texture and flavor.
- Enhances food safety by maintaining sufficient heat to kill pathogens.
- Helps in achieving professional cooking results with every meal.

Cooking Times

Timing is as crucial as temperature when cooking on your Blackstone Griddle. Here are strategies to perfect your timing:

1. **Know Your Food:** Different foods require different cooking times. Familiarize yourself with the recommended durations for various foods to avoid guesswork.

2. **Keep It Consistent:** For even cooking, cut your ingredients into uniform sizes. This is particularly important for meats and vegetables.

3. **Use Timers:** Don't rely solely on instinct; use a kitchen timer to help track cooking times, especially for foods that cook quickly or require precise timing.

4. **Rest Your Meat:** Allow meat to rest for a few minutes after cooking to let the juices redistribute. This results in a more flavorful and tender meal.

Benefits of precise cooking times:

- Ensures that foods are cooked just right, enhancing flavor and texture.
- Improves nutritional retention by preventing overcooking.
- Increases confidence in cooking, reducing stress for a more enjoyable experience.

By mastering temperature control and cooking times, you not only boost your grilling skills but also elevate the health and taste of your dishes, making every meal on your Blackstone Griddle a culinary success.

Tips for Cooking Meat, Fish, Vegetables, and Other Foods

- **Preheat Correctly:** Ensure your griddle is properly preheated to a high temperature before adding meat. This helps in searing the meat, locking in juices and flavor.

- **Pat Dry the Meat:** Before cooking, pat the meat dry with paper towels. This removes excess moisture and helps achieve a better sear.

- **Avoid Overcrowding:** Cook in batches if necessary to prevent the griddle from cooling down, which can lead to steaming rather than searing.

- **Let It Rest:** Allow the meat to rest after cooking. This helps the juices redistribute throughout the meat, making it more tender and flavorful.

- **Season Well:** Season the meat adequately just before placing it on the griddle to enhance its flavors. Use a combination of salt, pepper, and other spices according to your taste preference.

Tips for Cooking Fish

- **Gentle Heat:** Fish cooks best over medium heat. Too high heat can cause the delicate protein to become tough and dry.

- **Minimal Flipping:** Flip the fish only once during cooking to maintain its integrity. Use a thin spatula for best handling.

- **Skin Side Down:** Start with the skin side down to get it crispy. It also helps in holding the fish together.

- **Use Oil Wisely:** Lightly oil the fish instead of the griddle to prevent sticking and to control the amount of added fat.

- **Timing is Key:** Do not overcook; most fish will cook through in just a few minutes per side depending on thickness.

Tips for Cooking Vegetables

- **High Heat for Quick Cooking:** Vegetables like bell peppers, onions, and asparagus benefit from high heat that chars the outside while keeping the inside crispy.

- **Use Oil and Seasonings:** Toss vegetables in a light coating of oil and your favorite seasonings before cooking to enhance flavor.

- **Keep Moving:** Use tongs to keep vegetables moving on the griddle for an even char and to prevent them from burning.

- **Dense Vegetables:** For denser vegetables like potatoes or carrots, consider steaming them slightly before griddling to shorten cooking time and ensure they are cooked through.

Tips for Cooking Pancakes, Eggs, and Other Breakfast Foods

- **Consistent Medium Heat:** For pancakes and eggs, maintain a consistent medium heat. Too high heat can burn these delicate items quickly.

- **Non-stick Surface:** Ensure the griddle surface is well-seasoned or lightly greased to prevent sticking and allow for easy flipping.

- **Perfect Timing:** Cook pancakes until bubbles form on the surface and edges begin to look set before flipping. Eggs cook quickly; remove them from the heat just before they're fully set as they will continue to cook from residual heat.

General Tips for All Foods

- **Keep It Clean:** Start with a clean griddle for each type of food to avoid flavors transferring between items.

- **Temperature Zones:** Utilize different temperature zones on your griddle for cooking multiple types of foods at the same time efficiently.

- **Food Safety:** Always use separate utensils and plates for raw and cooked foods to prevent cross-contamination.

- **Experiment with Marinades and Sauces:** Enhance flavors with marinades, but apply sugary sauces towards the end of cooking to prevent burning.

By following these tailored tips for different types of foods, you can maximize the versatility of your Blackstone Griddle and enjoy a variety of healthy, flavorful dishes. Whether it's a hearty steak, a tender fillet of fish, crisp vegetables, or a fluffy pancake, each meal can be a testament to your culinary skills and the robust capabilities of the griddle.

Smoking Techniques

Smoking on a Blackstone Griddle adds a rich, aromatic depth to your dishes that can transform ordinary ingredients into extraordinary culinary delights. While the

Blackstone isn't a traditional smoker, with a bit of creativity and the right techniques, you can infuse smoky flavors into meats, vegetables, and even some cheeses. Here's how to master smoking on your Blackstone Griddle:

- **Choose the Right Equipment:** To smoke on a Blackstone Griddle, you'll need a smoker box or a heavy-duty aluminum foil to make a DIY smoker pouch. Fill the box or pouch with your choice of wood chips, like hickory for a strong flavor or apple for a sweeter touch.

- **Preparation of Wood Chips:** Soak the wood chips in water for at least an hour before use. This prevents them from burning too quickly and helps to produce more smoke for a longer duration.

- **Placement of the Smoker Box or Pouch:** Place the smoker box or foil pouch directly over one of the burners. Turn the burner to high to generate smoke. Once you see a steady stream of smoke, you can begin cooking.

- **Indirect Smoking Method:** Arrange the food on a part of the griddle that is not directly over the active burner. This method allows the food to cook slowly, absorbing the smoky flavors without burning. Close the lid or cover the food with a basting cover to trap the smoke around the food.

- **Managing Heat:** Maintain a low to medium heat to ensure that the food absorbs the smoke and cooks evenly. Smoking is a slower cooking process, and patience is key to allowing the flavors to develop fully.

- **Experiment with Flavors:** Different woods impart different flavors. Experiment with various types of wood chips to find the flavors that best complement your dishes. Mesquite, for example, works well with red meat due to its strong flavor, while alder is milder and suitable for fish.

- **Keep an Eye on Your Chips:** Depending on the duration of your cooking, you may need to replenish the wood chips. Keep additional pre-soaked chips on hand for longer smoking sessions.

Using these smoking techniques on your Blackstone Griddle will allow you to enjoy the nuanced flavors of smoked cuisine without the need for a dedicated smoker. It's a fantastic way to add complexity and a gourmet touch to your outdoor cooking repertoire, enhancing the overall experience with each smoky, savory bite.

CHAPTER 4:

Food Safety

Ensuring food safety on your Blackstone Griddle is crucial not just for the health and well-being of those enjoying your meals but also for enhancing the overall cooking experience. **Adhering to strict hygiene rules and maintaining safe cooking temperatures are foundational to this process.** This chapter provides essential guidelines and best practices for maintaining a safe cooking environment.

Hygiene Rules

Maintaining a high standard of cleanliness and following strict hygiene protocols can significantly reduce the risk of foodborne illnesses. Here are some essential hygiene rules to follow:

- **Keep Hands Clean:** Always wash your hands with soap and water before and after handling food, especially when switching between handling raw meats and other foods.

- **Avoid Cross-Contamination:** Use separate cutting boards and utensils for raw meat, poultry, seafood, and vegetables. Consider color-coding utensils and boards to help remember which is used for each type of food.

- **Regularly Clean Your Griddle:** Clean your Blackstone Griddle after each use. Remove food particles and grease that can harbor bacteria. Also, perform a deep clean periodically to maintain its condition and safety.

- **Sanitize Cooking Areas:** Regularly disinfect surfaces that come into contact with food. Use a kitchen sanitizer or a solution of bleach and water (1 tablespoon of unscented bleach per gallon of water).

- **Proper Food Storage:** Store raw meats, poultry, and seafood below other foods in the refrigerator to prevent accidental drips that could contaminate other items. Keep these items in sealed containers to contain any leaks.

- **Thaw Safely:** Always thaw frozen food in the refrigerator, in cold water, or in the microwave—

never at room temperature on the counter, as this can promote bacterial growth.

- **Keep Ingredients Fresh:** Use fresh ingredients whenever possible, and check expiration dates on packaged goods to avoid using spoiled items.

Adhering to these hygiene rules ensures that your outdoor cooking environment is as safe as it is enjoyable, allowing you to cook with confidence and peace of mind.

Cooking at Safe Temperatures

Cooking food to the right temperature is vital for safety, killing harmful bacteria that might be present. Here's how to ensure that foods reach safe internal temperatures:

- **Use a Food Thermometer:** This is the most reliable way to check if your food is cooked to a safe internal temperature. Insert the thermometer into the thickest part of the food, without touching any bone, fat, or griddle.

- **Know the Safe Temperatures:** Cook all poultry to an internal temperature of 165°F (74°C); ground meats, including beef and pork, to 160°F (71°C); and steaks, chops, and whole cuts of beef, pork, lamb, and veal to a minimum of 145°F (63°C) followed by a three-minute rest time.

- **Check Seafood for Opacity and Texture:** Cook fish until it's opaque and flakes easily with a fork; shellfish should be cooked until the shells open naturally.

- **Keep Hot Foods Hot and Cold Foods Cold:** Maintain hot cooked food at 140°F (60°C) or warmer and keep cold dishes at 40°F (4°C) or cooler. This prevents bacterial growth that can occur in the "danger zone" between these temperatures.

By strictly adhering to these temperature guidelines, you ensure that your meals are not only delicious but also safe for everyone to enjoy, preventing foodborne illnesses and making your cooking sessions a resounding success.

Food Preservation

Proper food preservation is crucial to maintaining the quality and safety of your ingredients. Here are essential tips to ensure your food remains safe and fresh:

- **Refrigeration:** Keep perishable items like meats, dairy, and certain vegetables refrigerated at or below 40°F (4°C) until ready to use. Rapid refrigeration of cooked leftovers is crucial to prevent bacterial growth.

- **Avoid Time in the Danger Zone:** Foods should not be left out at room temperature for more than two hours. In hot weather (above 90°F or 32°C), reduce this time to one hour.

- **Use Airtight Containers:** Store food in airtight containers to protect it from airborne contaminants and to preserve freshness. Label containers with the date of storage to keep track of freshness.

- **Monitor Shelf Life:** Regularly check expiration dates and the condition of stored foods. When in doubt, throw it out to avoid the risk of using spoiled ingredients.

Implementing these preservation techniques ensures that your food retains its quality and safety, reducing waste and minimizing health risks associated with spoiled foods.

Contamination Prevention

Preventing contamination is fundamental in cooking, especially when handling diverse food types on your Blackstone Griddle. Here's how to mitigate risks:

- **Separate Raw and Cooked Foods:** Always use separate utensils, plates, and cutting boards for raw and cooked foods. This avoids the transfer of bacteria from raw foods to cooked or ready-to-eat items.

- **Clean As You Go:** Regularly clean your cooking area, utensils, and hands to prevent the spread of bacteria. Use hot, soapy water for washing and sanitize surfaces where raw food has been prepared.

- **Proper Marinating:** Always marinate foods in the refrigerator, not on the counter. Additionally, never use sauce that was used to marinate raw meat on cooked food unless it is boiled first.

- **Handle Food Minimally:** Use utensils rather than hands for food handling as much as possible, especially when transferring food from the grill to serving dishes.

- **Cook to Proper Temperatures:** Use a food thermometer to ensure all food reaches a safe internal temperature, crucial for destroying harmful bacteria.

- **Be Aware of Allergen Cross-Contact:** Be vigilant about using separate utensils and cookware for allergen-free cooking to prevent cross-contact, an essential consideration for guests with food allergies.

By following these rigorous practices, you can greatly minimize the risk of foodborne illness and ensure a safe, enjoyable experience for everyone around your Blackstone Griddle. Effective contamination prevention helps maintain the integrity of your dishes, keeping them delicious and safe for consumption.

CHAPTER 5:

Meats and Cooking Tips

Cooking meats on the Blackstone Griddle transforms simple ingredients into savory masterpieces. This chapter delves into various types of meats, each offering unique flavors and textures suited for griddle cooking.

Understanding these differences and their preparation needs will help you maximize the culinary potential of your Blackstone Griddle.

Types of Meat

1. Beef:

- **Steaks:** Popular cuts such as ribeye, sirloin, and filet mignon are prized for griddling due to their rich marbling and tender textures. Preheat the griddle to high to achieve a delicious sear that locks in juices.

- **Ground Beef:** Ideal for burgers and meatballs, ground beef should be cooked to an internal temperature of 160°F to ensure safety. Mix in spices and a little fat for juicier, flavorful patties.

- **Brisket:** Known for its rich flavor, brisket requires slow cooking on low heat on the griddle to tenderize the tough fibers. It's perfect for smoking or making pastrami.

2. Pork:

- **Chops:** Pork chops cook quickly on the griddle and are best enjoyed when they reach an internal temperature of 145°F, followed by a three-minute rest. Season simply with salt, pepper, and a touch of garlic powder.

- **Bacon:** The griddle renders bacon perfectly crispy. Lay strips flat and watch the fat render evenly, turning occasionally until crisp.

- **Sausages:** Pre-cook sausages by simmering in water on the griddle before browning. This ensures they're cooked through and juicy.

3. Chicken:

- **Breasts and Thighs:** Chicken pieces should be cooked until they reach an internal temperature of 165°F. Consider pounding breasts for even thickness to ensure uniform cooking.

- **Wings:** A favorite for quick griddle meals, wings benefit from high heat and constant movement to achieve crispy skin without overcooking the delicate meat inside.

4. Lamb:

- **Chops:** Lamb chops are rich in flavor and benefit from quick searing over high heat. Marinate in rosemary, garlic, and olive oil to enhance the natural flavors.

- **Ground Lamb:** Excellent for burgers or koftas, ground lamb should be seasoned with Middle Eastern spices and cooked until it has a beautiful crust on the outside, ensuring it is not overdone to maintain moisture.

5. Fish and Seafood:

- **Salmon:** High in omega-3 fatty acids, salmon fillets cook quickly and are best when left slightly translucent in the center. Cook skin-side down first to render the fat and crisp the skin.

- **Shrimp:** Perfect for high-heat, quick cooking, shrimp are done as soon as they turn pink and opaque. Toss with garlic and lemon for a fresh flavor.

- **Scallops:** Require a high heat and quick sear to caramelize the outside while keeping the inside tender and moist. Do not overcrowd the griddle to allow for even cooking.

6. Game Meats:

- **Venison:** Leaner than beef, venison benefits from marinating and should be cooked quickly over high heat to avoid drying out.
- **Bison:** Similar to beef but leaner, bison steaks and burgers cook faster and should be monitored closely to prevent overcooking.

7. Exotic Meats:

- **Ostrich:** Extremely lean, best served medium-rare to keep it tender.
- **Alligator:** Often described as a cross between chicken and fish, it is excellent when marinated and quickly grilled.

Each type of meat offers a unique flavor profile and cooking requirements, making your Blackstone Griddle an incredibly versatile tool for outdoor cooking. Experiment with different cuts, marinades, and cooking techniques to fully explore the culinary possibilities of each meat type, turning every meal into a gourmet experience.

Beef Cuts

Each type of meat is divided into different cuts, each with its own characteristics in terms of texture, flavor, and fat content. Choosing the right cut of meat for each recipe is crucial for achieving optimal results.

1. Prime Cuts

TENDERLOIN: The most prized and tender cut of beef, perfect for:

- **Rare Steaks:** Grilling, pan-searing.
- **Carpaccio:** Slicing thinly and serving raw.
- **Roast Beef:** Oven-roasting with herbs.

RIB: A flavorful and versatile cut, ideal for:

- **Grilling:** Grilling over coals or in a skillet.
- **Roasts:** Oven-roasting with potatoes or vegetables.
- **Florentine Steaks:** Grilling over high flames.
- **Braises:** Slow cooking with red wine and spices.

TOP BLADE (ROAST BEEF): A lean and flavorful cut, perfect for:

- **Roasts:** Oven-roasting with herbs and vegetables.
- **Stuffed Steaks:** Stuffing and cooking in a skillet or oven.
- **Stews:** Cutting into cubes and stewing with tomatoes and vegetables.

2. Choice Cuts

INSIDE ROUND: A lean and versatile cut, ideal for:

- **Steaks:** Grilling, pan-searing.
- **Stews:** Cutting into cubes and stewing with vegetables and spices.
- **Carpaccio:** Slicing thinly and serving raw.

TOP ROUND: A lean and flavorful cut, perfect for:

- **Roast Beef:** Oven-roasting with herbs and vegetables.
- **Roasts:** Oven-roasting with potatoes or vegetables.
- **Stews:** Cutting into cubes and stewing with tomatoes and vegetables.

EYE OF ROUND: A very lean and tender cut, ideal for:

- **Steaks:** Grilling, pan-searing.
- **Carpaccio:** Slicing thinly and serving raw.
- **Pot Roasts:** Slow cooking in broth with vegetables and spices.

SIRLOIN: A lean and flavorful cut, perfect for:

- **Steaks:** Grilling, pan-searing.
- **Roasts:** Oven-roasting with herbs and vegetables.
- **Stews:** Cutting into cubes and stewing with tomatoes and vegetables.

3. Utility Cuts

CHUCK: A collagen-rich and flavorful cut, perfect for:

- **Braises:** Slow cooking with red wine and spices.
- **Stews:** Cutting into cubes and stewing with tomatoes and vegetables.
- **Stews:** Slow cooking with vegetables and spices.

BRISKET: A fatty and flavorful cut, perfect for:

- **Pastrami:** Marinating and smoking.
- **American Brisket:** Smoking at low temperature for several hours.
- **Beef Shank:** Baking or stewing with vegetables and spices.

SHOULDER: A versatile and flavorful cut, ideal for:

- **Braises:** Slow cooking with red wine and spices.
- **Roasts:** Oven-roasting with potatoes or vegetables.
- **Stews:** Cutting into cubes and stewing with tomatoes and vegetables.

- **Boiled Beef:** Long boiling to achieve a flavorful broth.

4. Lesser Cuts

SHANK: A collagen-rich and flavorful cut, perfect for:

- **Broths:** Long boiling to achieve a flavorful broth.
- **Sauces:** Slow cooking with vegetables and spices.
- **Beef Shank:** Baking or stewing with vegetables and spices.

FLANK: A lean and flavorful cut, perfect for:

- **Marinating:** Marinating with spices and herbs, then grilling or cooking in a skillet.
- **Fajitas:** Slicing into strips and cooking in a skillet with onions and peppers.
- **Roasts:** Oven-roasting with herbs and vegetables.

CROSS-CUT SHANK (Osso Buco): A collagen-rich and flavorful cut, perfect for:

- **Osso Buco Milanese:** Slow braising with white wine and vegetables.
- **Stews:** Cutting into cubes and stewing with tomatoes and vegetables.
- **Beef Shank:** Baking or stewing with vegetables and spices.

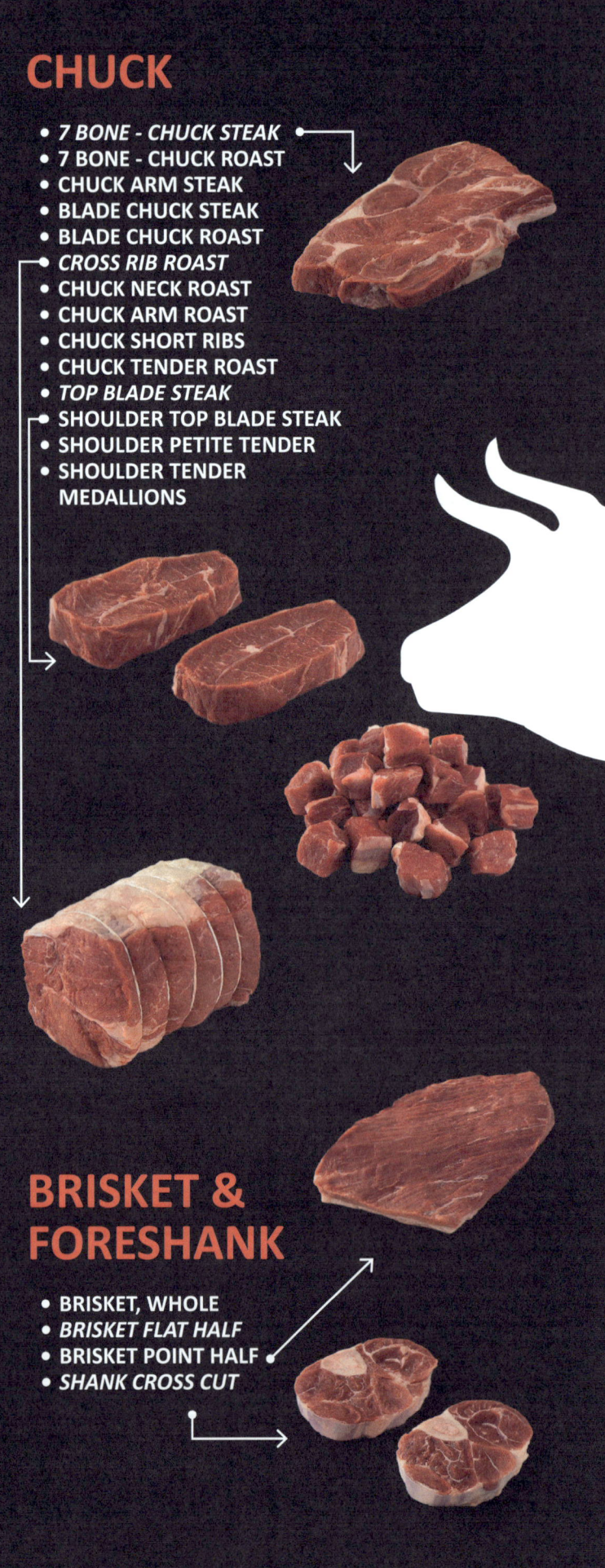

CHUCK

- *7 BONE - CHUCK STEAK*
- *7 BONE - CHUCK ROAST*
- CHUCK ARM STEAK
- BLADE CHUCK STEAK
- BLADE CHUCK ROAST
- *CROSS RIB ROAST*
- CHUCK NECK ROAST
- CHUCK ARM ROAST
- CHUCK SHORT RIBS
- CHUCK TENDER ROAST
- *TOP BLADE STEAK*
- SHOULDER TOP BLADE STEAK
- SHOULDER PETITE TENDER
- SHOULDER TENDER MEDALLIONS

BRISKET & FORESHANK

- BRISKET, WHOLE
- *BRISKET FLAT HALF*
- *BRISKET POINT HALF*
- *SHANK CROSS CUT*

MEATS AND COOKING TIPS

RIB
- RIB ROAST
- RIB STEAK
- RIBEYE ROAST
- RIBEYE STEAK
- *BACK RIBS*

SHORT LOIN
- TOP LOIN STEAK
- PORTERHOUSE STEAK
- TENDERLOIN ROAST
- *TENDERLOIN STEAK*
- *T-BONE STEAK*

SIRLOIN
- SIRLOIN STEAK, FLAT BONE
- SIRLOIN STEAK, ROUND BONE
- *TOP SIRLOIN STEAK*
- TRI-TIP STEAK
- *TRI-TIP ROAST*

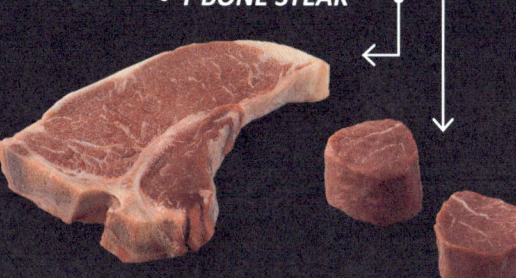

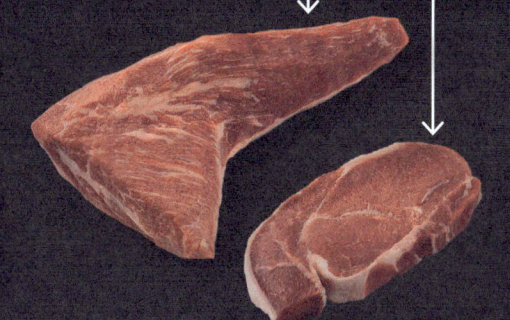

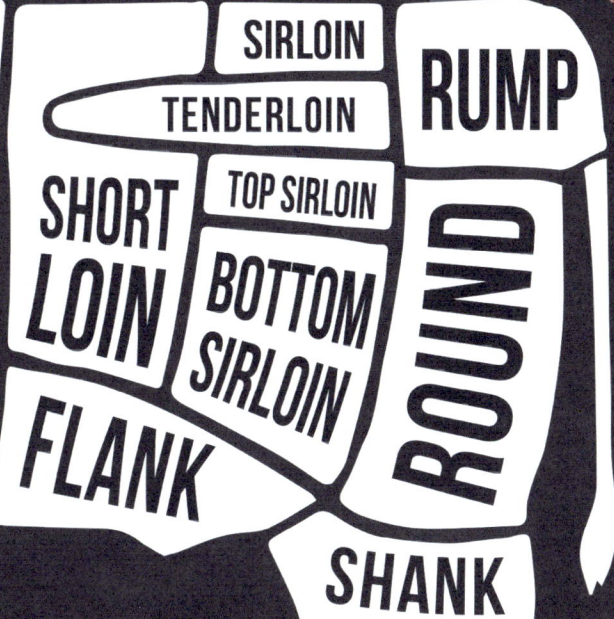

ROUND & RUMP
- *ROUND STEAK*
- BOTTOM ROUND ROAST
- BOTTOM ROUND STEAK
- *EYE OF ROUND ROAST*
- EYE OF ROUND STEAK
- TIP ROAST, CAP OFF
- TIP STEAK
- BONELESS RUMP ROAST

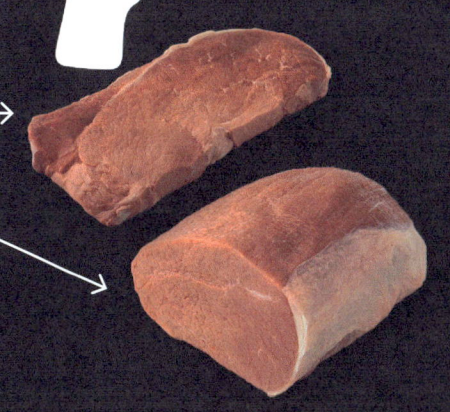

PLATE & FLANK
- *FLANKEN STYLE SHORT RIBS*
- PLATE SHORT RIBS
- SKIRT STEAK
- FLANK STEAK

MEATS AND COOKING TIPS

Pork Cuts

Pork is a versatile, economical, and flavorful meat that can be used to prepare a wide variety of dishes. Thanks to its varied texture and robust taste, pork lends itself to many preparations, from simple and quick to more elaborate and refined dishes.

In this complete guide, we will explore all the pork cuts, describing their characteristics, best cooking methods, and ideal recipes for each. Before we begin, it is important to understand the anatomical structure of the pig.

1. Prime Cuts

LOIN: The most prized part of the pig, characterized by lean and tender meat. Perfect for:

- **Chops:** Grilling, pan-searing.
- **Roast:** Oven-roasting.
- **Steaks:** Grilling, pan-searing.
- **Stew Meat:** Cutting into pieces and stewing.

TENDERLOIN: A very lean and tender cut, ideal for:

- **Rare Steaks:** Grilling, pan-searing.
- **Carpaccio:** Slicing thinly and serving raw.
- **Medallions:** Grilling, pan-searing.

HAM: A large and versatile cut, which can be used whole for:

- **Roasts:** Oven-roasting.
- **Steaks:** Cutting and grilling, pan-searing.
- **Chops:** Cutting and grilling, pan-searing.
- **Stew Meat:** Cutting and stewing.

2. Choice Cuts

SHOULDER: A collagen-rich and flavorful cut, perfect for:

- **Braises:** Slow cooking, stewing.
- **Stews:** Cutting and stewing.
- **Stew Meat:** Cutting and stewing.

BACON: A fatty and flavorful cut, used to prepare:

- **Classic Bacon:** Smoking, pan-cooking.
- **Smoked Bacon:** Smoking with aromatic woods.

COPPA: A fatty and marbled cut, ideal for charcuterie such as:

- **Coppa:** Curing and eating raw.
- **Lonza:** Curing and eating raw.

3. Utility Cuts

JOWL: A collagen-rich and flavorful cut, perfect for preparations such as:

- **Gricia:** Sautéing in a pan with guanciale, Pecorino Romano, and black pepper.
- **Roman-style Artichokes:** Cooking artichokes with guanciale, garlic, and parsley.

BELLY: A fatty and flavorful cut, used to prepare:

- **Lardo:** Curing and eating raw.
- **Salami:** Grinding and stuffing for the preparation of typical salamis.

HEAD: A collagen-rich and flavorful cut, used to prepare:

- **Broths:** Long boiling to obtain a richly flavored broth.
- **Sauces:** Slow cooking with vegetables and spices.
- **Regional Dishes:** Various regional preparations based on the head of the pig.

20 MEATS AND COOKING TIPS

SHOULDER (BOSTON BUTT & CLEAR PLATE)

- BLADE STEAK, BONE IN
- *SHOULDER ROAST, BONE IN*
- SHOULDER COUNTRY STYLE RIBS, BONE IN
- BLADE PORK ROAST
- *GROUND PORK*
- *PORK SAUSAGE*

LOIN

- *RACK OF PORK*
- PORK COUNTRY STYLE RIBS, BONELESS AND BONE-IN
- PORK BACK RIBS
- *PORK CHOPS*
- RIBEYE PORK CHOP
- RIBEYE PORK CHOP BONELESS
- PORTERHOUSE PORK CHOP
- SIRLOIN PORK CHOP, BONELESS
- *PORK ROAST OR LOIN ROAST*
- SIRLOIN PORK ROAST, BONELESS
- SIRLOIN PORK ROAST, BONE-IN
- *PORK TENDERLOIN*
- PORK RIBEYE ROAST
- LOIN CUBES

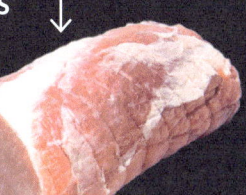

PICNIC HAM

- ARM PORK ROAST OR ARM PICNIC
- PICNIC ROAST, BONELESS

OTHER

- PIG'S CHEEKS
- SAUSAGES
- SNOUT
- PORK TRIPE
- PORK LIVER
- TAIL
- EARS
- HEAD
- PORK RIND
- PORK HOCK
- TROTTERS

SPARE RIBS & BACON

- PORK SPARE RIBS
- PORK BELLY, FRESH
- PORK ST.LOUS-STYLE RIBS
- LARD
- BACON

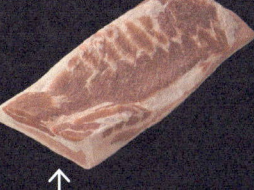

LEG OR HAM

- HAM, SHANK
- HAM, STEAK
- FRESH HAM, BONE IN
- SMOKED HAM, BONE IN
- LEG CUTLETS
- FRESH HAM ROAST, BONELESS
- SIRLOIN STEAK

MEATS AND COOKING TIPS

Chicken Cuts

Chicken is a versatile, economical, and protein-rich meat that is consumed worldwide. Thanks to its delicate flavor and ease of cooking, chicken lends itself to various preparations, from simple and quick to more elaborate and refined dishes. In this complete guide, we will explore all the cuts of chicken, describing their characteristics, best cooking methods, and ideal recipes for each.

Understanding Chicken Anatomy

To better understand the different cuts of chicken, it's important to know the anatomy of this bird. Chicken is divided into two main parts:

Front Part: Includes the wings, breast, and neck.

Back Part: Includes the thighs, drumsticks, and back.

1. Front Part Cuts

WINGS: Chicken wings are a versatile and flavorful cut, perfect for:

- **Grilling:** Seasoned and grilled over coals or in a skillet.
- **Frying:** Breaded and fried until golden.
- **Baking:** Roasted in the oven with herbs and vegetables.
- **Stewing:** Cut into pieces and used to make soups and stews.

CHICKEN BREAST: Chicken breast is a lean and protein-rich cut, ideal for:

- **Grilling:** Grilled whole or sliced, seasoned with herbs or spices.
- **Roasting:** Roasted in the oven with vegetables or stuffed.
- **Pan-frying:** Sautéed in a pan with oil, vegetables, and spices.
- **Steaks:** Cut into thick slices and cooked in a skillet or oven.
- **Carpaccio:** Thinly sliced and served raw with oil, lemon, and salt.

CHICKEN NECK: Chicken neck is a budget-friendly and collagen-rich cut, perfect for:

- **Broths:** Boiled long to obtain a richly flavored broth.
- **Stews:** Cut into pieces and cooked with vegetables and spices.
- **Stews:** Added to stews and soups to enhance flavor and texture.

2. Back Part Cuts

CHICKEN THIGHS: Chicken thighs are a juicy and flavorful cut, ideal for:

- **Roasting:** Roasted in the oven with herbs and vegetables.
- **Braising:** Braised slowly with red wine or broth.
- **Stews:** Cut into pieces and cooked with vegetables and spices.
- **Cacciatore:** Cooked in a skillet with onions, mushrooms, and tomato.

DRUMSTICKS: Drumsticks are the lower part of the thigh, leaner and more delicate, perfect for:

- **Grilling:** Grilled over coals or in a skillet, seasoned with herbs or spices.
- **Frying:** Breaded and fried until golden.
- **Baking:** Roasted in the oven with vegetables or stuffed.
- **Stewing:** Cut into pieces and used to make soups and stews.

CHICKEN BACK: Chicken back is a budget-friendly and flavorful cut, ideal for:

- **Broths:** Boiled long to obtain a richly flavored broth.
- **Stews:** Cut into pieces and cooked with vegetables and spices.
- **Stews:** Added to stews and soups to enhance flavor and texture.

Other Chicken Cuts: In addition to the main cuts, there are also less common cuts of chicken, such as:

CHICKEN WINGS: Chicken wings are the terminal part of the wings, small and crispy, perfect for:

- **Frying:** Breaded and fried until golden, seasoned with spicy or flavored sauces.
- **Grilling:** Grilled over coals or in a skillet, seasoned with herbs or spices.
- **Baking:** Roasted in the oven with vegetables or marinated in flavorful sauces.

BONELESS SKINLESS CHICKEN BREAST: Boneless skinless chicken breast is a lean and versatile cut, ideal for:

- **Scaloppine:** Cut into thin slices and cooked in a skillet with oil, lemon, and spices.
- **Roulades:** Stuffed with vegetables, cheese, or other ingredients and cooked in a skillet or oven.
- **Salads:** Grilled, baked, or boiled and added to fresh salads.

CHICKEN
- ENTIRE CHICKEN

WING
- DRUMETTE
- WINGETTE
- WINGTIP
- WHOLE WING

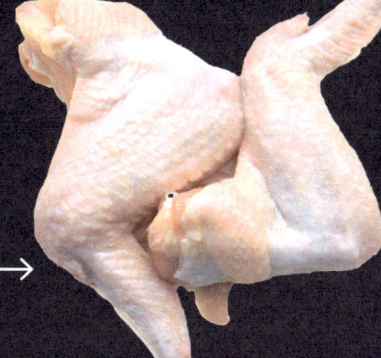

BACK
- BACK

THIGH
- THIGH FILLETS
- THIGH CUTLETS

BREAST & TENDERLION
- BONELESS BREAST
- BONE-IN BREAST
- SPLIT BREAST
- AIRLINE BREAST
- TENDERLOINS
- DICED CHICKEN

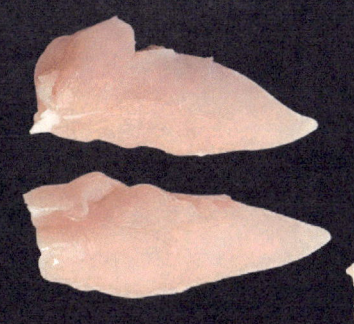

DRUMSTICK
- DRUMSTICK
- LEG QUARTER
- WHOLE LEG

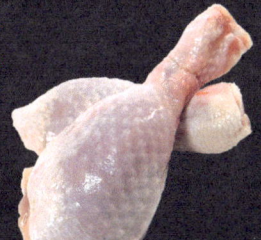

MEATS AND COOKING TIPS

- **Wraps and Sandwiches:** Cut into strips and used to stuff wraps and sandwiches.

BONELESS SKINLESS CHICKEN THIGHS: Boneless skinless chicken thighs are a juicy and flavorful cut, perfect for:

- **Steaks:** Cut into thick slices and cooked in a skillet or oven.
- **Stews:** Cut into pieces and cooked with vegetables and spices.
- **Cacciatore:** Cooked in a skillet with onions, mushrooms, and tomato.
- **Pan-frying:** Sautéed in a pan with oil, vegetables, and spices.

CHICKEN HEARTS: Chicken hearts are a budget-friendly and flavorful cut, ideal for:

- **Grilling:** Grilled over coals or in a skillet, seasoned with herbs or spices.
- **Roasting:** Roasted in the oven with vegetables or marinated in flavorful sauces.
- **Stews:** Cut into pieces and cooked with vegetables and spices.
- **Salads:** Grilled, baked, or boiled and added to fresh salads.

CHICKEN LIVER: Chicken liver is a cut rich in iron and other nutrients, ideal for:

- **Pan-frying:** Sautéed in a pan with oil, onions, and spices.
- **Pâté:** Ground and used to make a flavorful pâté.
- **Sauces:** Ground and used to make richly flavored sauces.
- **Roasting:** Roasted in the oven with onions and bacon.

Chicken Cooking:

- **Direct Grilling:** This method involves cooking the chicken directly on the heated surface of the grill. It's important to keep the grill at a medium-high temperature and flip the chicken regularly to ensure even cooking.
- **Marinating:** Before grilling the chicken, it's advisable to marinate the meat to add flavor and tenderness. You can use a marinade made with oil, vinegar, herbs, spices, and other flavors of your choice. Let the chicken marinate in the refrigerator for at least 30 minutes before cooking it on the Blackstone grill.
- **Indirect Grilling:** This method involves cooking the chicken on a part of the Blackstone grill that is not directly over the heat source. This is particularly useful for cooking thicker pieces of chicken evenly without burning them. You can cover the chicken with a lid to ensure even cooking.
- **Searing:** For smaller pieces of chicken, you can sear them on the Blackstone grill with a little oil. This method is quick and ideal for chicken cubes, thin slices, or chicken strips.

Here are some tips for cooking chicken:

- Chicken meat should always be thoroughly cooked before consumption.
- Leaner cuts of meat, such as chicken breast, require quicker cooking at higher temperatures to prevent them from drying out.
- Fattier cuts, such as chicken thighs, can be cooked at lower temperatures for a longer period.
- Use a meat thermometer to ensure that the chicken has reached the safe internal temperature of 165°F (74°C) before serving.

Meat Quality

The quality of meat is an important factor that influences the flavor and texture of the final dish. When choosing meat, look for the following signs of quality:

- **Color:** The meat should have a uniform and bright color.
- **Smell:** The meat should have a fresh and pleasant odor.
- **Marbling:** Beef and pork should have good marbling, which means streaks of fat.
- **Texture:** The meat should be firm and elastic to the touch.

Meat Storage

Fresh meat should be stored in the refrigerator at a temperature of 4°C (39°F) or lower. Frozen meat should be stored in the freezer at a temperature of -18°C (0°F) or lower.

- **Fresh Meat:** Fresh meat should be consumed within 2-3 days of purchase.
- **Frozen Meat:** Frozen meat can be stored for up to 6 months.

Meat Cooking

Direct Cooking on the Blackstone Outdoor Gas Griddle

Direct cooking on a Blackstone Outdoor Gas Griddle involves using high heat applied directly to the food, enabling quick cooking and a rich flavor profile through methods like grilling and searing. Here are detailed insights and tips for utilizing these techniques effectively on your Blackstone griddle.

GRILLING

Grilling is a cornerstone cooking technique for any outdoor chef, especially on a flat top like the Blackstone Outdoor Gas Griddle. This method is ideal for cooking a variety of foods, from breakfast items like pancakes and eggs to lunch and dinner favorites like burgers, steaks, and vegetables.

Key Benefits:

- **Even Cooking:** The large, flat surface of the Blackstone Griddle provides even heat distribution, avoiding hot spots typical of traditional wire grills.

- **Versatility:** Almost any food that can be cooked on a traditional grill can be cooked on a Blackstone Griddle, including delicate items that might fall through grill grates.

- **Flavor Enhancement:** The griddle surface allows for the development of a rich sear that enhances flavor, thanks to the Maillard reaction.

Tips for Grilling on a Blackstone Griddle:

1. **Preheat the Griddle:** Always start with a preheated griddle to ensure a good sear. The Blackstone should be heated to a medium-high temperature for about 10-15 minutes before adding food.
2. **Oil the Surface:** Lightly oil the griddle surface before cooking to prevent sticking and to add an extra layer of flavor. Use oils with a high smoke point like canola, vegetable, or avocado oil.
3. **Control the Temperature:** Use the temperature controls to adjust the heat under different parts of the griddle. This way, you can cook multiple foods at once, each at its ideal temperature.
4. **Use Zones:** Create different heat zones on the griddle for cooking and warming. This allows you to move food from hotter to cooler parts of the griddle as needed.
5. **Clean Regularly:** After each use, clean the griddle surface while it's still warm. Scrape off food residues with a metal spatula, then wipe down with a paper towel soaked in oil. This helps maintain the seasoning of the griddle surface.

SEARING

Searing involves cooking at a high temperature to form a tasty crust on the surface of the food, typically used for meats like steaks or burgers. It is perfect for locking in flavors and juices, making it a must-master technique for serious griddle users.

Key Benefits:

- **Flavor Lock:** Searing meats on the Blackstone seals in juices, ensuring that the food remains moist and flavorful.

- **Aesthetic Appeal:** Searing provides an appealing brown crust with improved texture and taste.

- **Speed:** Due to the high heat involved, searing cooks foods quickly, making it ideal for busy cooks.

Tips for Searing on a Blackstone Griddle:

1. **Very High Heat:** Ensure the griddle is extremely hot before adding your meat—this is crucial for a good sear. The surface should be around 400°F to 450°F.
2. **Do Not Overcrowd:** Give each piece of meat plenty of space on the griddle. Crowding can lower the surface temperature and cause steaming instead of searing.
3. **Pat Dry the Meat:** Moisture is the enemy of a good sear. Pat meat dry with paper towels before placing it on the griddle.
4. **Flip Once:** Let the meat develop a crust on one side before flipping it. This typically takes about 3-4 minutes. Flip only once to ensure a robust crust.
5. **Rest After Cooking:** Allow your seared meat to rest off the heat for a few minutes before cutting. This helps the juices redistribute throughout the meat, ensuring it's moist and flavorful when served.

BRAISING

Braising typically involves cooking food slowly in a covered pot with some amount of liquid. While not the first technique that comes to mind for a flat top griddle like the Blackstone, it is indeed possible with the right setup. Here's how you can adapt the braising method for your Blackstone Griddle to create tender, flavorful dishes.

Key Benefits:

- **Flavor Concentration:** Braising on a griddle allows for a unique sear before adding liquids, enhancing the depth of flavor in the food.

- **Versatility:** While unconventional, braising on a griddle can be achieved for dishes such as short ribs, pork belly, or even certain hearty vegetables like cabbage.

- **Outdoor Convenience:** Utilizing the Blackstone for braising lets you enjoy the benefits of slow-cooked dishes without being confined to the kitchen.

Tips for Braising on a Blackstone Griddle:

1. **Preheat and Sear:** Start by preheating your griddle to a high temperature. Sear the main ingredients (like meat or hearty vegetables) on all sides to develop a caramelized crust. This step adds a rich flavor base that is crucial for delicious braised dishes.

2. **Use a Cast Iron Skillet:** Since the Blackstone Griddle itself cannot hold liquids without a container, use a heavy-duty cast iron skillet or Dutch oven that can be placed directly on the griddle surface.

3. **Add Liquids and Aromatics:** After searing, add liquids such as stock, wine, or tomatoes, along with aromatics like garlic, onions, and herbs. The liquid should come up about halfway up the sides of the main ingredients, not covering them completely.

4. **Low and Slow Cooking:** Reduce the heat to low and cover the skillet with a lid or aluminum foil. Let the ingredients simmer gently. The heat from the griddle will circulate under and around the skillet, mimicking a traditional braising environment.

5. **Monitor and Stir:** Check periodically and stir gently to ensure that the food does not stick to the bottom. Depending on the dish, braising can take anywhere from 30 minutes to several hours.

6. **Finishing Touches:** Once the main ingredients are tender and the flavors melded, you can finish by adjusting the seasoning and perhaps adding a fresh herb for brightness.

Indirect Cooking on the Blackstone Outdoor Gas Griddle

Indirect cooking on a Blackstone Outdoor Gas Griddle allows you to employ techniques typically reserved for conventional kitchens, such as moist cooking and stewing. These methods involve cooking food at lower temperatures and often with added liquid, which makes them ideal for tenderizing tougher cuts of meat or for preparing complex, flavor-rich dishes.

ROASTING

Roasting involves cooking food, typically uncovered, in an environment where hot air circulates around the food. Roasting on a Blackstone Griddle is not traditional but can be accomplished with a setup that allows for indirect heat.

Key Benefits:

- **Even Cooking:** The consistent heat distribution of the Blackstone Griddle ensures that foods roast evenly.

- **Flavor Enhancement:** Roasting vegetables and meats on the griddle can add a delightful char and smokiness that you don't get in a conventional oven.

- **Outdoor Roasting:** Enjoy the benefits of roasting while engaging with family or guests outdoors, making it a social cooking experience.

Tips for Roasting on a Blackstone Griddle:

1. **Use a Grill Dome or Cover:** To mimic the effects of an oven, use a grill dome or a large metal bowl or pot to cover the food on the griddle. This will help to trap heat and circulate it around the food, similar to an oven.

2. **Preheat the Griddle:** Start with a medium-high heat to get a good initial sear on the food, then lower the temperature to maintain a steady, moderate heat that will cook the food through.

3. **Use a Cast Iron Pan:** For items that might benefit from a slower, more oven-like roasting, such as whole chickens or large roasts, use a cast iron pan. Place the food in the pan, and then cover it with foil or a lid to trap the heat.

4. **Rotate and Flip:** If not using a pan, make sure to rotate and flip your food items periodically to ensure even cooking and to prevent burning.

5. **Add Liquid if Needed:** A little bit of broth or water in the bottom of the pan can help keep the food moist and tender while it cooks.

MOIST COOKING

Moist cooking involves techniques that use water or another liquid to cook the food, generally at lower temperatures. This can include steaming, poaching, and simmering. While these methods are not traditional for a flat top grill, they can be adapted using the right accessories and approach.

Key Benefits:

- **Gentle Cooking Method:** Moist cooking methods are excellent for cooking delicate foods such as fish, vegetables, and certain cuts of meat without drying them out.
- **Flavor Enhancement:** Using broths or seasoned liquids can infuse the food with additional flavors.
- **Healthy Cooking Option:** Moist cooking uses little to no added fat, making it a healthier option for preparing various dishes.

Tips for Moist Cooking on a Blackstone Griddle:

1. **Use Suitable Cookware:** To effectively moist cook on a Blackstone Griddle, use a heavy-duty pot or pan that can handle the griddle's intense heat. Cast iron pots or high-grade stainless steel pans are ideal.
2. **Preheat Your Cookware:** Before adding your ingredients, preheat your pot or pan on the griddle. This helps in maintaining a consistent temperature once the food is added.
3. **Add Liquid and Ingredients:** Pour in your cooking liquid—water, broth, or a seasoned mixture—and bring it to a simmer. Then add your ingredients. The liquid should not boil vigorously as this can break down the ingredients too quickly.
4. **Cover to Retain Moisture:** Use a lid to cover your pot or pan. This keeps the steam contained, which helps in cooking the food evenly and retaining its moisture.
5. **Manage Heat Settings:** Keep the griddle's heat on a medium to low setting to maintain a gentle simmer and prevent the liquid from evaporating too quickly.

STEWING

Stewing involves slow cooking smaller pieces of food in a moderate amount of liquid at low temperatures. It is similar to braising but typically uses more liquid and smaller cuts of meat or vegetables.

Key Benefits:

- **Deep Flavor Development:** Stewing allows flavors to meld together over the extended cooking time, creating rich and layered taste profiles.
- **Tenderizes Tough Cuts:** The slow cooking process gently breaks down the fibers in tougher cuts of meat, making them incredibly tender.
- **Versatility:** You can stew a variety of ingredients, from meats and poultry to beans and hearty vegetables.

Tips for Stewing on a Blackstone Griddle:

1. **Suitable Cookware Is Key:** Use a heavy-duty pot or Dutch oven that can distribute heat evenly and maintain temperature throughout the long cooking process.
2. **Sear Ingredients First:** For added flavor, sear meats and some hearty vegetables on the griddle before stewing. This caramelization adds depth to the dish.
3. **Low and Slow Cooking:** After adding all ingredients and liquid into the pot, ensure the heat is low enough to maintain a gentle simmer. This slow cooking process is crucial for developing flavors and tenderizing meats.
4. **Stir Occasionally:** While the lid should mostly stay on to retain heat and moisture, lifting the lid occasionally to stir helps prevent sticking and ensures even cooking.
5. **Adjust Seasonings at the End:** As flavors concentrate, it's best to adjust salt and other seasonings towards the end of cooking to avoid over-seasoning.

SMOKING

Smoking is a technique often associated with traditional smokers or charcoal grills, but it can also be adapted for use on a Blackstone Outdoor Gas Griddle with some creativity and the right tools. This method involves cooking food at low temperatures in the presence of smoke from burning wood, adding a distinctive smoky flavor to the food.

Key Benefits:

- **Flavor Enhancement:** Smoking imparts a unique, smoky taste that can't be replicated with other cooking methods.
- **Versatility:** A variety of foods can be smoked, from meats and fish to cheeses and vegetables.

MEATS AND COOKING TIPS

Tenderness and Moisture Retention: The slow-cooking nature of smoking helps keep meats tender and moist.

Tips for Smoking on a Blackstone Griddle:

1. **Use a Smoke Box or Foil Packets:** Purchase a metal smoke box or make your own foil packets filled with wood chips. Soak the wood chips in water for at least 30 minutes before use to prevent them from burning too quickly.

2. **Preheat the Griddle and Place the Smoker Box:** Preheat your Blackstone Griddle to a low setting. Place the smoke box or foil packet directly over one of the burners. Wait until it starts producing smoke.

3. **Prepare Food for Smoking:** While the smoker box is heating up, prepare your food. Season as desired and place it on the griddle, away from direct heat if possible.

4. **Low and Slow Cooking:** Maintain a low temperature and let the food cook slowly, absorbing the flavors from the smoke. This can take several hours, depending on the thickness and type of food.

5. **Monitor and Adjust:** Keep an eye on your griddle's temperature and the amount of smoke. Add more soaked wood chips to the smoke box as needed to maintain consistent smoke.

SOUS VIDE COOKING

Sous vide is a French cooking technique that translates to "under vacuum." It involves cooking food sealed in airtight plastic bags in a water bath at very precise temperatures. This method is praised for its ability to cook food evenly and retain moisture, and it can be adapted to work with a Blackstone Griddle.

Key Benefits:

- **Precision Cooking:** Sous vide allows for precise temperature control, which results in perfectly cooked food every time.

- **Enhanced Flavors and Juiciness:** Foods cook in their own juices, which enhances flavor and prevents drying out.

- **Flexibility and Convenience:** Once set, sous vide cooking requires minimal supervision, freeing up time for other tasks.

Tips for Sous Vide Cooking on a Blackstone Griddle:

1. **Use a Portable Sous Vide Cooker:** Attach a portable sous vide cooker to a large pot filled with water. Set it on your Blackstone Griddle for stability and easy access to power.

2. **Water Bath Setup:** Ensure your water bath is large enough to accommodate the food you plan to cook and maintain the water level during cooking.

3. **Bag the Ingredients:** Place your ingredients and any marinades or seasonings into a vacuum-sealed bag or a high-quality resealable plastic bag. Remove as much air as possible to ensure even cooking.

4. **Set the Temperature and Time:** Follow specific recipes for the correct temperature and cooking time to achieve desired doneness.

5. **Finishing on the Griddle:** After sous vide cooking, you can quickly sear meats or vegetables on the griddle to develop a flavorful crust.

By integrating these advanced cooking techniques with your Blackstone Outdoor Gas Griddle, you enhance your culinary capabilities and enjoy a broader range of flavors and textures in your outdoor cooking adventure

Resting Meat After Cooking

After sizzling on a grill or roasting in an oven, meat needs a crucial but often overlooked step before it's served: resting. This seemingly simple process is vital to ensuring that your meat is as juicy and flavorful as possible. Whether it's a thick, hearty steak, a tender breast of chicken, or a succulent piece of lamb, allowing the meat to rest after cooking can dramatically improve its texture and taste.

Importance of Resting Meat

1. **Juice Redistribution:** During cooking, the heat causes the proteins in meat to contract, pushing the juices towards the center of the cut. When the meat rests after cooking, these juices redistribute and reabsorb throughout the meat, resulting in a moister, more evenly juicy bite.

2. **Continued Cooking (Carryover Cooking):** Most types of meat will continue to cook even after they are removed from the heat source, a phenomenon known as carryover cooking. Resting allows the temperature to equalize, preventing the outer edges from overcooking and the center from being undercooked.

3. **Improved Texture and Flavor:** Resting allows the fibers in the meat to relax and the juices that have been pushed out to seep back and be reabsorbed. This not only improves the texture, making it tender

and easier to cut, but also enhances the flavor, making each bite equally satisfying.

Recommended Resting Times for Different Types of Meat

1. Beef:

- **Steaks:** Depending on the thickness, steaks should rest for 5 to 10 minutes. A good rule of thumb is to allow the steak to rest for about 1 minute for every 10 degrees of internal temperature or every inch of thickness.
- **Roasts:** Larger cuts like roasts should rest longer, typically 20 to 30 minutes, to ensure that the juices have adequate time to redistribute.

2. Pork:

- **Chops:** Pork chops should rest for 5 to 10 minutes before slicing to ensure they retain their moisture and flavor.
- **Larger cuts (e.g., pork loin, tenderloin):** Allow these to rest for 10 to 20 minutes. The larger mass means more internal heat, which requires a longer resting time to achieve optimal juiciness.

3. Chicken:

- **Breasts:** Rest chicken breasts for 5 to 10 minutes so that the juices settle and the meat remains succulent upon cutting.
- **Whole Chickens:** A whole chicken should rest for 20 to 30 minutes. This not only helps with juice distribution but also makes it safer and easier to carve.

4. Turkey:

- **Whole Turkey:** Given its size, a whole turkey needs a significant resting period, usually about 20 to 30 minutes. This time allows the high internal heat to mellow out, ensuring that the meat is not only flavorful but also retains its moisture throughout.

5. Lamb:

- **Chops:** Like pork and beef chops, lamb chops benefit from a 5 to 10 minute rest.
- **Leg of Lamb or Larger Roasts:** These should rest for 15 to 25 minutes. The denser muscle structure and fattier content benefit from a longer resting period to achieve a tender texture.

6. Fish:

- While not often discussed in the context of resting, even fish benefits from a brief rest period. Delicate fillets should rest for about 3 to 5 minutes before serving. This helps the layers of the fish flesh settle and reabsorb some of the juices lost during cooking.

Additional Tips for Resting Meat

- **Use a Warm Place:** Rest meat in a warm part of your kitchen, but not so hot as to continue cooking significantly. Covering loosely with foil can help keep the meat warm without steaming it.
- **Don't Cover Tightly:** Covering meat too tightly with foil while it rests can create steam and moisture, which might make the surface soggy, especially for crispy skins like on chicken or turkey.
- **Resting Surface:** Rest meat on a cutting board or a warm plate. For roasts, use a rack so that air can circulate around the meat, maintaining its texture.

By understanding and implementing proper resting times for different types of meat, you ensure that every dish served is as delicious, tender, and juicy as possible, elevating both everyday meals and special occasion dishes to new heights.

Temperature Control on the Blackstone Grill

Effective temperature control is key to mastering the Blackstone Grill. It ensures foods are cooked perfectly to your desired doneness, enhances flavors, and can prevent burning or undercooking.

1. **Knowing Your Zones:**

- **Multiple Burners:** Utilize the multiple burners of your Blackstone Grill to create different heat zones. This can be crucial for preparing multiple dishes at once or for a single dish that requires both searing and slower cooking.
- **High Heat:** Use high heat for searing meats or quick-cooking foods. It's crucial for achieving a caramelized crust and sealing in flavors.
- **Medium Heat:** Ideal for general cooking, including frying eggs, cooking pancakes, or grilling chicken to completion.

MEATS AND COOKING TIPS

- **Low Heat:** Best for slow-cooking or keeping food warm. It's also great for delicate items like fish or for foods that have already been seared and need to finish cooking at a gentler pace.

2. **Preheating the Griddle:**

- Always preheat the griddle before cooking. This ensures the surface is evenly heated, which helps in cooking food uniformly. For most cooking, 10-15 minutes of preheating is adequate.

3. **Using a Thermometer:**

Use an infrared thermometer to check the surface temperature of your griddle. This helps in precisely managing the cooking temperature for different foods.

4. **Adjust as You Go:**

- Be prepared to adjust burner settings as you cook. If food is cooking too quickly or burning, turn down the heat. Conversely, if it's cooking too slowly, you may need to increase the heat.

Cooking Times for Different Types of Meat on the Blackstone Grill

Cooking times can vary based on the type of meat, its thickness, and desired level of doneness. Here's a general guide to help you achieve perfectly cooked meats on your Blackstone Grill.

1. **Beef:**

- **Steaks (1-inch thick):** Cook for 4-5 minutes on each side for medium-rare, 5-7 minutes for medium, and 8-10 minutes for well-done.
- **Burgers (1/2-inch thick):** Cook for 4-5 minutes on each side for medium.
- **Roasts:** Cook at a lower temperature for a longer period; approximately 20 minutes per pound for medium-rare.

2. **Pork:**

- **Chops (1-inch thick):** Cook for 7-8 minutes on each side.
- **Ribs:** Indirect heat is preferred. Cook for 1.5-2 hours at a lower heat until tender.
- **Bacon:** Cook for 5-7 minutes, flipping occasionally until crisp.

3. **Chicken:**

- **Breasts (boneless, 1/2-inch thick):** Cook for 6-8 minutes on each side.
- **Thighs:** Cook for 7-10 minutes on each side.
- **Wings:** Cook for 15-20 minutes, turning occasionally until fully cooked.

4. **Fish:**

- **Salmon Fillets (1-inch thick):** Cook for 3-4 minutes on each side.
- **Tuna Steaks (1-inch thick):** Sear for 1-2 minutes on each side for medium-rare.
- **Whole Trout:** Cook for 5-7 minutes on each side.

These times are approximate and can vary depending on the specific heat settings of your grill and external factors like wind and ambient temperature. Always use a meat thermometer to ensure meats reach their safe internal temperatures.

CHAPTER 6:

Recipes

In this Chapter you'll find a rich variety of recipes to cook in your Blackstone Grill.

Note: This recipes are designed for one serving. To accommodate more people, simply multiply the ingredients by the desired number of servings.

The words "tablespoon" and "teaspoon" have been shortened to "tbsp" and "tsp".

1. Classic American Burger

PREP TIME: 15 minutes	**COOKING TIME:** 10 minutes	**TOTAL TIME:** 25 minutes	**SERVINGS:** For 1 person
DIFFICULTY: Easy	**TEMPERATURE:** 375°F (190°C)	**COOKING TYPE:** Griddling	**SAUCE:** Ketchup & mustard

INGREDIENTS:
- Ground beef (80/20 mix): 6 oz (170 g)
- Salt: ½ tsp (2 g)
- Black pepper: ¼ tsp (1 g)
- Cheddar cheese, sliced: 1 oz (28 g)
- Lettuce, leaf: 1 large leaf
- Tomato, sliced: 2 slices
- Red onion, sliced: 2 rings
- Hamburger bun: 1 bun
- Ketchup: 1 tbsp (15 ml)
- Mustard: 1 tsp (5 ml)

(For multiple servings, simply multiply the ingredient quantities by the number of people you are serving.)

NUTRITIONAL VALUES PER SERVING:
Calories: 720kcal | Carbohydrates: 40g | Proteins: 40g | Fats: 40g | Fiber: 2g | Sodium: 950mg | Glucose: 6 g

PROCEDURE:
1. **Grill Preparation:** Preheat your Blackstone Griddle to a medium-high temperature.
2. **Forming and Cooking the Burger:** Shape the ground beef into a patty slightly larger than the bun to allow for shrinkage. Season both sides with salt and pepper. Place the patty on the grill and cook for about 5 minutes on each side for a medium finish.
3. **Adding the Cheese:** Place the slice of cheddar cheese on the patty during the last minute of cooking to allow it to melt.
4. **Toasting the Bun:** Lightly toast the hamburger bun on the griddle for 1-2 minutes until golden and crispy.
5. **Assembly:** Spread ketchup and mustard on the bottom bun, then layer the lettuce, tomato, and red onion. Top with the burger and cheese, and cover with the top bun.

TIPS FOR PERFECT COOKING:
- **Avoid Pressing the Patty:** Do not press down on the burger with a spatula while it cooks to keep all the flavorful juices inside.
- **Resting Time:** Let the burger rest for a couple of minutes after cooking to allow the juices to redistribute throughout the meat, ensuring a juicier burger.
- **Sauce Application:** For added flavor, brush some ketchup or mustard on the burger in the last minute of cooking.

POSSIBLE VARIATIONS:
1. **Less Spicy Variant:** Use mild cheddar or American cheese for a less intense flavor.
2. **Tastier Variant:** Add a layer of crispy bacon under the cheese for a smokey flavor boost.
3. **Light Variant:** Opt for a whole-grain bun and low-fat cheese, and skip the ketchup and mustard to reduce calories and sugars.

2. Bacon Cheeseburger

PREP TIME: 15 minutes	**COOKING TIME:** 10 minutes	**TOTAL TIME:** 25 minutes	**SERVINGS:** For 1 person
DIFFICULTY: Easy	**TEMPERATURE:** Medium-high About 375°F (190°C)	**COOKING TYPE:** Direct on the grill	**SAUCE:** Mayonnaise

INGREDIENTS:
- Ground beef (80/20 mix): 6 oz / 170 grams
- Salt: ½ tsp / 2 grams
- Black pepper: ¼ tsp / 1 gram
- Smoked bacon: 2 slices
- Cheddar cheese, sliced: 1 oz / 28 grams
- Hamburger bun: 1 bun
- Mayonnaise: 1 tbsp / 15 ml
- Lettuce, leaf: 1 large leaf

(For multiple servings, simply multiply the ingredient quantities by the number of people you are serving.)

NUTRITIONAL VALUES PER SERVING:
Calories: 750kcal | Carbohydrates: 32g | Proteins: 42g | Fats: 50g | Fiber: 1g | Sodium: 1100mg | Glucose: 5 g

PROCEDURE:
1. **Grill Preparation:** Preheat your Blackstone Griddle to a medium-high temperature.
2. **Cooking the Bacon:** Place the bacon slices on the griddle and cook until crispy, about 3-4 minutes per side. Remove from the griddle and set aside on a paper towel to drain excess fat.
3. **Forming and Cooking the Burger:** Shape the ground beef into a patty slightly larger than the bun to accommodate shrinkage. Season both sides with salt and pepper. Grill the patty for about 5 minutes on each side for a medium finish.
4. **Adding the Cheese:** Place the slice of cheddar cheese on the patty during the last minute of cooking to allow it to melt.
5. **Toasting the Bun:** Lightly toast the hamburger bun on the griddle for 1-2 minutes until golden and crispy.
6. **Assembly:** Spread mayonnaise on the bottom bun, then add the lettuce leaf. Place the cooked burger with melted cheese on the lettuce, top with crispy bacon, and cover with the top bun.

TIPS FOR PERFECT COOKING:
- **Render the Bacon Crispy:** Ensure the bacon is sufficiently crispy as it adds texture and a rich, smoky flavor to the burger.
- **Cheese Melting:** Use a dome or cover over the burger when melting the cheese for even heat distribution and a perfectly melted topping.
- **Resting the Burger:** Allow the burger to rest for a few minutes after cooking for the juices to redistribute, enhancing flavor and juiciness.

POSSIBLE VARIATIONS:
1. **Less Fatty Variant:** Use turkey bacon and low-fat cheese, and replace the mayonnaise with a light mayo or yogurt-based sauce.
2. **Tastier Variant:** Add a fried egg on top of the bacon for an extra layer of flavor and richness.
3. **Spicy Variant:** Mix a bit of chopped jalapeños into the ground beef before forming your patty for a spicy kick.

BEEF BURGERS RECIPES

3. BBQ Burger

PREP TIME: 20 minutes	COOKING TIME: 15 minutes	TOTAL TIME: 35 minutes	SERVINGS: For 1 person
DIFFICULTY: Easy	TEMPERATURE: Medium-high About 375°F (190°C)	COOKING TYPE: Direct on the grill	SAUCE: Barbecue Sauce

INGREDIENTS:
- Ground beef (80/20 mix): 6 oz / 170 grams
- Salt: ½ tsp / 2 grams
- Black pepper: ¼ tsp / 1 gram
- Barbecue Sauce: 2 tbsp / 30 ml
- Onion rings: 3 large rings
- Cheddar cheese, sliced: 1 oz / 28 grams
- Hamburger bun: 1 bun

(For multiple servings, simply multiply the ingredient quantities by the number of people you are serving.)

NUTRITIONAL VALUES PER SERVING:
Calories: 780kcal | Carbohydrates: 48g | Proteins: 35g | Fats: 45g | Fiber: 2g | Sodium: 1250mg | Glucose: 14 g

PROCEDURE:
1. **Grill Preparation:** Preheat your Blackstone Griddle to a medium-high temperature.
2. **Forming and Cooking the Burger:** Shape the ground beef into a patty slightly larger than the bun. Season both sides with salt and pepper. Grill the patty for about 5 minutes on each side or until the desired doneness is reached.
3. **Adding the Barbecue Sauce:** During the last few minutes of cooking, brush the patty generously with barbecue sauce on both sides, allowing it to caramelize slightly.
4. **Adding the Cheese:** Place the slice of cheddar cheese on the patty during the last minute of cooking to allow it to melt.
5. **Cooking the Onion Rings:** While the burger cooks, place the onion rings on the griddle and cook until they are crispy and golden, about 2-3 minutes per side.
6. **Toasting the Bun:** Lightly toast the hamburger bun on the griddle for 1-2 minutes until golden and crispy.
7. **Assembly:** Spread a layer of barbecue sauce on the bottom bun. Place the cooked burger with melted cheese on top, add the crispy onion rings, and cover with the top bun.

TIPS FOR PERFECT COOKING:
- **Caramelizing the** Sauce: Apply the barbecue sauce towards the end of cooking to prevent it from burning while still allowing it to caramelize and infuse the patty with its flavor.
- **Melting the Cheese:** Cover the burger with a dome or a lid to melt the cheese uniformly, creating a gooey, delicious topping.
- **Crispy Onion Rings:** Ensure the onion rings are spaced out on the griddle to cook evenly and become perfectly crispy.

POSSIBLE VARIATIONS:
1. **Spicy Variant:** Add a spicy barbecue sauce or include a few slices of jalapeños under the cheese for a fiery kick.
2. **Smoky Variant:** Use smoked cheddar cheese and add a slice of smoked bacon for deeper, more complex flavors.
3. **Lighter Variant:** Opt for a leaner cut of beef, low-fat cheese, and bake the onion rings instead of frying them for a healthier version.

4. Mushroom Swiss Burger

PREP TIME: 20 minutes	COOKING TIME: 15 minutes	TOTAL TIME: 35 minutes	SERVINGS: For 1 person
DIFFICULTY: Easy	TEMPERATURE: Medium-high - About 375°F (190°C)	COOKING TYPE: Direct on the grill	SAUCE: Mayonnaise

INGREDIENTS:
- Ground beef (80/20 mix): 6 oz / 170 grams
- Salt: ½ tsp / 2 grams
- Black pepper: ¼ tsp / 1 gram
- Champignon mushrooms, sliced: ½ cup / about 50 grams
- Swiss cheese, sliced: 1 oz / 28 grams
- Hamburger bun: 1 bun
- Mayonnaise: 1 tbsp / 15 ml

(For multiple servings, simply multiply the ingredient quantities by the number of people you are serving.)

NUTRITIONAL VALUES PER SERVING:
Calories: 750kcal | Carbohydrates: 40g | Proteins: 39g | Fats: 47g | Fiber: 2g | Sodium: 820mg | Glucose: 5 g

PROCEDURE:
1. **Grill Preparation:** Preheat your Blackstone Griddle to a medium-high temperature.
2. **Sautéing the Mushrooms:** Place the sliced mushrooms on the griddle and sauté with a little oil or butter, seasoning lightly with salt and pepper. Cook until they are golden and tender, about 5-7 minutes. Set aside.
3. **Forming and Cooking the Burger:** Shape the ground beef into a patty slightly larger than the bun. Season both sides with salt and pepper. Grill the patty for about 5 minutes on each side or until the desired doneness is reached.
4. **Adding the Cheese:** Place the slice of Swiss cheese on the patty during the last minute of cooking to allow it to melt.
5. **Toasting the Bun:** Lightly toast the hamburger bun on the griddle for 1-2 minutes until golden and crispy.
6. **Assembly:** Spread mayonnaise on the bottom bun. Place the cooked burger with melted cheese on top, add the sautéed mushrooms, and cover with the top bun.

TIPS FOR PERFECT COOKING:
- **Mushroom Sauté:** Cook the mushrooms until they release their moisture and start to brown for the best flavor and texture.
- **Cheese Melting:** Use a dome or cover over the burger when melting the cheese for even heat distribution and a perfectly melted topping.
- **Patty Preparation:** Do not overwork the meat mixture to ensure a tender and juicy burger.

POSSIBLE VARIATIONS:
1. **Garlic Lover's Variant:** Sauté the mushrooms with garlic and a splash of white wine for an aromatic and flavorful twist.
2. **Deluxe Variant:** Add caramelized onions to the burger for added sweetness and depth of flavor.
3. **Lighter Variant:** Use a whole grain bun and low-fat Swiss cheese, and substitute the mayonnaise with a yogurt-based spread for a healthier option.

BEEF AND PORK BURGERS

5. Spicy Jalapeño Burger

PREP TIME: 20 minutes	**COOKING TIME:** 10 minutes	**TOTAL TIME:** 30 minutes		**SERVINGS:** For 1 person
DIFFICULTY: Easy	**TEMPERATURE:** Medium-high About 375°F (190°C)	**COOKING TYPE:** Direct on the grill		**SAUCE:** Ranch Sauce

INGREDIENTS:
- Ground beef (80/20 mix): 6 oz / 170 grams
- Chopped jalapeños: 1 tbsp / 15 grams
- Salt: ½ tsp / 2 grams
- Black pepper: ¼ tsp / 1 gram
- Pepper jack cheese, sliced: 1 oz / 28 grams
- Lettuce, leaf: 1 large leaf
- Ranch Sauce: 1 tbsp / 15 ml
- Hamburger bun: 1 bun

(For multiple servings, simply multiply the ingredient quantities by the number of people you are serving.)

NUTRITIONAL VALUES PER SERVING:
Calories: 730kcal | Carbohydrates: 38g | Proteins: 38g | Fats: 45g | Fiber: 2g | Sodium: 910mg | Glucose: 5 g

PROCEDURE:
1. **Grill Preparation:** Preheat your Blackstone Griddle to a medium-high temperature.
2. **Mixing the Patty:** In a bowl, combine the ground beef with chopped jalapeños, salt, and black pepper. Mix gently to distribute the ingredients evenly without overworking the meat.
3. **Forming and Cooking the Burger:** Shape the beef mixture into a patty slightly larger than the bun to allow for shrinkage. Place the patty on the griddle and cook for about 5 minutes on each side or until the desired doneness is reached.
4. **Adding the Cheese:** Place the slice of pepper jack cheese on the patty during the last minute of cooking to allow it to melt.
5. **Toasting the Bun:** Lightly toast the hamburger bun on the griddle for 1-2 minutes until golden and crispy.
6. **Assembly:** Spread ranch sauce on the bottom bun, place the lettuce leaf, then add the cooked burger with melted cheese on top, and cover with the top bun.

TIPS FOR PERFECT COOKING:
- **Jalapeño Distribution:** Ensure the jalapeños are finely chopped and evenly mixed throughout the patty for consistent heat in every bite.
- **Cheese Melting:** Cover the burger with a dome or a lid to melt the cheese evenly, creating a gooey, delicious topping that complements the spicy jalapeños.
- **Control the Spice:** Adjust the amount of jalapeños based on your heat preference. Add more if you like it hot or reduce it for a milder flavor.

POSSIBLE VARIATIONS:
1. **Extra Spicy Variant:** Add a splash of hot sauce to the ranch or include additional chopped jalapeños in the mix.
2. **Smoky Variant:** Include smoked paprika in the patty mix to introduce a deep, smoky flavor that pairs well with the heat of the jalapeños.
3. **Cooling Variant:** Add a slice of avocado or a spoonful of guacamole on top of the burger for a creamy

6. Pork and Apple Burger

PREP TIME: 20 minutes	**COOKING TIME:** 10 minutes	**TOTAL TIME:** 30 minutes		**SERVINGS:** For 1 person
DIFFICULTY: Easy	**TEMPERATURE:** Medium-high About 375°F (190°C)	**COOKING TYPE:** Direct on the grill		**SAUCE:** Dijon Mustard

INGREDIENTS:
- Ground pork: 6 oz / 170 grams
- Chopped apples (preferably a sweet variety like Fuji or Honeycrisp): ¼ cup / about 40 grams
- Chopped onion: 2 tbsp / 30 grams
- Salt: ½ tsp / 2 grams
- Black pepper: ¼ tsp / 1 gram
- Hamburger bun: 1 bun
- Dijon mustard: 1 tbsp / 15 ml

(For multiple servings, simply multiply the ingredient quantities by the number of people you are serving.)

NUTRITIONAL VALUES PER SERVING:
Calories: 590kcal | Carbohydrates: 39g | Proteins: 26g | Fats: 34g | Fiber: 2g | Sodium: 750mg | Glucose: 6 g

PROCEDURE:
1. **Grill Preparation:** Preheat your Blackstone Griddle to a medium-high temperature.
2. **Mixing the Patty:** In a bowl, combine the ground pork with chopped apples, chopped onion, salt, and black pepper. Mix gently to integrate the ingredients without overworking the meat to maintain tenderness.
3. **Forming and Cooking the Burger:** Shape the pork mixture into a patty slightly larger than the bun to compensate for shrinkage during cooking. Place the patty on the griddle and cook for about 5 minutes on each side or until fully cooked and the internal temperature reaches at least 160°F.
4. **Toasting the Bun:** Lightly toast the hamburger bun on the griddle for 1-2 minutes until golden and slightly crispy.
5. **Assembly:** Spread Dijon mustard on the bottom bun, place the cooked patty on top, and then cap with the top bun.

TIPS FOR PERFECT COOKING:
- **Choosing Apples:** Use apples that are crisp and sweet, which will not only add flavor but also moisture to the patty, keeping it juicy.
- **Patty Thickness:** Make sure the patty is evenly thick to ensure uniform cooking. A slight indentation in the middle can prevent it from puffing up.
- **Final Cooking** Temperature: Pork needs to be well-cooked. Always check that the internal temperature of the patty reaches at least 160°F for safety.

POSSIBLE VARIATIONS:
1. **Herb Enhanced Variant:** Mix fresh herbs such as sage or thyme into the patty for an aromatic flavor that complements the apple.
2. **Spicy Variant:** Add a pinch of cayenne pepper or some finely chopped jalapeños to the mix for a spicy twist.
3. **Healthier Variant:** Serve the burger on a whole-grain bun and add a slice of low-fat cheese, such as mozzarella, for added protein without too much extra fat.

BEEF AND PORK BURGERS

7. Hawaiian Pork Burger

PREP TIME: 20 minutes
COOKING TIME: 15 minutes
TOTAL TIME: 35 minutes
SERVINGS: For 1 person
DIFFICULTY: Easy
TEMPERATURE: Medium-high; About 375°F (190°C)
COOKING TYPE: Direct on the grill
SAUCE: Teriyaki Sauce

INGREDIENTS:
- Ground pork: 6 oz / 170g
- Pineapple, sliced: 1 large ring
- Red onion, sliced: 2 rings
- Teriyaki Sauce: 2 tbsp / 30 ml
- Lettuce, leaf: 1 large leaf
- Hamburger bun: 1 bun

(For multiple servings, simply multiply the ingredient quantities by the number of people you are serving.)

NUTRITIONAL VALUES PER SERVING:
Calories: 650kcal | **Carbohydrates:** 42g | **Proteins:** 28g | **Fats:** 36g | **Fiber:** 3g | **Sodium:** 870mg | **Glucose:** 8 g

PROCEDURE:
1. **Grill Preparation:** Preheat your Blackstone Griddle to a medium-high temperature.
2. **Grilling the Pineapple:** Place the pineapple ring on the griddle and cook for about 2-3 minutes per side until it is caramelized and has grill marks. Set aside.
3. **Cooking the Onions:** Grill the red onion rings until they are slightly charred and soft, about 3-4 minutes per side. Set aside.
4. **Mixing the Patty:** In a bowl, season the ground pork lightly with salt and pepper if desired, though the teriyaki sauce will also add seasoning.
5. **Forming and Cooking the Burger:** Shape the pork into a patty slightly larger than the bun. Grill the patty for about 5-6 minutes on each side or until fully cooked and the internal temperature reaches 160°F.
6. **Glazing with Teriyaki:** In the last few minutes of cooking, brush the patty generously with teriyaki sauce, allowing it to glaze over the heat.
7. **Toasting the Bun:** Lightly toast the hamburger bun on the griddle for 1-2 minutes until crispy.
8. **Assembly:** Place a lettuce leaf on the bottom bun, followed by the teriyaki-glazed patty, grilled pineapple ring, and grilled onion. Drizzle a little more teriyaki sauce over the top, then cover with the bun.

TIPS FOR PERFECT COOKING:
- **Monitor the Glaze:** Keep an eye on the burger as you brush with teriyaki sauce, as the sugar content can cause it to burn if left unattended.
- **Achieving Perfect Grill Marks:** Ensure your griddle is hot before adding the pineapple and onions to achieve clear, appetizing grill marks.
- **Patty Thickness:** Flatten the patty a bit more than usual as pork tends to shrink more upon cooking.

POSSIBLE VARIATIONS:
1. **Spicy Variant:** Add a splash of sriracha or chili flakes to the teriyaki sauce for a spicy kick.
2. **Deluxe Variant:** Include a slice of smoked ham under the pineapple for an extra layer of flavor, enhancing the Hawaiian theme.
3. **Healthier Variant:** Opt for a whole grain bun and a low-sodium teriyaki sauce to reduce calories and enhance dietary fiber intake.

8. BBQ Pulled Pork Burger

PREP TIME: 20 minutes
COOKING TIME: 10 minutes
TOTAL TIME: 30 minutes
SERVINGS: For 1 person
DIFFICULTY: Easy
TEMPERATURE: Medium; About 350°F (177°C)
COOKING TYPE: Direct on the grill
SAUCE: Your favorite barbecue sauce

INGREDIENTS:
- Shredded pork (pre-cooked and pre-shredded): 6 oz / 170 grams
- Barbecue Sauce: ¼ cup / 60 ml
- Coleslaw (pre-made or homemade):
- Cabbage, finely shredded: ½ cup / 50 grams
- Carrot, finely shredded: 2 tbsp / 15 grams
- Coleslaw dressing: 2 tbsp / 30 ml
- Hamburger bun: 1 bun

NUTRITIONAL VALUES PER SERVING:
Calories: 720kcal | **Carbohydrates:** 58g | **Proteins:** 28g | **Fats:** 38g | **Fiber:** 3g | **Sodium:** 950mg | **Glucose:** 14 g

PROCEDURE:
1. **Grill Preparation:** Preheat your Blackstone Griddle to medium temperature.
2. **Warming the Pork:** Place the shredded pork on the griddle and gently spread it out for even heating. Pour the barbecue sauce over the pork, mixing well to ensure every piece is coated. Heat the mixture until it is thoroughly warm, about 5-7 minutes, stirring occasionally.
3. **Preparing the Coleslaw:** In a mixing bowl, combine the shredded cabbage, carrot, and coleslaw dressing. Toss well until the vegetables are evenly coated with the dressing.
4. **Toasting the Bun:** Lightly toast the hamburger bun on the griddle for 1-2 minutes until it's golden and slightly crispy.
5. **Assembly:** Spoon the warm BBQ pulled pork onto the bottom half of the bun. Top with a generous helping of coleslaw. Place the top half of the bun on top.

TIPS FOR PERFECT COOKING:
- **Keep the Pork Moist:** When heating the pulled pork on the griddle, ensure it does not dry out. Add a little water or more barbecue sauce if necessary to keep it moist and flavorful.
- **Crisp Coleslaw:** Prepare the coleslaw just before serving to maintain its crunchiness and prevent it from becoming soggy.
- **Balancing Flavors:** Adjust the amount of barbecue sauce according to your taste. Some prefer a more subtly flavored pork, while others may enjoy a richer, saucier finish.

POSSIBLE VARIATIONS:
- **Spicy Variant:** For those who like it hot, add chopped jalapeños to the pork while heating or mix a spicy barbecue sauce.
- **Smoky Variant:** Choose a smoky barbecue sauce or add a pinch of smoked paprika to the pork mixture for an extra smoky flavor.
- **Lighter Variant:** To reduce the overall calorie count, use a low-carbohydrate bun and a light dressing for the coleslaw.

9. Italian Pork Burger

PREP TIME:	COOKING TIME:	TOTAL TIME:	SERVINGS:
15 minutes	10 minutes	25 minutes	For 1 person
DIFFICULTY: Easy	TEMPERATURE: Medium-high 375-400°F (190-205°C)	COOKING TYPE: Direct on the grill	SAUCE: Pesto

INGREDIENTS:
- Ground pork: 6 oz / 170 grams
- Garlic powder: ½ tsp / 2.5 ml / 2 grams
- Chopped parsley: 1 tbsp / 15 ml / 3 grams
- Provolone cheese, sliced: 1 oz / 28 grams
- Tomato, sliced: 2 slices
- Hamburger bun: 1 bun
- Pesto: 1 tbsp / 15 ml

(For multiple servings, simply multiply the ingredient quantities by the number of people you are serving.)

NUTRITIONAL VALUES PER SERVING:
Calories: 780kcal | Carbohydrates: 38g | Proteins: 42g | Fats: 48g | Fiber: 2g | Sodium: 860mg | Glucose: 4 g

PROCEDURE:
1. **Grill Preparation:** Preheat the grill to medium-high temperature.
2. **Preparing the Patty:** In a bowl, mix the ground pork with garlic powder and chopped parsley. Form this mixture into a patty that is slightly wider than the bun to compensate for shrinkage during cooking.
3. **Cooking the Burger:** Place the burger on the grill and cook for about 5 minutes on each side or until the pork is thoroughly cooked and reaches an internal temperature of at least 160°F.
4. **Adding the Cheese:** In the last minute of cooking, place the slice of provolone cheese on the burger to allow it to melt.
5. **Toasting the Bun:** Lightly toast the hamburger bun on the grill for 1-2 minutes.
6. **Assembly:** Spread pesto on the bottom bun, place a slice of tomato, then add the cooked burger with melted cheese, and top with another slice of tomato. Cover with the top bun.

TIPS FOR PERFECT COOKING:
- **Do Not Overmix:** Avoid overmixing the pork mixture to ensure the patty remains tender and juicy.
- **Monitor Doneness:** Always use a meat thermometer to check that the pork has reached the safe internal temperature of 160°F to ensure it is fully cooked.
- **Enhance with Pesto:** For added flavor, consider brushing some additional pesto on the burger just before serving.

POSSIBLE VARIATIONS:
- **Less Garlic Variant:** For a milder flavor, reduce the garlic powder by half.
- **Tastier Variant:** Add a few basil leaves under the cheese for a fresh, herby flavor boost.
- **Lighter Variant:** Opt for a low-fat provolone cheese and use a whole grain bun to decrease the overall calorie and fat content.

10. Spicy Chorizo Burger

PREP TIME:	COOKING TIME:	TOTAL TIME:	SERVINGS:
20 minutes	10 minutes	30 minutes	For 1 person
DIFFICULTY: Medium	TEMPERATURE: Medium-high 375-400°F (190-205°C)	COOKING TYPE: Direct on the grill	SAUCE: Guacamole

INGREDIENTS:
- Ground chorizo: 3 oz / 85 grams
- Ground pork: 3 oz / 85 grams
- Bell peppers (finely diced, mixed colors): 2 tbsp / 30 grams
- Onion (finely diced): 1 tbsp / 15 grams
- Cheddar cheese, sliced: 1 oz / 28 grams
- Hamburger bun: 1 bun
- Guacamole: 2 tbsp / 30 ml

(For multiple servings, simply multiply the ingredient quantities by the number of people you are serving.)

NUTRITIONAL VALUES PER SERVING:
Calories: 790kcal | Carbohydrates: 38g | Proteins: 42g | Fats: 50g | Fiber: 3g | Sodium: 1200mg | Glucose: 3 g

PROCEDURE:
1. **Grill Preparation:** Preheat the grill to medium-high temperature.
2. **Preparing the Patty:** In a bowl, mix the ground chorizo and ground pork with diced bell peppers and onions. Form this mixture into a patty that is slightly wider than the bun to accommodate for shrinkage during cooking.
3. **Cooking the Burger:** Place the burger on the grill and cook for about 5 minutes on each side or until the meats are thoroughly cooked and reach an internal temperature of at least 160°F.
4. **Adding the Cheese:** In the last minute of cooking, place the slice of cheddar cheese on the burger to allow it to melt.
5. **Toasting the Bun:** Lightly toast the hamburger bun on the grill for 1-2 minutes until it's golden and slightly crispy.
6. **Assembly:** Spread guacamole on the bottom bun, add the cooked burger with melted cheese, and then cover with the top bun.

TIPS FOR PERFECT COOKING:
- **Even Mixing:** Ensure that the chorizo, pork, bell peppers, and onions are evenly mixed to distribute flavors throughout the patty.
- **Checking Doneness:** Use a meat thermometer to verify that the patty has reached the safe internal temperature of 160°F to ensure thorough cooking.
- **Balancing Flavors:** The spiciness of chorizo can be intense, so adjust the amount of guacamole to help balance the heat according to your preference.

POSSIBLE VARIATIONS:
- **Extra Spicy Variant:** For an additional heat boost, add chopped jalapeños to the patty mix or a spicy cheese like pepper jack instead of cheddar.
- **Smokey Variant:** Mix a bit of smoked paprika into the patty for a deeper, smoky flavor.
- **Cooler Variant:** Increase the amount of guacamole or add a layer of sour cream to the burger for more cooling elements to counteract the spice.

PORK BURGERS RECIPES

11. Salmon Burger

PREP TIME: 20 minutes	**COOKING TIME:** 8 minutes	**TOTAL TIME:** 28 minutes
SERVINGS: For 1 person	**DIFFICULTY:** Easy	**TEMPERATURE:** Medium: 350-375°F (177-190°C)
COOKING TYPE: Direct on the grill	**SAUCE:** Lemon Mayonnaise	

INGREDIENTS:
- **Ground salmon:** 6 oz / 170 grams
- **Dill, finely chopped:** 1 tbsp / 3 grams
- **Lemon juice:** 1 tbsp / 15 ml
- **Chopped onion:** 2 tbsp / 30 grams
- **Hamburger bun:** 1 bun
- **Lemon mayonnaise:** 2 tbsp / 30 ml

NUTRITIONAL VALUES PER SERVING:
Calories: 650kcal | Carbohydrates: 39g | Proteins: 38g | Fats: 36g | Fiber: 2g | Sodium: 580mg | Glucose: 5 g

PROCEDURE:
1. **Grill Preparation:** Preheat the grill to medium temperature.
2. **Preparing the Patty:** In a mixing bowl, combine ground salmon, dill, lemon juice, and chopped onion. Mix gently to combine without overworking the mixture, to keep the patty tender.
3. **Forming and Cooking the Burger:** Shape the mixture into a patty slightly larger than the bun. Oil the grill lightly and place the patty on the grill. Cook for about 4 minutes on each side or until the patty is firm and fully cooked.
4. **Toasting the Bun:** Lightly toast the hamburger bun on the grill for 1-2 minutes until it's lightly browned and crispy.
5. **Assembly:** Spread lemon mayonnaise on the bottom bun, place the cooked salmon patty on top, and cover with the top bun.

TIPS FOR PERFECT COOKING:
- **Patty Consistency:** Salmon can be quite moist; if the patty mixture feels too wet, you can add a small amount of breadcrumbs to help bind it.
- **Don't Overcook:** Salmon dries out quickly; keep an eye on the cooking time to ensure it remains moist and tender.
- **Enhance the Flavor:** Brush a little extra lemon juice on the patty during cooking for an added zesty flavor.

POSSIBLE VARIATIONS:
- **Herb Enhanced Variant:** Mix additional herbs such as parsley or chives into the salmon mixture for a fresh, herby flavor.
- **Spicy Variant:** Add a dash of hot sauce or a sprinkle of chili flakes to the salmon mixture for a spicy twist.
- **Healthier Variant:** Substitute the regular bun with a whole-grain bun and use a low-fat yogurt-based lemon dressing instead of mayonnaise for a lighter meal.

12. Tuna Burger

PREP TIME: 20 minutes	**COOKING TIME:** 6 minutes	**TOTAL TIME:** 26 minutes
SERVINGS: For 1 person	**DIFFICULTY:** Easy	**TEMPERATURE:** Medium-high: 375-400°F (190-205°C)
COOKING TYPE: Direct on the grill	**SAUCE:** Wasabi Mayonnaise	

INGREDIENTS:
- **Fresh ground tuna:** 6 oz / 170 grams
- **Soy Sauce:** 1 tbsp / 15 ml
- **Chopped ginger:** 1 tsp / 5 grams
- **Green onion, finely chopped:** 1 tbsp / 15 grams
- **Sesame seeds:** 1 tsp / 5 grams
- **Hamburger bun:** 1 bun
- **Wasabi mayonnaise:** 2 tbsp / 30 ml

NUTRITIONAL VALUES PER SERVING:
Calories: 640kcal | Carbohydrates: 38g | Proteins: 40g | Fats: 34g | Fiber: 2g | Sodium: 860mg | Glucose: 4 g

PROCEDURE:
1. **Grill Preparation:** Preheat the grill to medium-high temperature.
2. **Preparing the Patty:** In a mixing bowl, combine the ground tuna, soy sauce, chopped ginger, green onion, and sesame seeds. Mix gently to ensure even distribution of flavors without overworking the mixture.
3. **Forming and Cooking the Burger:** Form the tuna mixture into a patty slightly larger than the bun. Lightly oil the grill and place the patty on it. Cook for about 3 minutes on each side, or until the patty is firm and fully cooked, with a slightly pink center if preferred.
4. **Toasting the Bun:** Lightly toast the hamburger bun on the grill for 1-2 minutes until it's golden and crispy.
5. **Assembly:** Spread wasabi mayonnaise on the bottom bun, add the cooked tuna patty, and cover with the top bun.

TIPS FOR PERFECT COOKING:
- **Avoid Overcooking:** Tuna can become dry if overcooked. Keep an eye on the patty and remove it from the heat as soon as it's cooked through but still moist.
- **Patty Formation:** Press the center of the patty down slightly with your thumb before grilling to prevent it from puffing up in the middle.
- **Flavor Enhancement:** Brush the patty with a little extra soy sauce while cooking for added depth of flavor.

POSSIBLE VARIATIONS:
- **Extra Spicy Variant:** Mix additional wasabi into the mayonnaise for more heat.
- **Sesame Crust Variant:** Press additional sesame seeds onto the surface of the patty before grilling for a crunchy sesame crust.
- **Lighter Variant:** Serve on a lettuce wrap instead of a bun and use a low-fat mayonnaise alternative for the wasabi mayo.

FISH BURGERS RECIPES

13. Cod Burger Recipe

PREP TIME: 15 minutes	**COOKING TIME:** 8 minutes	**TOTAL TIME:** 23 minutes
SERVINGS: For 1 person	**DIFFICULTY:** Easy	**TEMPERATURE:** Medium: 350-375°F (177-190°C)
COOKING TYPE: Direct on the grill	**SAUCE:** Tartar Sauce	

INGREDIENTS:
- **Ground cod:** 6 oz / 170 grams
- **Parsley, finely chopped:** 1 tbsp / 3 grams
- **Lemon juice:** 1 tbsp / 15 ml
- **Garlic powder:** ½ tsp / 2.5 ml / 2 grams
- **Hamburger bun:** 1 bun
- **Tartar Sauce:** 2 tbsp / 30 ml

NUTRITIONAL VALUES PER SERVING:
Calories: 520kcal | Carbohydrates: 39g | Proteins: 35g | Fats: 20g | Fiber: 2g | Sodium: 700mg | Glucose: 3g

PROCEDURE:
1. **Grill Preparation:** Preheat the grill to medium temperature.
2. **Preparing the Patty:** In a bowl, mix the ground cod with parsley, lemon juice, and garlic powder. Gently form the mixture into a patty slightly larger than the bun to allow for slight shrinkage while cooking.
3. **Cooking the Burger:** Place the patty on a lightly oiled grill. Cook for about 4 minutes on each side or until the patty is firm and fully cooked through.
4. **Toasting the Bun:** Lightly toast the hamburger bun on the grill for 1-2 minutes until it's golden and slightly crispy.
5. **Assembly:** Spread tartar sauce on both halves of the bun, place the cooked cod patty on the bottom bun, and cover with the top bun.

TIPS FOR PERFECT COOKING:
- **Handling the Patty:** Cod is more delicate than other meats; handle the patty gently during preparation and turning to maintain its shape.
- **Don't Overcook:** Keep a close eye on the burger as fish cooks quickly and can dry out if overcooked.
- **Lemon for Freshness:** Squeeze a little extra lemon juice over the burger just before serving to enhance the fresh, zesty flavor.

POSSIBLE VARIATIONS:
- **Herb Enhancement:** Add finely chopped dill or chives to the patty mixture for an additional herby touch.
- **Spicy Kick:** Mix a small amount of finely chopped capers or a dash of hot sauce into the tartar sauce for an extra zing.
- **Healthier Option:** Use a whole wheat bun and a low-fat homemade tartar sauce to reduce calories and increase dietary fiber.

14. Shrimp Burger Recipe

PREP TIME: 15 minutes	**COOKING TIME:** 6 minutes	**TOTAL TIME:** 21 minutes
SERVINGS: For 1 person	**DIFFICULTY:** Easy	**TEMPERATURE:** Medium-high: 375-400°F (190-205°C)
COOKING TYPE: Direct on the grill	**SAUCE:** Cocktail Sauce	

INGREDIENTS:
- **Chopped shrimp:** 6 oz / 170 grams
- **Garlic, minced:** 1 tsp / 5 grams
- **Cayenne pepper:** ¼ tsp / 1.25 ml
- **Hamburger bun:** 1 bun
- **Cocktail Sauce:** 2 tbsp / 30 ml

NUTRITIONAL VALUES PER SERVING:
Calories: 490kcal | Carbohydrates: 38g | Proteins: 30g | Fats: 20g | Fiber: 2g | Sodium: 880mg | Glucose: 4 g

PROCEDURE:
1. **Grill Preparation:** Preheat the grill to medium-high temperature.
2. **Preparing the Patty:** In a bowl, combine the chopped shrimp, minced garlic, and cayenne pepper. Mix gently until well blended. Form the mixture into a patty slightly larger than the bun to compensate for any shrinkage during cooking.
3. **Cooking the Burger:** Place the patty on a lightly oiled grill. Cook for about 3 minutes on each side, or until the shrimp turn pink and are cooked through.
4. **Toasting the Bun:** Lightly toast the hamburger bun on the grill for 1-2 minutes until it's golden and crispy.
5. **Assembly:** Spread cocktail sauce on the bottom bun, add the cooked shrimp patty, and top with the other half of the bun.

TIPS FOR PERFECT COOKING:
- **Do Not Overmix:** When combining the shrimp with seasonings, mix just enough to incorporate the flavors to keep the texture of the shrimp intact.
- **Watch the Cooking Time:** Shrimp cook quickly and can become tough if overcooked. Remove from heat as soon as they're pink and firm.
- **Extra Flavor:** For an additional flavor boost, add a squeeze of fresh lemon juice to the shrimp mixture before forming the patty.

POSSIBLE VARIATIONS:
- **Herb Infusion:** Mix chopped fresh herbs like parsley or cilantro into the shrimp mixture for a fresh, herby flavor.
- **Spicy Upgrade:** Enhance the cayenne pepper or add chopped jalapeños to the patty for a spicier kick.
- **Lighter Touch:** For a healthier option, serve the burger on a lettuce wrap instead of a bun and use a low-calorie cocktail sauce.

FISH BURGERS RECIPES

15. Black Bean Veggie Burger

PREP TIME: 20 minutes	**COOKING TIME:** 8 minutes	**TOTAL TIME:** 28 minutes
SERVINGS: For 1 person	**DIFFICULTY:** Easy	**TEMPERATURE:** Medium: 350-375°F (177-190°C)
COOKING TYPE: Direct on the grill	**SAUCE:** Guacamole	

INGREDIENTS:
- Black beans, rinsed and drained: 1 cup / 170 grams
- Red bell pepper, finely chopped: ¼ cup / 40 grams
- Onion, finely chopped: ¼ cup / 40 grams
- Breadcrumbs: ¼ cup / 30 grams
- Cumin: ½ tsp / 2.5 ml
- Hamburger bun: 1 bun
- Guacamole: 2 tbsp / 30 ml

NUTRITIONAL VALUES PER SERVING:
Calories: 540kcal | Carbohydrates: 72g | Proteins: 19g | Fats: 20g | Fiber: 15g | Sodium: 480mg | Glucose: 3 g

PROCEDURE:
1. **Grill Preparation:** Preheat the grill to medium temperature.
2. **Forming the Patty:** In a bowl, mash the black beans until mostly smooth but still slightly chunky for texture. Stir in the red bell pepper, onion, breadcrumbs, and cumin until well combined. Form the mixture into a patty slightly larger than the bun.
3. **Cooking the Burger:** Lightly oil the grill and place the patty on it. Cook for about 4 minutes on each side, or until the patty is golden and heated through.
4. **Toasting the Bun:** Lightly toast the hamburger bun on the grill for 1-2 minutes until it's golden and slightly crispy.
5. **Assembly:** Spread guacamole on the bottom bun, add the cooked veggie patty, and then top with the other half of the bun.

TIPS FOR PERFECT COOKING:
- **Patty Consistency:** If the burger mixture feels too wet and doesn't hold together, add a bit more breadcrumbs to help bind it.
- **Don't Overflip:** Let the patty cook undisturbed on each side to develop a nice crust and prevent it from falling apart.
- **Enhance Flavors:** Adjust the level of cumin according to your taste or add other spices like smoked paprika or chili powder for extra flavor.

POSSIBLE VARIATIONS:
- **Spicy Variant:** Add finely chopped jalapeños or a dash of chili powder to the bean mixture for a spicy version.
- **Herb Freshness:** Mix in fresh cilantro or parsley for a bright herbal note.
- **Cheesy Delight:** Top the burger with a slice of your favorite vegan cheese during the last minute of grilling for a melty, cheesy experience.

16. Portobello Mushroom Burger

PREP TIME: 15 minutes	**COOKING TIME:** 10 minutes	**TOTAL TIME:** 25 minutes
SERVINGS: For 1 person	**DIFFICULTY:** Easy	**TEMPERATURE:** Medium: 350-375°F (177-190°C)
COOKING TYPE: Direct on the grill	**SAUCE:** Aioli	

INGREDIENTS:
- Large Portobello mushroom cap, stem removed: 1
- Caramelized onions: ¼ cup / 40 grams
- Provolone cheese, sliced: 1 oz / 28 grams
- Hamburger bun: 1 bun
- Aioli Sauce: 2 tbsp / 30 ml

NUTRITIONAL VALUES PER SERVING:
Calories: 460kcal | Carbohydrates: 40g | Proteins: 15g | Fats: 25g | Fiber: 3g | Sodium: 620mg | Glucose: 4 g

PROCEDURE:
1. **Grill Preparation:** Preheat the grill to medium temperature.
2. **Preparing the Mushroom:** Clean the Portobello mushroom by gently wiping it with a damp cloth. Brush the mushroom cap lightly with oil, and season with salt and pepper if desired.
3. **Grilling the Mushroom:** Place the mushroom cap on the grill, gill side down first. Grill for about 5 minutes on each side or until the mushroom is tender and juicy.
4. **Adding the Cheese:** In the last minute of cooking, place the slice of provolone cheese on top of the mushroom to allow it to melt.
5. **Toasting the Bun:** Lightly toast the hamburger bun on the grill for 1-2 minutes until it's golden and crispy.
6. **Assembly:** Spread aioli sauce on the bottom bun, place the grilled mushroom with melted cheese, top with caramelized onions, and cover with the top bun.

TIPS FOR PERFECT COOKING:
- **Mushroom Preparation:** Ensure the mushroom is cleaned properly but not washed under water as it absorbs moisture.
- **Enhance Flavors:** For added depth, marinate the mushroom in a mixture of balsamic vinegar, olive oil, garlic, and herbs before grilling.
- **Cheese Selection:** While provolone is recommended, feel free to experiment with other cheeses like Swiss or smoked gouda for different flavor profiles.

POSSIBLE VARIATIONS:
- **Garlic Lovers' Variant:** Enhance the aioli with extra minced garlic or roasted garlic for a more pronounced garlic flavor.
- **Spicy Kick:** Add a few slices of jalapeño to the burger or mix some hot sauce into the aioli for a spicy version.
- **Lighter Touch:** Opt for a low-fat cheese and a whole-grain bun to reduce the calorie and fat content.

VEGETARIAN BURGERS RECIPES

17. Chickpea Veggie Burger

| PREP TIME: 20 minutes | COOKING TIME: 10 minutes | TOTAL TIME: 30 minutes | SERVINGS: For 1 person |
| DIFFICULTY: Easy | TEMPERATURE: Medium: 350-375°F (177-190°C) | COOKING TYPE: Direct on the grill | SAUCE: Tzatziki |

INGREDIENTS:
- Chickpeas, rinsed and drained: 1 cup / 240 grams
- Cilantro, finely chopped: 2 tbsp / 8 grams
- Cumin: 1 tsp / 5 ml
- Garlic, minced: 1 tsp / 5 grams
- Hamburger bun: 1 bun
- Tzatziki: 2 tbsp / 30 ml

NUTRITIONAL VALUES PER SERVING:
Calories: 480kcal | **Carbohydrates:** 65g | **Proteins:** 18g | **Fats:** 15g | **Fiber:** 12g | **Sodium:** 620mg | **Glucose:** 4 g

PROCEDURE:
1. **Grill Preparation:** Preheat the grill to medium temperature.
2. **Preparing the Patty:** In a food processor, combine chickpeas, cilantro, cumin, and garlic. Pulse until the mixture is coarsely ground and holds together when pinched. If the mixture is too dry, add a little water or olive oil to help it bind.
3. **Forming and Cooking the Burger:** Form the chickpea mixture into a patty slightly larger than the bun. Lightly oil the grill and place the patty on it. Cook for about 5 minutes on each side, or until the patty is golden and firm.
4. **Toasting the Bun:** Lightly toast the hamburger bun on the grill for 1-2 minutes until it's golden and slightly crispy.
5. **Assembly:** Spread tzatziki on the bottom bun, add the cooked chickpea patty, and then cover with the top bun.

TIPS FOR PERFECT COOKING:
- **Avoid Overprocessing:** Pulse the chickpea mixture just until it's combined but still has some texture. Overprocessing can make the patty mushy.
- **Ensure Patty Integrity:** Chill the patty in the refrigerator for about 10-15 minutes before grilling if it feels too soft; this helps it hold together better during cooking.
- **Flavor Boost:** For extra flavor, add a pinch of smoked paprika or a squeeze of lemon juice to the chickpea mixture before forming the patty.

POSSIBLE VARIATIONS:
- **Herb Enhanced Variant:** Mix in additional fresh herbs such as parsley or mint to the chickpea mixture for a fresher taste.
- **Spicy Kick:** Incorporate a tbsp of finely chopped jalapeños or a dash of chili flakes into the patty mixture for a spicy version.
- **Creamier Tzatziki:** Enhance the tzatziki by adding chopped cucumber or a drizzle of olive oil for extra richness and flavor.

18. Quinoa Veggie Burger

| PREP TIME: 20 minutes | COOKING TIME: 10 minutes | TOTAL TIME: 30 minutes | SERVINGS: For 1 person |
| DIFFICULTY: Easy | TEMPERATURE: Medium: 350-375°F (177-190°C) | COOKING TYPE: Direct on the grill | SAUCE: Tomato Sauce |

INGREDIENTS:
- Cooked quinoa: 1/2 cup / 90 grams
- Spinach, finely chopped: 1/4 cup / 30 grams
- Feta cheese, crumbled: 1 oz / 28 grams
- Egg, beaten: 1 large
- Hamburger bun: 1 bun
- Tomato Sauce: 2 tbsp / 30 ml

NUTRITIONAL VALUES PER SERVING:
Calories: 450kcal | **Carbohydrates:** 55g | **Proteins:** 20g | **Fats:** 18g | **Fiber:** 6g | **Sodium:** 710mg | **Glucose:** 4 g

PROCEDURE:
1. **Grill Preparation:** Preheat the grill to medium temperature.
2. **Preparing the Patty:** In a mixing bowl, combine the cooked quinoa, chopped spinach, crumbled feta, and beaten egg. Mix well until the ingredients are thoroughly combined and the mixture can be formed into patties.
3. **Forming and Cooking the Burger:** Shape the mixture into a patty slightly larger than the bun. If the mixture is too moist, you can add a little more cooked quinoa or some breadcrumbs to help it hold together. Lightly oil the grill and place the patty on it. Cook for about 5 minutes on each side, or until the patty is golden and firm.
4. **Toasting the Bun:** Lightly toast the hamburger bun on the grill for 1-2 minutes until it's golden and slightly crispy.
5. **Assembly:** Spread tomato sauce on the bottom bun, add the cooked quinoa patty, and then cover with the top bun.

TIPS FOR PERFECT COOKING:
- **Consistency is Key:** If the burger mixture feels too wet, adding breadcrumbs or more quinoa will help absorb excess moisture and keep the patty together during cooking.
- **Keep It Gentle:** When flipping the burger, be gentle to prevent the patty from breaking apart. Using a wide spatula can help.
- **Flavorful Touch:** Consider sautéing the spinach with a little garlic before adding it to the burger mix for an extra flavor boost.

POSSIBLE VARIATIONS:
- **Vegan Variant:** Replace the feta cheese with vegan cheese and use a flaxseed meal mixed with water in place of the egg.
- **Spicy Version:** Add some finely diced jalapeño or a sprinkle of chili flakes to the burger mix for a bit of heat.
- **Extra Creamy:** Add a dollop of yogurt or sour cream on top of the patty under the tomato sauce for a creamy contrast.

19. Lentil Veggie Burger

| PREP TIME: 25 minutes | COOKING TIME: 10 minutes | TOTAL TIME: 35 minutes | SERVINGS: For 1 person |
| DIFFICULTY: Easy | TEMPERATURE: Medium 350-375°F (177-190°C) | COOKING TYPE: Direct on the grill | SAUCE: Spiced Mayonnaise |

INGREDIENTS:
- **Cooked lentils:** 1 cup / 200 grams
- **Carrots, grated:** 1/4 cup / 30 grams
- **Onion, finely chopped:** 1/4 cup / 40 grams
- **Garlic, minced:** 1 tsp / 5 grams
- **Oats, ground into flour:** 1/4 cup / 20 grams
- **Hamburger bun:** 1 bun
- **Spiced mayonnaise:** 2 tbsp / 30 ml

NUTRITIONAL VALUES PER SERVING:
Calories: 510kcal | Carbohydrates: 60g | Proteins: 21g | Fats: 20g | Fiber: 15g | Sodium: 620mg | Glucose: 5 g

PROCEDURE:
1. **Grill Preparation:** Preheat the grill to medium temperature.
2. **Preparing the Patty:** In a large bowl, mash the cooked lentils with a fork or potato masher until partially mashed for texture. Mix in the grated carrots, chopped onion, minced garlic, and ground oats until the mixture is well combined and holds together. If the mixture is too moist, add a little more ground oats.
3. **Forming and Cooking the Burger:** Shape the mixture into a patty slightly larger than the bun to compensate for shrinkage during cooking. Lightly oil the grill and place the patty on it. Cook for about 5 minutes on each side or until the patty is firm and has a golden crust.
4. **Toasting the Bun:** Lightly toast the hamburger bun on the grill for 1-2 minutes until it's golden and crispy.
5. **Assembly:** Spread spiced mayonnaise on the bottom bun, place the cooked lentil patty on top, and then cover with the top bun.

TIPS FOR PERFECT COOKING:
- **Binding the Patty:** Ground oats are great for binding the ingredients, but breadcrumbs can also be used if the mixture feels too loose.
- **Patty Formation:** Chill the patty in the refrigerator for 10-15 minutes before grilling to help it hold its shape better on the grill.
- **Flavor Enhancement:** For an extra flavor kick, add a pinch of cumin or smoked paprika to the lentil mixture before forming the patties.

POSSIBLE VARIATIONS:
- **Extra Spicy Variant:** Mix a little sriracha or hot sauce into the mayonnaise for an additional kick.
- **Herb Freshness:** Incorporate chopped fresh herbs like parsley or cilantro into the lentil mix for a refreshing herbal note.
- **Creamy Addition:** Top the burger with a slice of avocado along with the spiced mayonnaise for creamy richness and added nutrients.

20. Chili and Crispy Onion Hot Dog

| PREP TIME: 15 minutes | COOKING TIME: 10 minutes | TOTAL TIME: 25 minutes | SERVINGS: For 1 person |
| DIFFICULTY: Easy | TEMPERATURE: Medium 350-375°F (177-190°C) | COOKING TYPE: Direct on the grill | NOT EXPECTED |

INGREDIENTS:
- **Chili con carne:** 1/2 cup / 120 grams
- **White onions, thinly sliced:** 1/4 cup / 30 grams
- **Olive oil:** 1 tbsp / 15 ml
- **Hot dog bun:** 1 bun

NUTRITIONAL VALUES PER SERVING:
Calories: 410kcal | Carbohydrates: 45g | Proteins: 15g | Fats: 20g | Fiber: 5g | Sodium: 790mg | Glucose: 6 g

PROCEDURE:
1. **Grill Preparation:** Preheat the grill to medium temperature.
2. **Preparing the Onions:** In a small skillet or directly on the grill, heat the olive oil. Add the thinly sliced onions and cook, stirring frequently, until they are golden and crispy. This should take about 5-7 minutes.
3. **Warming the Chili:** Place the chili con carne in a saucepan on the grill or in a skillet. Stir occasionally and heat until it's hot and bubbly, about 5 minutes.
4. **Toasting the Bun:** Lightly toast the hot dog bun on the grill for 1-2 minutes until it's warm and slightly crispy.
5. **Assembly:** Place your hot dog in the toasted bun. Top with the hot chili con carne and sprinkle the crispy onions over the chili.

TIPS FOR PERFECT COOKING:
- **Achieving Crispy Onions:** Make sure the onions are sliced thinly for the best texture and to ensure they crisp up nicely on the grill.
- **Monitor the Chili:** Keep the chili stirring on a gentle heat to avoid burning while it warms up.
- **Enhance Your Dish:** For a smokier flavor, consider adding a dash of smoked paprika to the chili as it warms.

POSSIBLE VARIATIONS:
- **Cheesy Delight:** Add a sprinkle of shredded cheddar cheese over the chili before topping with onions for a cheesy version.
- **Spicy Kick:** Include slices of jalapeño in the onion mix while cooking to give an extra spicy flavor to the crispy onions.
- **Healthier Twist:** For a healthier option, opt for turkey chili and use a whole grain hot dog bun.

VEGETARIAN & HOT DOGS RECIPES

21. Guacamole, Pico de Gallo, and Cream Cheese Hot Dog

PREP TIME: 20 minutes	**COOKING TIME:** 5 minutes	**TOTAL TIME:** 25 minutes
SERVINGS: For 1 person	**DIFFICULTY:** Easy	**TEMPERATURE:** Medium 350-375°F (177-190°C)
COOKING TYPE: Direct on the grill	**Sauce:** Guacamole and Cream Cheese	

INGREDIENTS:
- **Avocado:** 1 medium
- **Tomato, finely diced:** 1/4 cup / 40 grams
- **Red onion, finely diced:** 2 tbsp / 30 grams
- **Cilantro, chopped:** 1 tbsp / 3 grams
- **Lime, juiced:** 1/2 lime
- **Pico de gallo:** 1/4 cup / 60 ml
- **Cream cheese, softened:** 2 tbsp / 30 grams
- **Hot dog bun:** 1 bun

NUTRITIONAL VALUES PER SERVING:
Calories: 490kcal | Carbohydrates: 45g | Proteins: 13g | Fats: 30g | Fiber: 7g | Sodium: 620mg | Glucose: 4 g

PROCEDURE:
1. **Grill Preparation:** Preheat the grill to medium temperature.
2. **Making the Guacamole:** In a bowl, mash the avocado. Add half of the diced tomatoes, half of the diced red onions, chopped cilantro, and lime juice. Mix well to combine and set aside.
3. **Preparing the Hot Dog:** While the grill is heating, spread the inside of the hot dog bun with cream cheese. Toast the bun lightly on the grill, cream cheese side up, being careful not to let it burn.
4. **Cooking the Hot Dog:** Grill the hot dog until heated through and slightly charred, about 3-5 minutes, turning occasionally.
5. **Assembly:** Place the cooked hot dog in the cream cheese-lined bun. Top with a generous amount of guacamole and then spoon the pico de gallo over the top.

TIPS FOR PERFECT COOKING:
- **Cream Cheese Spread:** Soften the cream cheese before spreading to ensure a smooth application without tearing the bun.
- **Balance Flavors:** Adjust the amount of lime juice in the guacamole according to taste; the right amount will brighten the flavors without overpowering them.
- **Fresh Ingredients:** Use fresh ingredients for the guacamole and pico de gallo to maximize the vibrant, fresh flavors.

POSSIBLE VARIATIONS:
- **Spicy Variant:** Add diced jalapeños to the pico de gallo or include a dash of hot sauce in the guacamole for a spicy kick.
- **Deluxe Topping:** Include crispy bacon bits or fried onions on top for added crunch and flavor.
- **Lighter Version:** Substitute the cream cheese with a lighter or fat-free version and use a whole grain hot dog bun to reduce the overall calorie count.

22. Chili Sauce, Pepper Jack Cheese, and Crispy Onion Hot Dog

PREP TIME: 15 minutes	**COOKING TIME:** 10 minutes	**TOTAL TIME:** 25 minutes
SERVINGS: For 1 person	**DIFFICULTY:** Easy	**TEMPERATURE:** Medium 350-375°F (177-190°C)
COOKING TYPE: Direct on the grill	**SAUCE:** Chili Sauce	

INGREDIENTS:
- **Chili Sauce:** 2 tbsp / 30 ml
- **Pepper jack cheese, sliced:** 1 oz / 28 grams
- **White onions, thinly sliced:** 1/4 cup / 30 grams
- **Olive oil:** 1 tbsp / 15 ml
- **Hot dog bun:** 1 bun

NUTRITIONAL VALUES PER SERVING:
Calories: 520kcal | Carbohydrates: 45g | Proteins: 15g | Fats: 30g | Fiber: 2g | Sodium: 880mg | Glucose: 6 g

PROCEDURE:
1. **Grill Preparation:** Preheat the grill to medium temperature.
2. **Preparing the Crispy Onions:** In a small skillet or directly on the grill, heat the olive oil. Add the thinly sliced onions and cook, stirring frequently, until they are golden brown and crispy. This should take about 5-7 minutes.
3. **Cooking the Hot Dog:** Grill the hot dog until heated through and slightly charred, about 3-5 minutes, turning occasionally.
4. **Toasting the Bun:** Lightly toast the hot dog bun on the grill for 1-2 minutes until it's warm and slightly crispy.
5. **Assembly:** Place the cooked hot dog in the toasted bun. Top with slices of pepper jack cheese so it melts slightly from the heat of the hot dog. Generously drizzle chili sauce over the cheese, then top with the crispy onions.

TIPS FOR PERFECT COOKING:
- **Cheese Melting:** If you prefer the cheese more melted, place the cheese slices on the hot dog during the last minute of grilling and close the grill lid to trap the heat.
- **Onion Preparation:** Ensure the onions are sliced very thinly for the best crispy texture. A mandoline slicer can be helpful for getting consistently thin slices.
- **Sauce Selection:** Choose a high-quality chili sauce for the best flavor. You can adjust the amount of sauce based on how spicy and moist you like your hot dog.

POSSIBLE VARIATIONS:
- **Extra Spicy Variant:** Add sliced jalapeños to the hot dog along with the chili sauce for an additional heat boost.
- **Smoky Flavor:** Include a splash of smoked paprika in the onions while they cook to add a subtle smoky flavor to the crispy onions.
- **Lighter Option:** Use a reduced-fat pepper jack cheese and a whole-grain hot dog bun to cut down on calories without sacrificing flavor.

VEGETARIAN & HOT DOGS RECIPES

23. French Fries and Melted Cheddar Cheese Hot Dog

| PREP TIME: 10 minutes | COOKING TIME: 15 minutes | TOTAL TIME: 25 minutes | SERVINGS: For 1 person |
| DIFFICULTY: Easy | TEMPERATURE: Medium: 350-375°F (177-190°C) | COOKING TYPE: Direct on the grill | NOT EXPECTED |

INGREDIENTS:
- French fries: 1/2 cup / 75 grams (pre-cooked weight)
- Cheddar cheese, shredded: 1 oz / 28 grams
- Hot dog bun: 1 bun
- Hot dog: 1

NUTRITIONAL VALUES PER SERVING:
Calories: 550kcal | Carbohydrates: 45g | Proteins: 20g | Fats: 30g | Fiber: 3g | Sodium: 980mg | Glucose: 2 g

PROCEDURE:
1. **Grill Preparation:** Preheat the grill to medium temperature.
2. **Cooking the French Fries:** If using frozen French fries, spread them on the grill (or a grill-safe pan) and cook according to package instructions, usually about 10-15 minutes, turning occasionally until they are golden and crispy.
3. **Cooking the Hot Dog:** Grill the hot dog until heated through and slightly charred, about 3-5 minutes, turning occasionally.
4. **Toasting the Bun:** Lightly toast the hot dog bun on the grill for 1-2 minutes until it's warm and slightly crispy.
5. **Assembling the Hot Dog:** Place the cooked hot dog in the toasted bun. Top with the hot, crispy French fries. Generously sprinkle shredded cheddar cheese over the fries. If desired, close the grill lid for a minute or two to help the cheese melt.
6. **Serving:** Serve immediately while the cheese is melty and the fries are still crispy.

TIPS FOR PERFECT COOKING:
- **Cheese Melting:** To ensure the cheddar melts perfectly, consider placing the hot dog with fries and cheese back on the grill for a couple of minutes, or use a small kitchen torch to melt the cheese directly.
- **Fries Texture:** For the crispiest French fries, make sure they aren't overcrowded on the grill or in the pan. The more surface area each fry has, the crispier it will get.
- **Enhancements:** For added flavor, you can season the French fries with garlic powder, paprika, or your favorite seasoning blend before grilling.

POSSIBLE VARIATIONS:
- **Extra Spicy Variant:** Drizzle some hot sauce over the cheese before serving or mix some chopped jalapeños into the shredded cheese for a spicy kick.
- **BBQ Twist:** Swap the cheddar for smoked gouda and drizzle some barbecue sauce over the top for a smoky, tangy flavor.
- **Healthier Option:** Use oven-baked sweet potato fries instead of regular fries and a low-fat cheese alternative to reduce calories.

24. Bourbon BBQ Sauce and Crispy Bacon Hot Dog

| PREP TIME: 20 minutes | COOKING TIME: 10 minutes | TOTAL TIME: 30 minutes | SERVINGS: For 1 person |
| DIFFICULTY: Medium | TEMPERATURE: Medium: 350-375°F (177-190°C) | COOKING TYPE: Direct on the grill | Sauce: Bourbon BBQ Sauce |

INGREDIENTS:
- Barbecue Sauce: 1/4 cup / 60 ml
- Bourbon: 1 tbsp / 15 ml
- Apple cider vinegar: 1 tsp / 5 ml
- Honey: 1 tsp / 5 ml
- Smoked paprika: 1/2 tsp / 2.5 ml
- Smoked bacon: 2 slices
- Hot dog bun: 1 bun
- Hot dog: 1

NUTRITIONAL VALUES PER SERVING:
Calories: 620kcal | Carbohydrates: 45g | Proteins: 22g | Fats: 35g | Fiber: 2g | Sodium: 1280mg | Glucose: 8 g

PROCEDURE:
1. **Making the Bourbon BBQ Sauce:** In a small saucepan, combine the barbecue sauce, bourbon, apple cider vinegar, honey, and smoked paprika. Bring to a simmer over low heat, stirring frequently. Allow the sauce to simmer for about 10 minutes until it thickens slightly and the flavors meld together.
2. **Grill Preparation:** Preheat the grill to medium temperature.
3. **Cooking the Bacon:** Place the bacon slices on the grill and cook until crispy, about 3-5 minutes per side. Once done, set aside on paper towels to drain excess fat.
4. **Cooking the Hot Dog:** Grill the hot dog until heated through and slightly charred, about 3-5 minutes, turning occasionally.
5. **Toasting the Bun:** Lightly toast the hot dog bun on the grill for 1-2 minutes until it's warm and slightly crispy.
6. **Assembling the Hot Dog:** Place the cooked hot dog in the toasted bun. Brush the hot dog generously with the bourbon BBQ sauce. Add the crispy bacon slices on top.
7. **Serving:** Serve the hot dog immediately, drizzled with additional bourbon BBQ sauce if desired.

TIPS FOR PERFECT COOKING:
- **Balance the Flavors:** Adjust the amount of bourbon and honey in the BBQ sauce according to your taste. More bourbon for a stronger whiskey flavor, or more honey for sweetness.
- **Watch the Bacon:** Keep an eye on the bacon as it cooks quickly and can burn easily on the grill. Flip it frequently to ensure even cooking and crispiness.
- **Enhance Your Dish:** For added texture, consider topping the hot dog with some crispy fried onions or a sprinkle of fresh chopped chives.

POSSIBLE VARIATIONS:
- **Spicy Kick:** Add a few drops of hot sauce to the bourbon BBQ sauce for a spicy version.
- **Deluxe Topping:** Layer some pickled jalapeños or crispy fried jalapeños on top for extra spice and crunch.
- **Healthier Twist:** Use turkey bacon instead of regular bacon and a whole-grain hot dog bun to lower the fat content and increase dietary fiber.

25. Steak with Sweet Potatoes and Caramelized Onions

- **PREP TIME:** 20 minutes
- **COOKING TIME:** 30 minutes
- **TOTAL TIME:** 50 minutes
- **SERVINGS:** For 1 person
- **DIFFICULTY:** Medium
- **TEMPERATURE:** Medium 375-400°F (190-205°C)
- **COOKING TYPE:** Direct on the grill
- **NOT EXPECTED**

INGREDIENTS:
- Steak (your choice of cut, such as ribeye or sirloin): 8 oz / 225 grams
- Sweet potatoes, peeled and cubed: 1 cup / 200 grams
- White onions, thinly sliced: 1/2 cup / 75 grams
- Butter: 2 tbsp / 30 grams
- Balsamic vinegar: 1 tbsp / 15 ml
- Salt and pepper to taste

NUTRITIONAL VALUES PER SERVING:
Calories: 850kcal | Carbohydrates: 45g | Proteins: 55g | Fats: 50g | Fiber: 6g | Sodium: 720mg | Glucose: 12 g

PROCEDURE:
1. **Preparation:** Preheat your grill to the appropriate temperatures for steak (medium-high) and vegetables (medium).
2. **Cooking the Sweet Potatoes:** Toss the sweet potato cubes with 1 tbsp of melted butter, salt, and pepper. Wrap them in aluminum foil and place them on the grill. Cook for about 20-25 minutes or until tender, turning the packet occasionally.
3. **Caramelizing the Onions:** In a skillet over medium heat on the grill, melt the remaining butter. Add the sliced onions, a pinch of salt, and cook, stirring occasionally, until the onions begin to soften and brown. Add the balsamic vinegar and continue to cook until the onions are well caramelized, about 15-20 minutes.
4. **Grilling the Steak:** Season the steak with salt and pepper. Place the steak on the grill and cook for about 4-5 minutes per side for medium-rare, or adjust the cooking time according to your preferred doneness. Let the steak rest for a few minutes after grilling.
5. **Assembly:** Slice the steak against the grain. Serve with the grilled sweet potatoes and top with the caramelized onions.

TIPS FOR PERFECT COOKING:
- **Rest the Steak:** Allow your steak to rest for at least 5 minutes after cooking to ensure the juices redistribute throughout the meat for a juicier, more flavorful steak.
- **Monitor the Sweet Potatoes:** Ensure the sweet potatoes don't overcook. You want them tender but not mushy.
- **Enhance the Onions:** For extra flavor depth, a sprinkle of sugar can be added to the onions during caramelization to enhance their natural sweetness.

POSSIBLE VARIATIONS:
- **Herb Infusion:** Add rosemary or thyme to the steak or sweet potatoes for a herby flavor.
- **Spicy Kick:** Incorporate a sprinkle of chili flakes over the sweet potatoes before wrapping them for a spicy twist.
- **Cheese Topping:** Garnish the dish with a sprinkle of blue cheese or goat cheese for a creamy texture and a punch of flavor.

26. Steak with Grilled Asparagus and Chimichurri Sauce

- **PREP TIME:** 15 minutes
- **COOKING TIME:** 15 minutes
- **TOTAL TIME:** 30 minutes
- **SERVINGS:** For 1 person
- **DIFFICULTY:** Easy
- **TEMPERATURE:** Medium-high: 375-400°F (190-205°C)
- **COOKING TYPE:** Direct on the grill
- **SAUCE:** Chimichurri

INGREDIENTS:
- Steak (preferably a cut like ribeye or sirloin): 8 oz / 225g
- Asparagus, trimmed: 1 cup / 100 g
- Olive oil: 2 tbsp / 30 ml
- Salt and pepper: to taste

Chimichurri sauce (store-bought or homemade):
- Fresh parsley, finely chopped: 1/2 cup / 30 g
- Garlic, minced: 1 clove
- Red wine vinegar: 2 tbsp / 30 ml
- Olive oil: 1/4 cup / 60 ml
- Red pepper flakes: 1/2 tsp / 2.5 ml
- Salt and pepper: to taste

NUTRITIONAL VALUES PER SERVING:
Calories: 800kcal | Carbohydrates: 6g | Proteins: 55g | Fats: 65g | Fiber: 3g | Sodium: 690mg | Glucose: 1 g

PROCEDURE:
1. **Prepare the Chimichurri Sauce:** If making homemade, combine parsley, minced garlic, red wine vinegar, olive oil, red pepper flakes, salt, and pepper in a bowl. Mix well and let sit to blend the flavors while you prepare the rest of the meal.
2. **Grill Preparation:** Preheat your grill to medium-high temperature.
3. **Season and Grill the Asparagus:** Toss the asparagus with 1 tbsp of olive oil, salt, and pepper. Grill the asparagus for about 6-8 minutes, turning occasionally, until they are tender and charred in spots.
4. **Cook the Steak:** Rub the steak with the remaining olive oil and season generously with salt and pepper. Grill the steak for about 4-5 minutes on each side for medium-rare, or adjust according to your preference. Let the steak rest for 5 minutes after grilling.
5. **Assembly:** Slice the steak against the grain. Arrange the sliced steak and grilled asparagus on a plate. Drizzle the chimichurri sauce over the steak or serve on the side.

TIPS FOR PERFECT COOKING:
- **Rest the Meat:** Allowing the steak to rest after grilling helps the juices redistribute throughout the meat, ensuring it is juicy and flavorful when you cut into it.
- **Don't Overcook Asparagus:** Keep a close eye on the asparagus to ensure it doesn't overcook. It should be tender but still have a slight crunch.
- **Freshness is Key for Chimichurri:** For the best flavor, use fresh herbs in your chimichurri. This sauce can be made in advance and stored in the refrigerator to enhance its flavors.

POSSIBLE VARIATIONS:
- **Herb Variations:** Try different herbs like cilantro or oregano in the chimichurri for a different flavor profile.
- **Spicy Chimichurri:** Add more red pepper flakes or a chopped fresh chili to the chimichurri sauce for extra heat.
- **Lemon Twist:** Add a squeeze of lemon juice to the asparagus before grilling for a bright, citrusy note.

HOT DOGS & STEAKS RECIPES

27. Steak with Porcini Mushrooms and Black Truffle

PREP TIME: 20 minutes	**COOKING TIME:** 20 minutes	**TOTAL TIME:** 40 minutes
SERVINGS: For 1 person	**DIFFICULTY:** Medium	**TEMPERATURE:** Medium-high: 375-400°F (190-205°C)
COOKING TYPE: Direct on the grill	**NOT EXPECTED**	

INGREDIENTS:
- Steak (preferably a high-quality cut like ribeye or filet mignon): 8 oz / 225 grams
- Porcini mushrooms, fresh or rehydrated if dried: 1/2 cup / 50 grams
- Butter: 2 tbsp / 30 grams
- Garlic, minced: 1 clove
- White wine: 1/4 cup / 60 ml
- Black truffle, thinly shaved or truffle oil: 1 tsp / 5 ml
- Salt and pepper to taste

NUTRITIONAL VALUES PER SERVING:
Calories: 950kcal | Carbohydrates: 6g | Proteins: 55g | Fats: 75g | Fiber: 2g | Sodium: 610mg | Glucose: 2 g

PROCEDURE:
1. **Prepare the Mushrooms:** If using dried porcini mushrooms, soak them in warm water until rehydrated, about 15-20 minutes, then drain. Slice fresh or rehydrated mushrooms.

2. **Cook the Mushrooms:** In a skillet over medium heat on the grill or stovetop, melt 1 tbsp of butter. Add the garlic and sauté for about 1 minute until fragrant. Add the porcini mushrooms and cook until they begin to soften, about 5-7 minutes. Pour in the white wine and let the mixture simmer until the liquid is reduced by half. Season with salt and pepper.

3. **Grill the Steak:** While the mushrooms are cooking, season the steak generously with salt and pepper. Grill the steak to your desired doneness, about 4-5 minutes per side for medium-rare, depending on thickness. Let it rest for at least 5 minutes after grilling.

4. **Final Assembly:** Place the cooked steak on a plate. Spoon the porcini mushroom mixture over the steak. Garnish with shaved black truffle or drizzle with truffle oil for an added touch of luxury.

TIPS FOR PERFECT COOKING:
- **Mushroom Preparation:** Ensure that any grit is thoroughly cleaned from fresh or rehydrated porcini mushrooms to avoid any unpleasant texture in the dish.
- **Rest the Meat:** Allowing the steak to rest helps the juices redistribute throughout the meat, enhancing flavor and ensuring a tender bite.
- **Truffle Enhancement:** If using truffle oil instead of fresh truffle, add it to the mushrooms right after removing them from the heat to preserve its aroma and flavor.

POSSIBLE VARIATIONS:
- **Herb Infusion:** Add a few sprigs of thyme or rosemary to the mushrooms while cooking for an aromatic depth.
- **Creamy Addition:** Stir a splash of heavy cream into the mushrooms right before serving for a richer, more decadent sauce.
- **Wine Selection:** Experiment with different types of white wine, such as Chardonnay or Sauvignon Blanc, to see how they subtly alter the flavor of the sauce.

28. Steak with Macaroni and Cheese and Crispy Bacon

PREP TIME: 15 minutes	**COOKING TIME:** 20 minutes	**TOTAL TIME:** 35 minutes
SERVINGS: For 1 person	**DIFFICULTY:** Easy	**TEMPERATURE:** Medium-high: 375-400°F (190-205°C)
COOKING TYPE: Direct on the grill	**NOT EXPECTED**	

INGREDIENTS:
- Steak (preferably a cut like ribeye or sirloin): 8 oz / 225 grams
- Macaroni and cheese, prepared: 1 cup / 240 ml
- Smoked bacon, strips: 2
- Salt and pepper to taste

NUTRITIONAL VALUES PER SERVING:
Calories: 950kcal | Carbohydrates: 30g | Proteins: 60g | Fats: 65g | Fiber: 1g | Sodium: 950mg | Glucose: 4 g

PROCEDURE:
1. **Prepare the Macaroni and Cheese:** If not already prepared, cook macaroni according to package instructions, then mix with your favorite cheese sauce until creamy and smooth. Keep warm.

2. **Cook the Bacon:** In a skillet over medium heat on the grill or stovetop, cook the bacon until crispy. Drain on paper towels and then crumble or chop into bits.

3. **Grill the Steak:** Season the steak generously with salt and pepper. Place the steak on the preheated grill and cook for about 4-5 minutes per side for medium-rare, or adjust the cooking time based on your preference. Let the steak rest for 5 minutes after grilling.

4. **Assembly:** Slice the steak against the grain. Serve the sliced steak with a generous portion of warm macaroni and cheese. Sprinkle the crispy bacon bits over the macaroni and cheese for added flavor and texture.

TIPS FOR PERFECT COOKING:
- **Cheese Choice:** Use a blend of cheeses for the macaroni such as sharp cheddar, Gouda, or Parmesan for a rich and complex flavor.
- **Steak Doneness:** Use a meat thermometer to ensure the steak is cooked to your desired doneness; 135°F for medium-rare, 145°F for medium.
- **Enhance Macaroni:** For an extra creamy and luxurious macaroni and cheese, add a splash of cream to the cheese sauce.

POSSIBLE VARIATIONS:
- **Spicy Kick:** Add a dash of cayenne pepper or diced jalapeños to the macaroni and cheese for a spicy version.
- **Garlic Flavor:** Sauté minced garlic in the pan before adding the bacon for a subtle garlic flavor.
- **Herb Infusion:** Mix fresh chopped herbs like parsley or chives into the macaroni and cheese for a fresh flavor boost.

STEAKS AND RIBS RECIPES

29. Steak with Tomato, Mozzarella, and Basil Salad

PREP TIME: 15 minutes
COOKING TIME: 10 minutes
TOTAL TIME: 25 minutes
SERVINGS: For 1 person
DIFFICULTY: Easy
TEMPERATURE: Medium-high; 375-400°F (190-205°C)
COOKING TYPE: Direct on the grill
SAUCE: NOT EXPECTED

INGREDIENTS:
- Steak (preferably a high-quality cut like ribeye or filet mignon): 8 oz / 225 grams
- Tomato, sliced: 1 medium
- Fresh mozzarella, sliced: 4 oz / 115 grams
- Fresh basil leaves: A handful
- Olive oil: 2 tbsp / 30 ml
- Balsamic vinegar: 1 tbsp / 15 ml
- Salt and pepper to taste

PROCEDURE:
1. **Grill the Steak:** Season the steak with salt and pepper. Preheat the grill to medium-high and grill the steak to your desired doneness, about 4-5 minutes per side for medium-rare. Remove from the grill and let it rest for at least 5 minutes.

2. **Prepare the Salad:** Arrange the sliced tomatoes and mozzarella on a plate, alternating them for a pleasing presentation. Tuck fresh basil leaves between the slices.

3. **Dressing:** In a small bowl, whisk together the olive oil and balsamic vinegar with a pinch of salt and pepper. Drizzle this dressing over the tomato and mozzarella slices.

4. **Serve:** Slice the rested steak against the grain. Serve alongside the tomato, mozzarella, and basil salad. Drizzle any remaining dressing over the steak if desired.

NUTRITIONAL VALUES PER SERVING:
Calories: 800kcal | Carbohydrates: 10g | Proteins: 55g | Fats: 60g | Fiber: 2g | Sodium: 560mg | Glucose: 6 g

TIPS FOR PERFECT COOKING:
- **Quality Ingredients:** Use the best quality tomatoes, mozzarella, and fresh basil you can find, as the simplicity of the salad relies on the quality of its ingredients.
- **Steak Doneness:** Use a meat thermometer to ensure the steak is cooked to your preferred level of doneness; 135°F for medium-rare, 145°F for medium.
- **Rest the Meat:** Allowing the steak to rest before slicing helps retain its juices, making it more flavorful and tender.

POSSIBLE VARIATIONS:
- **Herb-Infused Oil:** Instead of plain olive oil, use a basil-infused olive oil for an extra burst of basil flavor.
- **Cheese Variety:** Experiment with different types of mozzarella, such as smoked mozzarella, for a unique twist on the classic caprese.
- **Spicy Kick:** Add a sprinkle of red chili flakes to the dressing for a bit of heat.

30. Ribs with Bourbon BBQ Sauce

PREP TIME: 30 minutes + marinating time
COOKING TIME: 3 hours
TOTAL TIME: About 3.5 hours
SERVINGS: For 1 person
DIFFICULTY: Medium
TEMPERATURE: Low and slow; About 275°F (135°C)
COOKING TYPE: Direct on the grill
SAUCE: Bourbon BBQ Sauce

INGREDIENTS:
- Pork ribs: 1 rack (about 2 to 3 pounds)
- Barbecue Sauce: 1 cup / 240 ml
- Bourbon: 1/4 cup / 60 ml
- Apple cider vinegar: 2 tbsp / 30 ml
- Honey: 2 tbsp / 30 ml
- Smoked paprika: 1 tsp / 5 ml
- Salt and pepper to taste

NUTRITIONAL VALUES PER SERVING:
Calories: 1200kcal | Carbohydrates: 50g | Proteins: 70g | Fats: 70g | Fiber: 1g | Sodium: 1300 mg

PROCEDURE:
1. **Prepare the Bourbon BBQ Sauce:** In a saucepan, combine the barbecue sauce, bourbon, apple cider vinegar, honey, and smoked paprika. Bring to a simmer over medium heat, stirring frequently. Let the sauce simmer for about 10 minutes until it thickens slightly and the flavors are well combined. Set aside some sauce for serving.

2. **Prepare the Ribs:** Preheat your grill or oven to 275°F (135°C). If using an oven, line a baking sheet with aluminum foil for easier cleanup. Remove the membrane from the back of the ribs if it is still attached. Season the ribs generously with salt, pepper, and a bit of smoked paprika. Apply a generous coating of the bourbon BBQ sauce all over the ribs.

3. **Cook the Ribs:** If grilling, place the ribs on the cooler part of the grill (indirect heat), and cover. Grill for about 2.5 to 3 hours, basting with the BBQ sauce every hour. Keep the grill temperature steady at about 275°F. If baking, place the ribs on the prepared baking sheet and cover tightly with aluminum foil. Bake in the oven for about 2.5 to 3 hours, basting with more sauce every hour.

4. **Final Glaze and Serve:** In the last 30 minutes of cooking, remove the cover or foil and apply another layer of the bourbon BBQ sauce to the ribs. Continue cooking uncovered to let the sauce caramelize slightly. Once the ribs are tender and the meat easily pulls away from the bone, remove them from the heat. Let them rest for about 10 minutes. Slice the ribs between the bones, and serve with the reserved bourbon BBQ sauce on the side.

TIPS FOR PERFECT COOKING:
- **Low and Slow:** The key to tender ribs is cooking them at a low temperature for a long time, which breaks down the connective tissue without drying out the meat.
- **Basting:** Regular basting not only adds flavor but also helps to keep the ribs moist throughout the cooking process.
- **Resting Time:** Allowing the ribs to rest before cutting into them gives the juices time to redistribute, ensuring that each bite is moist and flavorful.

POSSIBLE VARIATIONS:
- **Spicy Version:** Add a tsp of cayenne pepper to the BBQ sauce for a spicy kick.
- **Herb Infusion:** Introduce a blend of dried herbs such as thyme, rosemary, and garlic powder to the rub for added flavor complexity.
- **Sweet Twist:** Mix in a bit of maple syrup with the BBQ sauce for a sweeter, stickier finish.

STEAKS AND RIBS RECIPES

31. Ribs with Teriyaki Sauce and Grilled Pineapple

PREP TIME: 30 minutes + marinating time | **COOKING TIME:** 3 hours | **TOTAL TIME:** About 3.5 hours | **SERVINGS:** For 1 person
DIFFICULTY: Medium | **TEMPERATURE:** Low and slow About 275°F (135°C) | **COOKING TYPE:** Direct on the grill | **SAUCE:** Teriyaki

INGREDIENTS:
- Pork ribs: 1 rack (about 2 to 3 pounds)
- Teriyaki Sauce: 1 cup / 240 ml (store-bought or homemade)
- Pineapple, sliced into rings: 1/2 pineapple
- Olive oil: 2 tbsp / 30 ml
- Salt and pepper to taste

NUTRITIONAL VALUES PER SERVING:
Calories: 1200kcal | Carbohydrates: 55g | Proteins: 70g | Fats: 75g | Fiber: 2g | Sodium: 1500 mg

PROCEDURE:
1. **Marinate the Ribs:** Remove the membrane from the back of the ribs if it is still attached. Season the ribs generously with salt and pepper. Coat the ribs thoroughly with about half of the teriyaki sauce. Let them marinate in the refrigerator for at least 2 hours, or overnight for deeper flavor.
2. **Prepare the Grill or Oven:** Preheat your grill or oven to 275°F (135°C). If using an oven, line a baking sheet with aluminum foil for easier cleanup.
3. **Cook the Ribs:** If grilling, place the ribs on the cooler part of the grill (indirect heat), and cover. Grill for about 2.5 to 3 hours, turning occasionally, until the ribs are tender. If baking, place the ribs on the prepared baking sheet and cover tightly with aluminum foil. Bake in the oven for about 2.5 to 3 hours.
4. **Grill the Pineapple:** During the last 30 minutes of the ribs cooking, brush the pineapple rings with olive oil and place them on the grill. Grill each side for 2-3 minutes or until you have nice grill marks. Alternatively, if using an oven, broil the pineapple rings for a few minutes on each side until charred.
5. **Final Glaze and Serve:** In the last 30 minutes of rib cooking, baste them with the remaining teriyaki sauce every 10 minutes to create a nice glaze. Once the ribs are tender and the pineapple is grilled, remove from heat. Let the ribs rest for about 10 minutes. Slice the ribs between the bones, and serve with the grilled pineapple rings on the side.

TIPS FOR PERFECT COOKING:
- **Marinating Time:** The longer you can marinate the ribs, the more flavorful they will be.
- **Low and Slow Cooking:** Keeping the temperature low and cooking the ribs slowly ensures they will be tender and juicy.
- **Basting Frequently:** Frequent basting during the last hours of cooking will enhance the flavor and help create a sticky, caramelized exterior.

POSSIBLE VARIATIONS:
- **Spicy Kick:** Add a bit of chili paste or sriracha to the teriyaki sauce for a spicy version.
- **Sesame Flavor:** Sprinkle sesame seeds on the ribs before the final set of basting to add a nutty flavor and texture.
- **Citrus Twist:** Add a splash of orange juice to the teriyaki marinade for a citrusy note.

32. Ribs with Spicy Mango Sauce and Caramelized Onions

PREP TIME: 30 minutes + marinating time | **COOKING TIME:** 3 hours | **TOTAL TIME:** About 3.5 hours | **SERVINGS:** For 1 person
DIFFICULTY: Medium | **TEMPERATURE:** Low and slow: About 275°F (135°C) | **COOKING TYPE:** Direct on the grill | **SAUCE:** Spicy Mango Sauce

INGREDIENTS:
- Pork ribs: 1 rack (2 to 3 pounds)
- Spicy mango sauce (store-bought or homemade):
- Mango, peeled and cubed: 1 large
- Garlic, minced: 2 cloves
- Jalapeño, seeded and chopped: 1
- Honey: 2 tbsp / 30 ml
- Apple cider vinegar: 2 tbsp / 30 ml
- White onions, thinly sliced: 1 cup / 150 grams
- Butter: 2 tbsp / 30 grams
- Balsamic vinegar: 1 tbsp / 15 ml
- Salt and pepper to taste

NUTRITIONAL VALUES PER SERVING:
Calories: 1250kcal | Carbohydrates: 65g | Proteins: 70g | Fats: 80g | Fiber: 3g | Sodium: 1300 mg

PROCEDURE:
1. **Prepare the Spicy Mango Sauce:** If making homemade, blend the mango, garlic, jalapeño, honey, and apple cider vinegar in a blender until smooth. Adjust seasoning with salt and a little more honey if needed for sweetness.
2. **Marinate the Ribs:** Remove the membrane from the back of the ribs if it is still attached. Season the ribs generously with salt and pepper. Coat the ribs thoroughly with about half of the spicy mango sauce. Let them marinate in the refrigerator for at least 2 hours, or overnight for deeper flavor.
3. **Prepare the Grill or Oven:** Preheat your grill or oven to 275°F (135°C). If using an oven, line a baking sheet with aluminum foil for easier cleanup.
4. **Cook the Ribs:** Place the ribs on the cooler part of the grill (indirect heat), and cover. Grill for about 2.5 to 3 hours, turning occasionally, until the ribs are tender. If baking, place the ribs on the prepared baking sheet and cover tightly with aluminum foil. Bake in the oven for about 2.5 to 3 hours.
5. **Caramelize the Onions:** While the ribs are cooking, melt the butter in a skillet over medium heat. Add the sliced onions and cook, stirring occasionally, until they start to soften and brown. Add balsamic vinegar and continue to cook until onions are fully caramelized, about 15-20 minutes. Set aside.
6. **Final Glaze and Serve:** In the last 30 minutes of rib cooking, baste them with the remaining spicy mango sauce every 10 minutes to create a nice glaze. Once the ribs are tender, remove from heat and let them rest for about 10 minutes. Slice the ribs between the bones, and serve with the caramelized onions on top.

TIPS FOR PERFECT COOKING:
- **Low and Slow Cooking:** Keeping the temperature low and cooking the ribs slowly ensures they will be tender and juicy.
- **Marinating Time:** The longer you can marinate the ribs, the more flavorful they will be.
- **Basting Frequency:** Frequent basting during the last hours of cooking will enhance the flavor and help create a sticky, caramelized exterior.

POSSIBLE VARIATIONS:
- **Extra Spicy Variant:** Add more jalapeño or a dash of hot sauce to the mango sauce for a spicier kick.
- **Sweet and Sour Twist:** Include a splash of lime juice in the mango sauce for a tangy contrast.
- **Herbal Touch:** Add some chopped cilantro to the mango sauce for an herbal freshness.

RIBS RECIPES

33. Ribs with Chimichurri Sauce and Sweet Potatoes

PREP TIME: 20 minutes + marinating time
COOKING TIME: 3 hours
TOTAL TIME: About 3 hours and 20 minutes
SERVINGS: For 1 person
DIFFICULTY: Medium
TEMPERATURE: Low and slow About 275°F (135°C)
COOKING TYPE: Direct on the grill
SAUCE: Chimichurri

INGREDIENTS:
- Pork ribs: 1 rack (about 2 to 3 pounds)
- Chimichurri sauce (store-bought or homemade):
- Fresh parsley, finely chopped: 1 cup / 60 grams
- Fresh garlic, minced: 3 cloves
- Red wine vinegar: 3 tbsp / 45 ml
- Olive oil: 1/2 cup / 120 ml
- Red pepper flakes: 1 tsp / 5 ml
- Salt and pepper to taste
- Sweet potatoes, peeled and cubed: 2 medium
- Olive oil: 2 tbsp / 30 ml

NUTRITIONAL VALUES PER SERVING:
Calories: 1300kcal | Carbohydrates: 55g | Proteins: 70g | Fats: 85g | Fiber: 6g | Sodium: 1200 mg

PROCEDURE:
1. **Prepare the Chimichurri Sauce:** If making homemade, combine parsley, garlic, red wine vinegar, olive oil, red pepper flakes, salt, and pepper in a bowl. Whisk until well blended. Let it sit for at least 30 minutes to allow the flavors to meld.
2. **Marinate the Ribs:** Remove the membrane from the back of the ribs if it is still attached. Season the ribs generously with salt and pepper. Coat the ribs thoroughly with about one-third of the chimichurri sauce. Reserve the rest for serving. Let the ribs marinate in the refrigerator for at least 2 hours, or overnight for deeper flavor.
3. **Prepare the Grill or Oven:** Preheat your grill or oven to 275°F (135°C). If using an oven, line a baking sheet with aluminum foil for easier cleanup.
4. **Cook the Ribs:** Place the ribs on the cooler part of the grill (indirect heat), and cover. Grill for about 2.5 to 3 hours, turning occasionally, until the ribs are tender. If baking, place the ribs on the prepared baking sheet and cover tightly with aluminum foil. Bake in the oven for about 2.5 to 3 hours.
5. **Prepare the Sweet Potatoes:** Toss the cubed sweet potatoes with olive oil, salt, and pepper. Spread them on a separate baking sheet. If using the oven for the ribs, roast the sweet potatoes in the last 45 minutes of the ribs' cooking time. If grilling, place them in a grill basket or wrap in foil and cook on the grill.
6. **Final Serve:** Once the ribs are tender, remove from heat and let them rest for about 10 minutes. Slice the ribs between the bones and serve with the roasted sweet potatoes. Drizzle the remaining chimichurri sauce over the ribs or serve on the side for dipping.

TIPS FOR PERFECT COOKING:
- **Low and Slow Cooking:** Keeping the temperature low and cooking the ribs slowly ensures they will be tender and juicy.
- **Marinating Time:** The longer you can marinate the ribs, the more flavorful they will be.
- **Fresh Chimichurri:** Freshly made chimichurri sauce is preferable for the best flavor. Letting it sit allows the flavors to develop fully.

POSSIBLE VARIATIONS:
- **Extra Spicy Variant:** Add more red pepper flakes to the chimichurri sauce for a spicier kick.
- **Herb Variety:** Try adding cilantro or oregano to the chimichurri for a different herb profile.
- **Citrus Twist:** Include a splash of lemon or lime juice in the chimichurri for a citrusy note.

34. Ribs with Honey BBQ Sauce and Crispy Onions

PREP TIME: 20 minutes + marinating time
COOKING TIME: 3 hours
TOTAL TIME: About 3 hours and 20 minutes
SERVINGS: For 1 person
DIFFICULTY: Medium
TEMPERATURE: Low and slow: About 275°F (135°C)
COOKING TYPE: Direct on the grill
SAUCE: Honey BBQ Sauce

INGREDIENTS:
- Pork ribs: 1 rack (about 2 to 3 pounds)
- Barbecue Sauce: 1 cup / 240 ml
- Honey: 1/4 cup / 60 ml
- White onions, thinly sliced: 1 cup / 150 grams
- Olive oil: for frying
- Salt and pepper to taste

NUTRITIONAL VALUES PER SERVING:
Calories: 1250kcal | Carbohydrates: 65g | Proteins: 70g | Fats: 80g | Fiber: 3g | Sodium: 1300 mg

PROCEDURE:
1. **Prepare the Honey BBQ Sauce:** In a small saucepan, combine the barbecue sauce and honey. Heat over medium-low, stirring until well combined and the mixture just begins to bubble. Remove from heat and set aside.
2. **Marinate the Ribs:** Remove the membrane from the back of the ribs if it is still attached. Season the ribs generously with salt and pepper. Coat the ribs thoroughly with about half of the honey BBQ sauce. Reserve the rest for basting and serving. Let the ribs marinate in the refrigerator for at least 2 hours, or overnight for deeper flavor.
3. **Prepare the Grill or Oven:** Preheat your grill or oven to 275°F (135°C). If using an oven, line a baking sheet with aluminum foil for easier cleanup.
4. **Cook the Ribs:** Place the ribs on the cooler part of the grill (indirect heat), and cover. Grill for about 2.5 to 3 hours, turning occasionally, until the ribs are tender. If baking, place the ribs on the prepared baking sheet and cover tightly with aluminum foil. Bake in the oven for about 2.5 to 3 hours.
5. **Prepare the Crispy Onions:** While the ribs are nearing completion, heat olive oil in a frying pan over medium heat. Fry the thinly sliced onions until they are golden and crispy. Remove with a slotted spoon and drain on paper towels.
6. **Final Baste and Serve:** In the last 30 minutes of cooking, baste the ribs with some of the remaining honey BBQ sauce. Continue to cook uncovered to allow the sauce to caramelize. Once the ribs are tender, remove from heat and let them rest for about 10 minutes. Slice the ribs between the bones, and serve topped with the crispy onions and drizzled with more honey BBQ sauce if desired.

TIPS FOR PERFECT COOKING:
- **Low and Slow Cooking:** Keeping the temperature low and cooking the ribs slowly ensures they will be tender and juicy.
- **Frequent Basting:** Basting the ribs during the last hour of cooking helps develop a rich, caramelized coating.
- **Crispiness of Onions:** Ensure the oil is hot enough before adding the onions for frying to get them perfectly crispy without absorbing too much oil.

POSSIBLE VARIATIONS:
- **Spicy Kick:** Add a bit of cayenne pepper to the honey BBQ sauce for a spicy twist.
- **Garlic Flavor:** Saute some minced garlic in the frying oil before adding the onions to infuse them with garlic flavor.
- **Smoky Touch:** Include a bit of liquid smoke in the BBQ sauce to enhance the smoky barbecue feel.

RIBS RECIPES

35. Lemon Chicken with Chives and Sweet Potatoes

PREP TIME: 15 minutes	**COOKING TIME:** 30 minutes	**TOTAL TIME:** 45 minutes	**SERVINGS:** For 1 person	
DIFFICULTY: Easy	**TEMPERATURE:** Oven at 375°F (190°C) or grill at medium-high	**COOKING TYPE:** Direct on the grill	**NOT EXPECTED**	

INGREDIENTS:
- **Chicken breast:** 1 large (about 6 oz / 170 grams)
- **Lemon juice:** 2 tbsp / 30 ml
- **Olive oil:** 2 tbsp / 30 ml
- **Fresh chives, chopped:** 2 tbsp / 8 grams
- **Sweet potatoes, peeled and cubed:** 1 large
- **Salt and pepper to taste**

NUTRITIONAL VALUES PER SERVING:
Calories: 550kcal | Carbohydrates: 45g | Proteins: 40g | Fats: 22g | Fiber: 6g | Sodium: 300 mg

PROCEDURE:
1. **Marinate the Chicken:** In a bowl, combine 1 tbsp of olive oil, lemon juice, salt, and pepper. Place the chicken breast in the marinade, ensuring it is well coated. Let it marinate in the refrigerator for at least 15 minutes, or up to 2 hours for more flavor.
2. **Prepare the Sweet Potatoes:** Toss the cubed sweet potatoes with the remaining tbsp of olive oil, salt, and pepper. Spread them out on a baking sheet in a single layer.
3. **Cooking:** Preheat your oven to 375°F (190°C). Alternatively, preheat your grill to medium-high. If using an oven, place the chicken breast on the same baking sheet as the sweet potatoes, or use a separate tray if needed. Bake in the oven for about 25-30 minutes, or until the chicken is thoroughly cooked and the sweet potatoes are tender. If grilling, grill the chicken over medium-high heat for about 6-7 minutes per side or until fully cooked. Grill the sweet potatoes in a grill basket, stirring occasionally, until tender and slightly charred, about 15-20 minutes.
4. **Garnish and Serve:** Once the chicken is cooked, let it rest for a few minutes, then slice or serve whole. Sprinkle chopped chives over the chicken. Serve the grilled or roasted chicken alongside the sweet potatoes.

TIPS FOR PERFECT COOKING:
- **Marinating Time:** To enhance the chicken's flavor, marinate it for as long as possible within the safe refrigeration time.
- **Chicken Doneness:** To confirm it's fully cooked, ensure the chicken reaches an internal temperature of 165°F (74°C).
- **Sweet Potatoes:** For extra flavor, consider sprinkling some paprika or garlic powder on the sweet potatoes before roasting.

POSSIBLE VARIATIONS:
- **Herb Variations:** Substitute chives with other fresh herbs like parsley or dill for a different flavor profile.
- **Spicy Kick:** For a bit of heat, add a pinch of chili flakes to the marinade or the sweet potatoes.
- **Citrus Twist:** Include a bit of grated lemon zest in the chicken marinade for an enhanced citrus flavor.

---

36. Chicken Fajitas with Onions and Peppers

PREP TIME: 20 minutes	**COOKING TIME:** 20 minutes	**TOTAL TIME:** 40 minutes	**SERVINGS:** For 1 person	
DIFFICULTY: Easy	**TEMPERATURE:** Stovetop over medium-high heat	**COOKING TYPE:** Direct on the grill	**SAUCE:** Guacamole	

INGREDIENTS:
- **Chicken breast:** 1 large (about 6 oz / 170 grams), thinly sliced
- **Flour tortillas:** 2
- **Red onions:** 1 medium, thinly sliced
- **Green peppers:** 1 medium, thinly sliced
- **Fajita spices:** 1 tbsp (a blend of cumin, chili powder, paprika, garlic powder, salt, and pepper)
- **Olive oil:** 2 tbsp
- **Guacamole:** 2 tbsp
- **Sour cream:** 2 tbsp
- **Salsa:** 2 tbsp

NUTRITIONAL VALUES PER SERVING:
Calories: 700kcal | Carbohydrates: 50g | Proteins: 40g | Fats: 35g | Fiber: 6g | Sodium: 700 mg

PROCEDURE:
1. **Marinate the Chicken:** In a bowl, combine the thinly sliced chicken breast with the fajita spices and 1 tbsp of olive oil. Mix well to ensure the chicken is evenly coated with the spices. Let it marinate for at least 15 minutes.
2. **Cook the Vegetables:** Heat 1 tbsp of olive oil in a large skillet over medium-high heat. Add the sliced onions and green peppers. Cook, stirring occasionally, until the vegetables are soft and slightly charred, about 8-10 minutes. Remove from the skillet and set aside.
3. **Cook the Chicken:** In the same skillet, add the marinated chicken. Cook over medium-high heat, stirring frequently, until the chicken is fully cooked and golden brown, about 8-10 minutes.
4. **Warm the Tortillas:** Warm the flour tortillas in a dry skillet over medium heat for about 30 seconds on each side or until they are soft and pliable.
5. **Assemble and Serve:** Lay the warm tortillas on a plate. Divide the cooked chicken and vegetables evenly among the tortillas. Top with guacamole, sour cream, and salsa. Fold the tortillas over the fillings, or serve them open-faced with the toppings.

TIPS FOR PERFECT COOKING:
- **Marinating Time:** For even more flavor, marinate the chicken for a few hours or overnight in the refrigerator.
- **Customize Your Vegetables:** Feel free to add other vegetables like yellow or red bell peppers, or even some spicy jalapeños for extra heat.
- **Keep It Moist:** To prevent the chicken from drying out, make sure not to overcook it. Keep the heat high, and cook quickly.

POSSIBLE VARIATIONS:
- **Lime and Cilantro:** Add a squeeze of lime and some chopped cilantro to the chicken while cooking for a zesty flavor boost.
- **Different Proteins:** Substitute chicken with thinly sliced beef or shrimp for a different take on fajitas.
- **Cheese Option:** Sprinkle some shredded cheddar or Monterey Jack cheese on the tortillas before adding the chicken and vegetables for a cheesy touch.

37. Chicken Thighs with Spicy BBQ Sauce and Potatoes

PREP TIME: 20 minutes	**COOKING TIME:** 45 minutes	**TOTAL TIME:** 65 minutes
SERVINGS: For 1 person	**DIFFICULTY:** Easy	**TEMPERATURE:** Oven at 400°F (200°C)
COOKING TYPE: Direct on the grill	**SAUCE:** Spicy BBQ Sauce	

INGREDIENTS:
- **Chicken thighs:** 2 (about 1 lb / 450 grams total)
- **Spicy barbecue Sauce:** 1/2 cup / 120 ml
- **Potatoes, cubed:** 2 medium
- **Onion powder:** 1 tsp / 5 ml
- **Garlic powder:** 1 tsp / 5 ml
- **Smoked paprika:** 1 tsp / 5 ml
- **Salt:** 1/2 tsp / 2.5 ml
- **Pepper:** 1/2 tsp / 2.5 ml
- **Olive oil:** 2 tbsp / 30 ml

NUTRITIONAL VALUES PER SERVING:
Calories: 850kcal | Carbohydrates: 50g | Proteins: 60g | Fats: 45g | Fiber: 6g | Sodium: 900 mg

PROCEDURE:
1. **Prepare the Potatoes:** Preheat your oven to 400°F (200°C). In a large bowl, toss the cubed potatoes with 1 tbsp of olive oil, onion powder, garlic powder, smoked paprika, salt, and pepper until evenly coated. Spread the potatoes in a single layer on one half of a large baking sheet.

2. **Prepare the Chicken:** Pat the chicken thighs dry with paper towels. Season both sides with a little salt and pepper. Place the chicken thighs on the other half of the baking sheet. Brush each thigh generously with the spicy barbecue sauce.

3. **Roast the Chicken and Potatoes:** Place the baking sheet in the preheated oven and roast for about 45 minutes, or until the chicken is thoroughly cooked and the potatoes are tender and golden. Halfway through cooking, stir the potatoes and add an additional brush of barbecue sauce on the chicken thighs.

4. **Final Glaze and Serve:** Five minutes before the end of cooking, brush the chicken thighs with more barbecue sauce for a final glaze. Remove from the oven and let rest for a few minutes before serving.

TIPS FOR PERFECT COOKING:
- **Ensure Even Cooking:** Keep the potato cubes roughly the same size for even roasting.
- **Internal Temperature Check:** Use a meat thermometer to ensure the chicken thighs reach an internal temperature of 165°F (74°C).
- **Maximize Flavor:** For a deeper flavor, consider marinating the chicken thighs in the barbecue sauce for a few hours or overnight before cooking.

POSSIBLE VARIATIONS:
- **Vegetable Additions:** Toss in some bell peppers or carrots with the potatoes for extra vegetables.
- **Different Spices:** Experiment with different spices such as cumin or chili powder for a change in flavor profile.
- **Citrus Twist:** Add a squeeze of lime or lemon over the chicken just before serving for a fresh citrusy note.

38. Italian Marinated Chicken Breast with Grilled Vegetables

PREP TIME: 25 minutes + marinating time	**COOKING TIME:** 20 minutes	**TOTAL TIME:** 45 minutes
SERVINGS: For 1 person	**DIFFICULTY:** Easy	**TEMPERATURE:** Grill at medium-high heat
COOKING TYPE: Direct on the grill	**NOT EXPECTED**	

INGREDIENTS:
- **Chicken breast:** 1 large (about 6 oz / 170 grams)
- **Olive oil:** 3 tbsp / 45 ml
- **Balsamic vinegar:** 2 tbsp / 30 ml
- **Fresh basil, chopped:** 1/4 cup / 15 grams
- **Sun-dried tomatoes, chopped:** 1/4 cup / 30 grams
- **Garlic, minced:** 1 clove
- **Mixed bell peppers (red, yellow, green), sliced:** 1 cup / 150 grams
- **Zucchini, sliced:** 1/2 medium
- **Eggplant, sliced:** 1/2 small
- **Salt and pepper to taste**

NUTRITIONAL VALUES PER SERVING:
Calories: 650kcal | Carbohydrates: 30g | Proteins: 40g | Fats: 40g | Fiber: 6g | Sodium: 600 mg

PROCEDURE:
1. **Marinate the Chicken:** In a bowl, whisk together 2 tbsps of olive oil, balsamic vinegar, chopped basil, sun-dried tomatoes, minced garlic, salt, and pepper. Place the chicken breast in the marinade, ensuring it is fully coated. Cover and refrigerate to marinate for at least 30 minutes, preferably a few hours.

2. **Prepare the Vegetables:** Toss the sliced bell peppers, zucchini, and eggplant with the remaining 1 tbsp of olive oil, salt, and pepper.

3. **Grill the Chicken and Vegetables:** Preheat the grill to medium-high heat. Grill the marinated chicken breast for about 6-7 minutes on each side, or until fully cooked with an internal temperature of 165°F (74°C). At the same time, place the vegetables on the grill, either directly on the grate or in a grill basket. Grill for about 10-15 minutes, turning occasionally, until they are tender and have grill marks.

4. **Serve:** Let the chicken rest for a few minutes after grilling, then slice it. Arrange the grilled vegetables on a plate, and place the sliced chicken on top. Optionally, drizzle some of the remaining marinade (bring it to a boil first for safety) or a little extra virgin olive oil and balsamic vinegar over the top before serving.

TIPS FOR PERFECT COOKING:
- **Marinating Time:** Allow enough time for the chicken to marinate to enhance the flavors deeply.
- **Vegetable Slicing:** Slice vegetables uniformly to ensure even cooking.
- **Rest the Chicken:** Resting the chicken after grilling helps retain juices, making the meat tender and juicy.

POSSIBLE VARIATIONS:
- **Herb Variations:** Add other fresh herbs such as thyme or rosemary to the marinade for different flavor profiles.
- **Cheesy Delight:** Sprinkle grated Parmesan or crumbled feta over the vegetables just before serving for a cheesy twist.
- **Heat Kick:** Add chili flakes to the marinade if you prefer a bit of spice.

39. Chicken Quesadillas with Green Sauce and Cheese

- **PREP TIME:** 15 minutes
- **COOKING TIME:** 10 minutes
- **TOTAL TIME:** 25 minutes
- **SERVINGS:** For 1 person
- **DIFFICULTY:** Easy
- **TEMPERATURE:** Stovetop over medium heat
- **COOKING TYPE:** Griddling
- **SAUCE:** Green Sauce

INGREDIENTS:
- Cooked and shredded chicken breast: 1 cup (about 6 oz / 170 grams)
- Corn tortillas: 4
- Green sauce (salsa verde): 1/4 cup / 60 ml
- Grated cheddar cheese: 1/2 cup / 50 grams
- Sour cream: 2 tbsp / 30 ml
- Avocado, sliced: 1/2 of a medium avocado

NUTRITIONAL VALUES PER SERVING:
Calories: 750kcal | Carbohydrates: 55g | Proteins: 40g | Fats: 40g | Fiber: 8g | Sodium: 800 mg

PROCEDURE:
1. **Assemble the Quesadillas:** Lay two corn tortillas flat on a clean surface. Spread each tortilla with half of the green sauce. Top each sauced tortilla with half of the shredded chicken and half of the grated cheddar cheese. Place another tortilla on top of each, pressing gently to compact the fillings slightly.
2. **Cook the Quesadillas:** Heat a non-stick skillet or griddle over medium heat. Carefully transfer one quesadilla to the skillet and cook for about 2-3 minutes on each side, or until the tortilla is golden brown and the cheese has melted. Repeat with the second quesadilla.
3. **Serve:** Cut each quesadilla into quarters using a pizza cutter or a sharp knife. Serve hot, topped with slices of avocado and a dollop of sour cream.

TIPS FOR PERFECT COOKING:
- **Cheese Options:** You can substitute cheddar with Monterey Jack, mozzarella, or any other melting cheese of your choice for different flavors.
- **Green Sauce:** For an authentic taste, consider using homemade or high-quality store-bought salsa verde.
- **Cooking Quesadillas:** Ensure the heat is not too high to avoid burning the tortillas before the cheese melts.

POSSIBLE VARIATIONS:
- **Meat Variations:** You can add cooked bacon or ham along with the chicken for an extra layer of flavor.
- **Vegetarian Option:** Replace chicken with grilled vegetables such as bell peppers, onions, and zucchini for a vegetarian version.
- **Spicy Kick:** Add sliced jalapeños inside the quesadillas or use a spicy green sauce to enhance the heat.

40. Chicken Burger with Guacamole and Bacon

- **PREP TIME:** 20 minutes
- **COOKING TIME:** 10 minutes
- **TOTAL TIME:** 30 minutes
- **SERVINGS:** For 1 person
- **DIFFICULTY:** Easy
- **TEMPERATURE:** Grill or skillet over medium-high heat
- **COOKING TYPE:** Direct on the grill
- **SAUCE:** Guacamole

INGREDIENTS:
- Ground chicken breast: 6 oz / 170 grams
- Hamburger bun: 1
- Guacamole: 1/4 cup / 60 ml
- Crispy bacon: 2 slices
- Lettuce: 1 leaf
- Tomato, sliced: 1 medium
- Red onion, sliced: 2 rings
- Mayonnaise: 1 tbsp / 15 ml
- Salt and pepper to taste

NUTRITIONAL VALUES PER SERVING:
Calories: 800kcal | Carbohydrates: 40g | Proteins: 45g | Fats: 50g | Fiber: 5g | Sodium: 950 mg

PROCEDURE:
1. **Prepare the Chicken Patty:** Season the ground chicken with salt and pepper. Form it into a patty that is slightly larger than your bun because it will shrink a bit while cooking.
2. **Cook the Chicken Patty:** Heat a grill or skillet over medium-high heat. If using a skillet, add a small amount of oil to prevent sticking. Cook the chicken patty for about 5 minutes on each side, or until fully cooked and the internal temperature reaches 165°F (74°C).
3. **Prepare the Bacon:** In a skillet over medium heat, cook the bacon until crispy. Drain on paper towels.
4. **Assemble the Burger:** Toast the hamburger bun lightly on the grill or in a skillet. Spread mayonnaise on the bottom bun. Layer the lettuce, tomato slices, and red onion on top of the mayonnaise. Place the cooked chicken patty on top of the vegetables. Spread the guacamole on the chicken patty and top it with crispy bacon. Cap with the top half of the bun.

TIPS FOR PERFECT COOKING:
- **Patty Cooking:** Ensure not to press down on the patty while it cooks, as this can cause it to lose its juices and become dry.
- **Guacamole Freshness:** Use fresh, ripe avocados for the guacamole for the best flavor and texture.
- **Bun Choices:** You can opt for whole grain or brioche buns depending on your preference for a different taste and texture experience.

POSSIBLE VARIATIONS:
- **Cheese Addition:** Add a slice of your favorite cheese, such as pepper jack or cheddar, on top of the patty just before it finishes cooking to add a creamy texture.
- **Spicy Mayo:** Mix some chipotle or sriracha into the mayonnaise for an extra kick.
- **Vegetable Variations:** Feel free to add or substitute other vegetables like spinach or cucumber for a different crunch and freshness.

CHICKEN AND FISH RECIPES

41. Salmon with Chimichurri Sauce and Lime

PREP TIME: 15 minutes	COOKING TIME: 10 minutes	TOTAL TIME: 25 minutes	SERVINGS: For 1 person
DIFFICULTY: Easy	TEMPERATURE: Grill or pan over medium-high heat	COOKING TYPE: Direct on the grill	SAUCE: Chimichurri

INGREDIENTS:
- **Salmon fillet:** 6 oz / 170 grams
- **Salt:** 1/2 tsp
- **Black pepper:** 1/4 tsp
- **Olive oil:** 1 tbsp for salmon + 2 tbsp for chimichurri
- **Fresh parsley:** 1/2 cup, finely chopped
- **Fresh cilantro:** 1/2 cup, finely chopped
- **Garlic:** 2 cloves, minced
- **White vinegar:** 1 tbsp
- **Lime juice:** 2 tbsp
- **Smoked paprika:** 1/2 tsp
- **Lemon:** 1, for serving

NUTRITIONAL VALUES PER SERVING:
Calories: 520kcal | **Carbohydrates:** 5g | **Proteins:** 34g | **Fats:** 40g | **Fiber:** 1g | **Sodium:** 600 mg

PROCEDURE:
1. **Prepare the Chimichurri Sauce:** In a small bowl, combine the finely chopped parsley, cilantro, minced garlic, 2 tbsps olive oil, white vinegar, lime juice, smoked paprika, salt, and pepper. Mix well to combine all the ingredients. Set aside to let the flavors meld.

2. **Cook the Salmon:** Season the salmon fillet with salt and pepper. Heat 1 tbsp of olive oil in a grill pan or skillet over medium-high heat. Place the salmon skin-side down (if skin-on) and cook for about 4-5 minutes on each side, or until the salmon is fully cooked and flakes easily with a fork.

3. **Serve:** Transfer the cooked salmon to a plate. Generously spoon the chimichurri sauce over the salmon. Cut the lemon into wedges and serve alongside the salmon for added freshness.

TIPS FOR PERFECT COOKING:
- **Don't Overcook the Salmon:** Salmon should be cooked just until it's opaque throughout. Overcooking will dry it out.
- **Rest the Chimichurri:** Allow the chimichurri sauce to sit for at least 10 minutes before serving to enhance the melding of flavors.
- **Skin Crispiness:** If you enjoy crispy skin, make sure the skin is dry before seasoning and place it skin-side down first in a very hot pan.

POSSIBLE VARIATIONS:
- **Herb Variations:** While parsley and cilantro are classic, feel free to experiment with other herbs like mint or oregano.
- **Spicy Kick:** Add a finely chopped chili or a dash of chili flakes to the chimichurri for a spicy version.
- **Citrus Options:** Replace lime juice with orange or grapefruit juice for a different citrus profile.

42. Trout with Teriyaki Sauce and Grilled Vegetables

PREP TIME: 20 minutes	COOKING TIME: 20 minutes	TOTAL TIME: 40 minutes	SERVINGS: For 1 person
DIFFICULTY: Easy	TEMPERATURE: Grill or skillet over medium-high heat	COOKING TYPE: Direct on the grill	SAUCE: Teriyaki Sauce

INGREDIENTS:
- **Trout fillet:** 6 oz / 170g
- **Salt:** 1/4 tsp
- **Pepper:** 1/4 tsp
- **Olive oil:** 1 tbsp for trout + 1 tbsp for vegetables

Teriyaki Sauce
- **Soy Sauce:** 2 tbsp
- **Rice vinegar:** 1 tbsp
- **Sugar:** 1 tsp
- **Fresh ginger, grated:** 1 tsp
- **Red bell pepper, sliced:** 1/2 bell pepper
- **Red onion, sliced:** 1/4 onion
- **Zucchini, sliced:** 1/2 zucchini

NUTRITIONAL VALUES PER SERVING:
Calories: 450kcal | **Carbohydrates:** 20g | **Proteins:** 35g | **Fats:** 25g | **Fiber:** 3g | **Sodium:** 800 mg

PROCEDURE:
1. **Prepare the Teriyaki Sauce:** In a small saucepan, combine soy sauce, rice vinegar, sugar, and grated ginger. Heat over medium heat, stirring until the sugar dissolves. Bring to a simmer and cook for about 2-3 minutes or until slightly thickened. Set aside to cool.

2. **Marinate the Trout:** Season the trout fillet with salt and pepper, and brush both sides with a little olive oil. Spoon some of the cooled teriyaki sauce over the trout, reserving the rest for serving. Let the trout marinate for about 10-15 minutes.

3. **Grill the Vegetables:** Toss the sliced red bell pepper, red onion, and zucchini with 1 tbsp of olive oil. Place the vegetables on a grill pan or directly on a preheated grill over medium-high heat. Grill for about 10-15 minutes, turning occasionally, until they are tender and have char marks.

4. **Cook the Trout:** Heat a non-stick skillet or grill over medium-high heat. Add the marinated trout, skin side down first if skin-on, and cook for about 3-4 minutes per side, or until the trout is opaque and flakes easily with a fork.

5. **Serve:** Arrange the grilled vegetables on a plate. Place the cooked trout on top of the vegetables. Drizzle the remaining teriyaki sauce over the trout and vegetables.

TIPS FOR PERFECT COOKING:
- **Monitor Sauce Thickness:** Be careful not to over-thicken the teriyaki sauce; it should be just syrupy enough to coat the back of a spoon.
- **Avoid Overcooking Trout:** Trout cooks quickly, especially if the fillets are thin. Keep an eye on it to ensure it remains tender and moist.
- **Vegetable Doneness:** For softer vegetables, extend the grilling time; for crisper vegetables, reduce it.

POSSIBLE VARIATIONS:
- **Spicy Teriyaki:** Add a squirt of sriracha or a pinch of chili flakes to the teriyaki sauce to add some heat.
- **Different Vegetables:** Feel free to swap out or add other vegetables like eggplant, asparagus, or mushrooms.
- **Citrus Twist:** Add a splash of orange juice to the teriyaki sauce for a hint of citrus that complements the fish beautifully.

CHICKEN AND FISH RECIPES

43. Shrimp with Spicy Mango Salsa and Caramelized Onions

PREP TIME: 20 minutes
COOKING TIME: 30 minutes
TOTAL TIME: 50 minutes
SERVINGS: For 1 person
DIFFICULTY: Easy
TEMPERATURE: Grill over medium-high heat for shrimp, low for onions
COOKING TYPE: Direct on the grill
SAUCE: Spicy Mango Salsa

INGREDIENTS:
- **Shrimp, peeled and deveined:** 6 oz / 170 grams
- **Salt:** 1/4 tsp
- **Pepper:** 1/4 tsp
- **Olive oil:** 2 tbsp (1 tbsp for shrimp + 1 tbsp for onions)

Mango Salsa:
- **Ripe mango, peeled and diced:** 1 medium
- **Red chili, finely chopped** (adjust according to heat preference)**:** 1 small
- **Red bell pepper, finely diced:** 1/4 cup
- **Cilantro, chopped:** 2 tbsp
- **Lime juice:** 1 tbsp
- **Salt and pepper to taste**
- **White onions, thinly sliced:** 1 medium
- **Butter:** 1 tbsp
- **Balsamic vinegar:** 1 tbsp

PROCEDURE:
1. **Prepare the Mango Salsa:** In a medium bowl, combine diced mango, chopped red chili, diced red bell pepper, chopped cilantro, and lime juice. Season with salt and pepper to taste. Mix well and set aside for the flavors to meld.
2. **Caramelize the Onions:** In a skillet, melt butter with 1 tbsp of olive oil over medium-low heat. Add the thinly sliced onions and cook, stirring occasionally, for about 20-25 minutes, or until they are deeply golden and caramelized. Near the end of cooking, add balsamic vinegar and cook for an additional 5 minutes to deglaze the pan and enhance the flavors. Remove from heat and set aside.
3. **Cook the Shrimp:** Season the shrimp with salt and pepper. Heat the remaining 1 tbsp of olive oil in another skillet over medium-high heat. Add the shrimp and cook for about 2-3 minutes on each side, or until they are pink and opaque.
4. **Serve:** Arrange the cooked shrimp on a plate. Spoon the caramelized onions over the shrimp and top with a generous amount of spicy mango salsa.

TIPS FOR PERFECT COOKING:
- **Avoid Overcooking Shrimp:** Shrimp cook very quickly and can become rubbery if overcooked. Keep an eye on them and remove from heat as soon as they turn pink.
- **Let Salsa Sit:** Allowing the mango salsa to sit for at least 10-20 minutes before serving helps the flavors develop more fully.
- **Consistent Onion Slices:** Ensure the onions are evenly sliced to promote even caramelization.

POSSIBLE VARIATIONS:
- **Spice Variations:** Adjust the amount of red chili in the salsa according to your spice tolerance.
- **Protein Swap:** Replace shrimp with grilled chicken or fish for a different protein option.
- **Additional Vegetables:** Add diced cucumber or avocado to the mango salsa for extra freshness and texture.

NUTRITIONAL VALUES PER SERVING:
Calories: 550kcal | Carbohydrates: 45g | Proteins: 25g | Fats: 30g | Fiber: 4g | Sodium: 600 mg

44. Mixed Seafood Skewers with Aioli Sauce

PREP TIME: 20 minutes
COOKING TIME: 10 minutes
TOTAL TIME: 30 minutes
SERVINGS: For 1 person
DIFFICULTY: Easy
TEMPERATURE: Grill over medium-high heat
COOKING TYPE: Direct on the grill
SAUCE: Aioli Sauce

INGREDIENTS:
For the Skewers:
- **Assorted fish fillets (salmon, trout, cod), cut into cubes:** 6 oz total
- **Shrimp, peeled and deveined:** 4-6 large
- **Onions, cut into chunks:** 1/2 large
- **Bell peppers (red and green), cut into chunks:** 1/2 of each
- **Olive oil:** 2 tbsp
- **Garlic, minced:** 1 clove
- **Lemon juice:** 1 tbsp
- **Fresh parsley, chopped:** 1 tbsp
- **Salt and pepper to taste**

For the Aioli Sauce:
- **Garlic, minced:** 2 cloves
- **Egg yolk:** 1
- **Lemon juice:** 1 tbsp
- **Olive oil:** 1/2 cup
- **Salt and pepper to taste**

PROCEDURE:
1. **Marinate the Seafood:** In a bowl, combine olive oil, lemon juice, minced garlic, chopped parsley, salt, and pepper. Add the cubed fish and shrimp to the marinade, tossing gently to coat. Let sit for 15-20 minutes.
2. **Prepare the Aioli Sauce:** In a mixing bowl, whisk together the egg yolk, lemon juice, and minced garlic. Gradually whisk in the olive oil until the mixture emulsifies and becomes thick and creamy. Season with salt and pepper to taste. Set aside in the refrigerator.
3. **Assemble the Skewers:** Thread the marinated fish, shrimp, onion chunks, and bell pepper pieces alternately onto skewers.
4. **Grill the Skewers:** Preheat the grill to medium-high heat. Grill the skewers for about 2-3 minutes per side, or until the seafood is cooked through and the vegetables are slightly charred.
5. **Serve:** Serve the seafood skewers hot, accompanied by the freshly made aioli sauce for dipping.

TIPS FOR PERFECT COOKING:
- **Don't Overcook the Seafood:** Keep an eye on the skewers as fish and shrimp cook quickly and can dry out if overcooked.
- **Prevent Sticking:** Ensure the grill is well-oiled to prevent the seafood and vegetables from sticking.
- **Consistency in Aioli:** If the aioli fails to emulsify, you can start over with another egg yolk and slowly whisk in the broken sauce to salvage it.

POSSIBLE VARIATIONS:
- **Spice it Up:** Add a dash of cayenne pepper or chili flakes to the aioli for a spicy kick.
- **Different Vegetables:** Try adding zucchini, cherry tomatoes, or mushrooms to the skewers for variety.
- **Herb Variations:** Use different herbs such as dill or tarragon in the marinade for a different flavor profile.

NUTRITIONAL VALUES PER SERVING:
Calories: 700kcal | Carbohydrates: 15g | Proteins: 45g | Fats: 50g | Fiber: 3g | Sodium: 600 mg

45. Fish Burgers with Bacon and Tartar Sauce

PREP TIME: 30 minutes	**COOKING TIME:** 15 minutes	**TOTAL TIME:** 45 minutes
SERVINGS: For 1 person	**DIFFICULTY:** Medium	**TEMPERATURE:** Pan-fry over medium heat
COOKING TYPE: Direct on the grill	**SAUCE:** Tartar Sauce	

INGREDIENTS:

For the Fish Burgers:
- Ground white fish fillets (cod, hake): 6 oz / 170 grams
- Bacon: 2 slices
- Breadcrumbs: 1/4 cup / 60 ml
- Egg: 1, beaten
- Onion, finely chopped: 1/4 cup / 40 grams
- Fresh parsley, chopped: 1 tbsp / 15 ml
- Salt and pepper to taste
- Olive oil: for frying

For the Tartar Sauce:
- Mayonnaise: 1/2 cup / 120 ml
- Pickled cucumbers (gherkins), finely chopped: 2 tbsp / 30 ml
- Capers, finely chopped: 1 tbsp / 15 ml
- Chives, finely chopped: 1 tbsp / 15 ml
- Lemon juice: 1 tsp / 5 ml

PROCEDURE:

1. **Prepare the Fish Patties:** In a mixing bowl, combine ground fish, breadcrumbs, beaten egg, chopped onion, chopped parsley, salt, and pepper. Mix well until the mixture is homogeneous. Form the mixture into burger patties, about the size of your bun.
2. **Cook the Bacon:** In a skillet, cook the bacon slices over medium heat until crispy. Remove from the skillet and set aside on paper towels to drain.
3. **Cook the Fish Burgers:** In the same skillet, add a little olive oil if needed. Place the fish patties in the skillet and cook for about 4-5 minutes on each side or until golden brown and cooked through.
4. **Prepare the Tartar Sauce:** In a small bowl, mix mayonnaise, chopped pickled cucumbers, chopped capers, chopped chives, and lemon juice. Stir well to combine all the ingredients.
5. **Assemble the Burgers:** Place each cooked fish patty on a burger bun. Top with crispy bacon, a generous dollop of tartar sauce, and any additional toppings you might like such as lettuce or tomato slices.

NUTRITIONAL VALUES PER SERVING:
Calories: 850kcal | **Carbohydrates:** 45g | **Proteins:** 35g | **Fats:** 55g | **Fiber:** 2g | **Sodium:** 1300 mg

TIPS FOR PERFECT COOKING:
- **Patty Formation:** Chill the fish patty mixture in the refrigerator for about 10-15 minutes before forming patties to help them hold together better during cooking.
- **Avoid Overcooking:** Fish cooks quickly. Keep an eye on the patties to ensure they do not overcook and dry out.
- **Consistency of Tartar** Sauce: Adjust the tartar sauce's consistency with a little more lemon juice or mayonnaise depending on your taste.

POSSIBLE VARIATIONS:
- **Spicy Twist:** Add a splash of hot sauce or a bit of mustard to the tartar sauce for an extra kick.
- **Different Fish:** Try using salmon or a mix of different fish types for varied flavors and textures.
- **Additional Veggies:** Incorporate finely grated carrot or zucchini into the fish burger mix for added moisture and nutrition.

46. Grilled Zucchini and Bell Peppers with Olive Oil and Balsamic Vinegar

PREP TIME: 10 minutes	**COOKING TIME:** 10 minutes	**TOTAL TIME:** 20 minutes
SERVINGS: For 1 person	**DIFFICULTY:** Easy	**TEMPERATURE:** Grill over medium-high heat
COOKING TYPE: Direct on the grill	**SAUCE:** Balsamic Vinegar	

INGREDIENTS:
- Zucchini: 1 large, sliced into 1/4 inch thick rounds
- Bell peppers (mix of red, yellow, and green): 1 of each, seeded and cut into wide strips
- Olive oil: 2 tbsp
- Balsamic vinegar: 1 tbsp
- Salt: 1/4 tsp
- Pepper: 1/4 tsp

NUTRITIONAL VALUES PER SERVING:
Calories: 250kcal | **Carbohydrates:** 18g | **Proteins:** 3g | **Fats:** 20g | **Fiber:** 5g | **Sodium:** 150 mg

PROCEDURE:

1. **Preheat the Grill:** Preheat your grill to medium-high heat, ensuring it's hot before you start cooking the vegetables.
2. **Prepare the Vegetables:** In a large bowl, toss the sliced zucchini and bell pepper strips with olive oil, salt, and pepper until they are evenly coated.
3. **Grill the Vegetables:** Arrange the zucchini slices and bell pepper strips in a single layer on the grill. Avoid overcrowding to ensure each piece gets nicely charred. Grill the vegetables for about 4-5 minutes on each side, or until they have nice grill marks and are tender.
4. **Drizzle with Balsamic Vinegar:** Once the vegetables are grilled, transfer them to a serving plate. Drizzle balsamic vinegar over the warm vegetables to enhance their flavors.
5. **Serve:** Serve the grilled zucchini and bell peppers immediately, optionally garnished with fresh herbs like basil or parsley if desired.

TIPS FOR PERFECT COOKING:
- **Uniform Slices:** Cut the vegetables into uniform pieces to ensure they cook evenly.
- **Preventing Sticking:** Ensure your grill is clean and well-oiled before adding the vegetables to prevent sticking.
- **Balsamic Timing:** Drizzle balsamic vinegar over the vegetables immediately after removing them from the grill so they absorb the flavor while still hot.

POSSIBLE VARIATIONS:
- **Marinated Vegetables:** For more flavor, marinate the vegetables in olive oil, balsamic vinegar, and your choice of herbs for at least 30 minutes before grilling.
- **Cheesy Delight:** Sprinkle grated Parmesan or crumbled feta cheese over the grilled vegetables just before serving.
- **Spicy Kick:** Add a pinch of chili flakes to the olive oil before tossing with the vegetables for a spicy version.

47. Grilled Onions and Mushrooms with Butter and Chives

PREP TIME: 10 minutes	**COOKING TIME:** 15 minutes
TOTAL TIME: 25 minutes	**SERVINGS:** For 1 person
DIFFICULTY: Easy	**TEMPERATURE:** Grill or skillet over medium heat
COOKING TYPE: Direct on the grill	**NOT EXPECTED**

INGREDIENTS:
- **White onions:** 2 medium, sliced into thick rings
- **Mushrooms:** 8 oz (about 225 grams), sliced
- **Butter:** 2 tbsp
- **Fresh chives, chopped:** 2 tbsp
- **Salt:** 1/4 tsp
- **Pepper:** 1/4 tsp

NUTRITIONAL VALUES PER SERVING:
Calories: 300kcal | Carbohydrates: 20g | Proteins: 4g | Fats: 23g | Fiber: 3g | Sodium: 300 mg

PROCEDURE:
1. **Preheat the Grill or Skillet:** If using a grill, preheat it to medium heat. For indoor cooking, heat a skillet over medium heat.
2. **Prepare the Vegetables:** Clean the mushrooms with a damp cloth and slice them. Peel the onions and cut them into thick rings.
3. **Grill the Onions and Mushrooms:** Melt 1 tbsp of butter on the grill or in the skillet. Add the onions and mushrooms, season with salt and pepper, and grill or sauté for about 10-15 minutes, stirring occasionally, until the onions are caramelized and the mushrooms are golden and tender.
4. **Finish with Butter and Chives:** Once the onions and mushrooms are cooked, add the remaining tbsp of butter and allow it to melt over the vegetables. Stir in the chopped chives for an additional burst of flavor.
5. **Serve:** Transfer the grilled onions and mushrooms to a serving dish. They are perfect as a side to steaks, grilled chicken, or a vegetarian main dish.

TIPS FOR PERFECT COOKING:
- **Don't Overcrowd the Pan:** When grilling or sautéing, ensure the onions and mushrooms are not overcrowded. This helps them caramelize rather than steam.
- **Adjust Heat if Necessary:** Keep an eye on the heat level; if the onions or mushrooms begin to burn, reduce the heat.
- **Freshness of Chives:** Add the chives towards the end of cooking to preserve their delicate flavor and vibrant color.

POSSIBLE VARIATIONS:
- **Garlic Twist:** For garlic lovers, add minced garlic along with the onions for a robust garlic flavor.
- **Herb Variations:** Experiment with different herbs such as thyme or parsley instead of chives for variety.
- **Spicy Kick:** Sprinkle some crushed red pepper flakes when adding the salt and pepper for a spicy version.

48. Grilled Asparagus and Tomatoes with Pesto and Parmesan Cheese

PREP TIME: 10 minutes	**COOKING TIME:** 10 minutes
TOTAL TIME: 20 minutes	**SERVINGS:** For 1 person
DIFFICULTY: Easy	**TEMPERATURE:** Grill over medium-high heat
COOKING TYPE: Direct on the grill	**SAUCE:** Pesto

INGREDIENTS:
- **Asparagus:** 8-10 spears, trimmed
- **Cherry tomatoes:** 1 cup
- **Pesto:** 2 tbsp
- **Grated Parmesan cheese:** 2 tbsp
- **Olive oil:** 1 tbsp
- **Salt and pepper to taste**

NUTRITIONAL VALUES PER SERVING:
Calories: 300kcal | Carbohydrates: 12g | Proteins: 10g | Fats: 23g | Fiber: 4g | Sodium: 500 mg

PROCEDURE:
1. **Prepare the Grill:** Preheat your grill to medium-high heat. Make sure the grates are clean and lightly oiled to prevent sticking.
2. **Prepare the Vegetables:** Lightly coat the asparagus spears and cherry tomatoes with olive oil. Season with salt and pepper to taste.
3. **Grill the Vegetables:** Place the asparagus and cherry tomatoes on the grill. Grill the asparagus for about 6-8 minutes, turning occasionally, until they are tender and have visible grill marks. Grill the tomatoes for about 4-5 minutes or until they start to burst and get charred spots.
4. **Add Pesto and Parmesan:** Once the vegetables are grilled, transfer them to a serving platter. Drizzle the pesto evenly over the asparagus and tomatoes. Sprinkle grated Parmesan cheese on top while the vegetables are still hot, allowing the cheese to melt slightly.
5. **Serve:** Serve the vegetables immediately, garnished with additional Parmesan or fresh herbs if desired.

TIPS FOR PERFECT COOKING:
- **Preventing Overcooking:** Keep a close eye on the vegetables as they grill quickly. Remove them from the grill as soon as they are tender to avoid overcooking.
- **Pesto Variations:** You can use homemade or store-bought pesto. Consider trying different types of pesto, such as sun-dried tomato or arugula pesto, for a variation in flavor.
- **Cheese Choices:** While Parmesan is classic, you can also try using other hard cheeses like Pecorino Romano or a blend for different nuances in flavor.

POSSIBLE VARIATIONS:
- **Add Nuts:** Sprinkle toasted pine nuts or slivered almonds over the top for added crunch and nuttiness.
- **Spicy Kick:** Add a few dashes of crushed red pepper to the vegetables before grilling for a spicy version.
- **Additional Vegetables:** Include slices of bell pepper or zucchini on the grill for more variety and color.

49. Sweet Potatoes and Beets with Chimichurri Sauce

PREP TIME: 20 minutes	**COOKING TIME:** 30 minutes	**TOTAL TIME:** 50 minutes
SERVINGS: For 1 person	**DIFFICULTY:** Easy	**TEMPERATURE:** Oven at 400°F (200°C) or grill over medium heat
COOKING TYPE: Direct on the grill	**SAUCE:** Chimichurri	

INGREDIENTS:
- **Sweet potatoes:** 2 medium, peeled and cubed
- **Pre-cooked beets:** 2 medium, cubed
- **Fresh parsley:** 1/2 cup, finely chopped
- **Fresh cilantro:** 1/2 cup, finely chopped
- **Garlic:** 3 cloves, minced
- **Olive oil:** 1/4 cup for chimichurri + 2 tbsp for vegetables
- **White vinegar:** 2 tbsp
- **Lime juice:** 1 tbsp
- **Smoked paprika:** 1 tsp
- **Salt:** 1/2 tsp or to taste
- **Black pepper:** 1/2 tsp or to taste

NUTRITIONAL VALUES PER SERVING:
Calories: 500kcal | Carbohydrates: 65g | Proteins: 5g | Fats: 27g | Fiber: 10g | Sodium: 600 mg

PROCEDURE:
1. **Roast the Vegetables:** Preheat your oven to 400°F (200°C). Toss the cubed sweet potatoes and beets with 2 tbsps of olive oil, salt, and pepper. Spread them in a single layer on a baking sheet. Roast in the preheated oven for about 30 minutes, or until the vegetables are tender and starting to caramelize. Stir halfway through to ensure even cooking.

2. **Prepare the Chimichurri Sauce:** In a bowl, combine the finely chopped parsley, cilantro, minced garlic, 1/4 cup olive oil, white vinegar, lime juice, smoked paprika, salt, and pepper. Whisk together until well mixed. Let the sauce sit for at least 10 minutes to allow the flavors to meld.

3. **Serve:** Once the sweet potatoes and beets are roasted, transfer them to a serving dish. Drizzle the chimichurri sauce over the hot vegetables, tossing gently to coat.

TIPS FOR PERFECT COOKING:
- **Uniform Pieces:** Cut the sweet potatoes and beets into even-sized pieces to ensure they cook uniformly.
- **Freshness of Ingredients:** Use fresh herbs for the chimichurri to maximize the flavor and aroma.
- **Adjust Seasonings:** Taste and adjust the seasoning of the chimichurri sauce according to your preference. Some might prefer more vinegar or lime juice for extra tanginess.

POSSIBLE VARIATIONS:
- **Herb Variations:** Feel free to experiment with different herbs in the chimichurri, such as mint or basil, for a different flavor profile.
- **Spicy Version:** Add a chopped chili pepper or a dash of cayenne pepper to the chimichurri for a spicy kick.
- **Additional Texture:** Sprinkle roasted nuts like almonds or walnuts on top for added crunch.

50. Grilled Eggplant and Bell Peppers with Spicy Mango Salsa

PREP TIME: 20 minutes	**COOKING TIME:** 15 minutes	**TOTAL TIME:** 35 minutes
SERVINGS: For 1 person	**DIFFICULTY:** Easy	**TEMPERATURE:** Grill over medium-high heat
COOKING TYPE: Direct on the grill	**SAUCE:** Spicy Mango Salsa	

INGREDIENTS:
For the Grilled Vegetables:
- **Eggplant:** 1 medium, sliced into 1/2 inch thick rounds
- **Bell peppers:** 1 red and 1 yellow, seeded and quartered
- **Olive oil:** 2 tbsp
- **Balsamic vinegar:** 1 tbsp
- Salt and pepper to taste

For the Spicy Mango Salsa:
- **Ripe mango, peeled and diced:** 1 large
- **Red chili, finely chopped (adjust to heat preference):** 1 small
- **Red onion, finely chopped:** 1/4 cup
- **Fresh cilantro, chopped:** 2 tbsp
- **Lime juice:** 1 tbsp
- Salt to taste

PROCEDURE:
1. **Prepare the Spicy Mango Salsa:** In a medium bowl, combine the diced mango, chopped red chili, chopped red onion, chopped cilantro, and lime juice. Season with salt to taste and mix well. Set aside for the flavors to meld while you grill the vegetables.

2. **Grill the Vegetables:** Preheat your grill to medium-high heat. Brush the eggplant slices and bell pepper quarters with olive oil and balsamic vinegar. Season with salt and pepper. Place the vegetables on the grill and cook for about 7-8 minutes on each side, or until they are tender and have nice grill marks.

3. **Serve:** Arrange the grilled eggplant and bell peppers on a serving platter. Spoon the spicy mango salsa generously over the grilled vegetables.

TIPS FOR PERFECT COOKING:
- **Even Cooking:** Ensure the eggplant and bell peppers are cut uniformly for even grilling.
- **Resting the Salsa:** Let the salsa rest for at least 10 minutes before serving to allow the flavors to develop more fully.
- **Preventing Stickiness:** Make sure the grill is well-oiled to prevent the vegetables from sticking.

POSSIBLE VARIATIONS:
- **Add Protein:** For a protein boost, consider adding grilled shrimp or chicken on top of the vegetables before topping with salsa.
- **Different Vegetables:** Try adding zucchini or squash to the grill for more variety.
- **Heat Adjustments:** Customize the heat level in the salsa with more or fewer chilies according to your spice preference.

NUTRITIONAL VALUES PER SERVING:
Calories: 400kcal | Carbohydrates: 58g | Proteins: 5g | Fats: 20g | Fiber: 10g | Sodium: 300 mg

GRILLED VEGETABLES RECIPES

51. Barbecue Sauce

Prep Time:	20 minutes
Cooking Time:	15 minutes
Total Time:	35 minutes
Servings:	For 1 person
Difficulty:	Easy
Temperature:	Grill over medium-high heat
Cooking Type:	Prepared on the stove (NOT grilled)
	NOT EXPECTED

INGREDIENTS:
- Ketchup: 1 cup (240 ml)
- Apple cider vinegar: 1/4 cup (60 ml)
- Brown sugar: 1/4 cup (50 g)
- Worcestershire sauce: 2 tbsps (30 ml)
- Lemon juice: 1 tbsp (15 ml)
- Soy sauce: 1 tbsp (15 ml)
- Smoked paprika: 1 tsp (5 ml)
- Garlic powder: 1/2 tsp (2.5 ml)
- Onion powder: 1/2 tsp (2.5 ml)
- Black pepper: 1/2 tsp (2.5 ml)
- Cayenne pepper: A Pinch (optional)

INSTRUCTIONS:
1. **Combine ingredients:** In a medium saucepan, whisk together ketchup, apple cider vinegar, brown sugar, Worcestershire sauce, lemon juice, soy sauce, smoked paprika, garlic powder, onion powder, black pepper, and cayenne pepper (if using).
2. **Simmer:** Bring the mixture to a boil over medium heat, then reduce heat to low and simmer, stirring occasionally, for about 20-30 minutes, or until the sauce has thickened to your desired consistency.
3. **Let rest:** Remove the sauce from heat and let it cool. This allows the flavors to meld further and the sauce to thicken slightly.
4. **Store or use immediately:** You can use the sauce right away or store it in an airtight container in the refrigerator for up to 2 weeks.

TIPS:
- For a sweeter barbecue sauce, increase the amount of brown sugar.
- For a spicier sauce, add more cayenne pepper or a few drops of hot sauce.
- This sauce is great for marinating meats before grilling or as a finishing condiment on burgers, ribs, or grilled chicken.

NUTRITIONAL VALUES PER SERVING:
Calories: 70kcal | Carbohydrates: 18g | Proteins: 0g | Fats: 0g | Fiber: 1g | Sodium: 290mg | Glucose: 14g

52. Chimichurri Sauce

Prep Time:	10 minutes
Cooking Time:	0 minutes
Total Time:	10 minutes
Servings:	For 1 person
Difficulty:	Easy
Temperature:	Serve at room temperature
Cooking Type:	Prepared fresh, served cold (NOT grilled)
	NOT EXPECTED

INGREDIENTS:
- Fresh parsley: 1 cup (packed), finely chopped
- Fresh cilantro: 1/2 cup (packed), finely chopped
- Fresh oregano: 2 tbsps, finely chopped (or 2 tsps dried oregano)
- Garlic: 3 cloves, minced
- Red wine vinegar: 1/4 cup (60 ml)
- Lemon juice: 2 tbsps (30 ml)
- Olive oil: 1/2 cup (120 ml)
- Red chili flakes: 1 tsp (or to taste)
- Salt: 1/2 tsp
- Black pepper: 1/4 tsp

INSTRUCTIONS:
1. **Combine Herbs and Seasonings:** In a medium bowl, mix together the finely chopped parsley, cilantro, oregano, and minced garlic.
2. **Add Liquids:** Stir in the red wine vinegar, lemon juice, and olive oil. Mix thoroughly to combine.
3. **Season:** Add the red chili flakes, salt, and black pepper. Adjust the seasoning according to taste.
4. **Let Rest:** Allow the sauce to sit for at least 10-20 minutes before serving to let the flavors meld together. For best results, let it sit for a couple of hours at room temperature.
5. **Serve or Store:** Use the chimichurri sauce immediately, or store it in an airtight container in the refrigerator for up to a week. It may separate slightly, so stir it before use.

TIPS:
- **Herb Variations:** While parsley, cilantro, and oregano are traditional, you can experiment with different proportions or even try adding other herbs like basil for a unique twist.
- **Spice Adjustments:** If you prefer a less spicy sauce, reduce the amount of red chili flakes, or omit them entirely.
- **Acidity Balance:** If the sauce is too tart for your liking, adjust the acidity by adding more olive oil or a touch of water to mellow the flavors.

NUTRITIONAL VALUES PER SERVING:
Calories: 130kcal | Carbohydrates: 1g | Proteins: 0g | Fats: 14g | Fiber: 1g | Sodium: 580mg | Glucose: 0g

SAUCES FOR FISH DISHES

53. Teriyaki Sauce

| Prep Time: 5 minutes | Cooking Time: 10 minutes | Total Time: 15 minutes | Servings: For 1 person |
| Difficulty: Easy | Temperature: Over medium heat for cooking | Cooking Type: Prepared on the stove (NOT grilled) | NOT EXPECTED |

INGREDIENTS:
- **Soy Sauce:** 1/2 cup (120 ml)
- **Water:** 1/4 cup (60 ml)
- **Mirin (sweet rice wine):** 1/4 cup (60 ml)
- **Sugar:** 3 tbsps
- **Brown sugar:** 2 tbsps (for a deeper flavor)
- **Garlic, minced:** 1 clove
- **Fresh ginger, grated:** 1 tsp
- **Cornstarch:** 1 tbsp
- **Cold water:** 2 tbsps (to mix with cornstarch)

NUTRITIONAL VALUES PER SERVING:
Calories: 80kcal | **Carbohydrates:** 18g | **Proteins:** 1g | **Fats:** 0g | **Fiber:** 1g | **Sodium:** 780mg | **Glucose:** 15 g

INSTRUCTIONS:
1. **Combine Ingredients:** In a small saucepan, mix together the soy sauce, 1/4 cup water, mirin, sugar, brown sugar, minced garlic, and grated ginger. Stir well to dissolve the sugars.
2. **Simmer:** Place the saucepan over medium heat and bring the mixture to a simmer, stirring occasionally.
3. **Thicken the Sauce:** In a small bowl, dissolve the cornstarch in 2 tbsps of cold water to make a slurry. Slowly stir the slurry into the simmering sauce. Continue cooking, stirring continuously, until the sauce thickens and becomes glossy, about 2-3 minutes.
4. **Cool and Store:** Remove the sauce from heat and let it cool to room temperature. The sauce will thicken further as it cools. Store in an airtight container in the refrigerator for up to a week.

TIPS:
- **Adjusting Sweetness:** Depending on your preference, you can adjust the levels of sugar and mirin. Reduce the sugar for a less sweet sauce, or add more for extra sweetness.
- **Variation for Thickness:** If you prefer a thinner sauce, reduce the amount of cornstarch or omit it entirely for a more traditional, runnier sauce.
- **Using the Sauce:** Teriyaki sauce is excellent for marinating or glazing chicken, beef, pork, or seafood. It can also be brushed on vegetables before grilling or roasting.

54. Spicy Mango Salsa

| Prep Time: 15 minutes | Cooking Time: 0 minutes | Total Time: 15 minutes | Servings: For 1 person |
| Difficulty: Easy | Temperature: Served Chilled or at room temperature | Cooking Type: Prepared fresh, served cold (NOT grilled) | NOT EXPECTED |

INGREDIENTS:
- **Ripe mangoes:** 2 large, peeled and finely diced
- **Red bell pepper:** 1 medium, finely diced
- **Red onion:** 1 small, finely diced
- **Jalapeño or serrano chili:** 1, seeded and minced (adjust more or less depending on heat preference)
- **Cilantro:** 1/4 cup, chopped
- **Lime juice:** from 2 limes
- **Salt:** 1/2 tsp
- **Pepper:** 1/4 tsp

NUTRITIONAL VALUES PER SERVING:
Calories: 40kcal | **Carbohydrates:** 10g | **Proteins:** 1g | **Fats:** 0g | **Fiber:** 1g | **Sodium:** 150mg | **Glucose:** 8 g

INSTRUCTIONS:
1. **Prepare the Ingredients:** Ensure all the fruits and vegetables are finely chopped to help meld the flavors together more cohesively.
2. **Mix the Salsa:** In a large bowl, combine the diced mangoes, red bell pepper, red onion, and minced chili pepper. Add the chopped cilantro and pour over the lime juice. Season with salt and pepper to taste. Gently mix all the ingredients until well combined.
3. **Let It Marinate:** Allow the salsa to sit at room temperature for about 30 minutes before serving. This resting period lets the flavors combine and develop more fully. Alternatively, you can refrigerate it for a few hours; just be sure to bring it back to room temperature before serving to enhance the flavors.

TIPS:
- **Mango Selection:** Choose mangoes that are ripe but still firm, as they will hold up better in the salsa.
- **Adjusting Heat:** For a milder salsa, remove the seeds and membrane of the chili before mincing. For extra heat, include some of the seeds.
- **Lime Juice Balance:** Adjust the amount of lime juice according to how juicy your limes are and your taste preferences. More lime juice can add a refreshing tartness that balances the sweetness of the mango.

SAUCES FOR FISH DISHES

55. Tartar Sauce

- **Prep Time:** 10 minutes
- **Cooking Time:** 0 minutes
- **Total Time:** 10 minutes
- **Servings:** For 1 person
- **Difficulty:** Easy
- **Temperature:** Serve at room temperature
- **Cooking Type:** Prepared fresh, served cold (NOT grilled)
- **NOT EXPECTED**

INGREDIENTS:
- **Mayonnaise:** 1 cup (240 ml)
- **Pickles (or relish):** 1/4 cup, finely chopped
- **Capers:** 1 tbsp, chopped
- **Fresh parsley:** 2 tbsps, finely chopped
- **Lemon juice:** 2 tbsps (30 ml)
- **Dijon mustard:** 1 tsp
- **Onion, finely minced:** 1 tbsp
- **Salt:** 1/4 tsp
- **Black pepper:** 1/4 tsp

NUTRITIONAL VALUES PER SERVING:
Calories: 150kcal | **Carbohydrates:** 1g | **Proteins:** 0g | **Fats:** 16g | **Fiber:** 0g | **Sodium:** 360mg | **Glucose:** 1 g

INSTRUCTIONS:
1. **Combine Ingredients:** In a medium bowl, mix together the mayonnaise, finely chopped pickles (or relish), chopped capers, finely chopped parsley, lemon juice, Dijon mustard, and finely minced onion. Stir all the ingredients until they are well combined.

2. **Season:** Season with salt and black pepper to taste. Adjust the seasoning according to your preferences.

3. **Chill:** Cover and refrigerate the tartar sauce for at least 30 minutes before serving. This chilling time allows the flavors to meld together and intensify.

TIPS:
- **Consistency Adjustment:** If you prefer a thinner sauce, you can add a bit more lemon juice or a splash of pickle juice to achieve your desired consistency.
- **Flavor Variations:** Add a dash of hot sauce or Worcestershire sauce for an extra layer of flavor.
- **Freshness:** For the best flavor, use fresh lemon juice rather than bottled, and fresh herbs if possible.

56. Tomato Sauce

- **Prep Time:** 10 minutes
- **Cooking Time:** 20 minutes
- **Total Time:** 30 minutes
- **Servings:** For 1 person
- **Difficulty:** Easy
- **Temperature:** Simmer on medium-low heat
- **Cooking Type:** Cooked on the stove (NOT grilled)
- **NOT EXPECTED**

INGREDIENTS:
- **Ripe tomatoes:** 2 pounds (about 900 grams), peeled and diced
- **Olive oil:** 2 tbsps
- **Onion:** 1 medium, finely chopped
- **Garlic:** 3 cloves, minced
- **Carrot:** 1 small, grated (optional for sweetness)
- **Celery stalk:** 1, finely chopped (optional for depth of flavor)
- **Tomato paste:** 1 tbsp
- **Fresh basil leaves:** 1/4 cup, chopped
- **Salt:** 1 tsp
- **Black pepper:** 1/2 tsp
- **Sugar:** 1 tsp (optional, to balance acidity)
- **Red wine:** 1/4 cup (optional, for richness)

INSTRUCTIONS:
1. **Prepare Ingredients:** If using fresh tomatoes, blanch them first to peel easily. Cut a small "x" at the bottom of each tomato, immerse them in boiling water for about 30 seconds, and then transfer to ice water. The skin should peel off easily. Then, dice the tomatoes.

2. **Cook the Aromatics:** In a large saucepan, heat the olive oil over medium heat. Add the chopped onion, minced garlic, grated carrot, and chopped celery. Sauté until the onion is translucent and the vegetables are starting to soften, about 5-7 minutes.

3. **Add Tomatoes and Simmer:** Stir in the diced tomatoes and tomato paste. If using, pour in the red wine. Bring the mixture to a simmer. Reduce the heat to low and let simmer gently, uncovered, for about 30 minutes to an hour, stirring occasionally. The longer it simmers, the more the flavors will develop.

4. **Season and Finish:** Add the chopped basil, salt, black pepper, and sugar (if using). Adjust the seasoning to taste. Continue to simmer for another 10 minutes. For a smoother sauce, use an immersion blender to puree the sauce directly in the pot to your desired consistency.

5. **Serve or Store:** Use the sauce immediately, or let it cool and store it in airtight containers. It can be refrigerated for up to a week or frozen for up to six months.

TIPS:
- **Depth of Flavor:** Simmering the sauce for a longer period helps develop a richer flavor. If you have the time, a slow simmer of up to two hours can significantly enhance the sauce.
- **Acidity Balance:** Adjust the sugar according to the acidity of the tomatoes. Some tomatoes may need more sugar to achieve the perfect balance.
- **Herb Variations:** While basil is traditional, you can experiment with other herbs like oregano or thyme to customize the flavor profile.

NUTRITIONAL VALUES PER SERVING:
Calories: 80kcal | **Carbohydrates:** 9g | **Proteins:** 2g | **Fats:** 4g | **Fiber:** 2g | **Sodium:** 480mg | **Glucose:** 6 g

57. Ponzu Sauce

Prep Time: 5 minutes
Cooking Time: 0 minutes
Total Time: 5 minutes
Servings: For 1 person
Difficulty: Easy
Temperature: Serve at room temperature
Cooking Type: Prepared fresh, served cold (NOT grilled)
NOT EXPECTED

INGREDIENTS:
- **Soy Sauce:** 1/2 cup (120 ml)
- **Citrus juice (mix of lemon, lime, and orange):** 1/4 cup (60 ml)
- **Mirin (sweet rice wine):** 2 tbsps
- **Rice vinegar:** 2 tbsps
- **Kombu (dried kelp):** one small piece, approximately 2x2 inches
- **Katsuobushi (dried bonito flakes):** 1/4 cup
- **Sugar:** 1 tsp (optional, adjust to taste)

NUTRITIONAL VALUES PER SERVING:
Calories: 35kcal | Carbohydrates: 7g | **Proteins:** 1g | **Fats:** 0g | **Fiber:** 0g | **Sodium:** 800mg | **Glucose:** 3 g

INSTRUCTIONS:
1. **Combine Liquids:** In a bowl, combine the soy sauce, citrus juices, mirin, and rice vinegar. Stir well to mix.
2. **Add Kombu and Katsuobushi:** Add the piece of kombu and the katsuobushi flakes to the liquid mixture. Let this sit for about 30 minutes at room temperature to allow the flavors to infuse.
3. **Strain and Finish:** After 30 minutes, remove the kombu and strain out the katsuobushi to clear the sauce of any solids. If desired, add sugar at this point to balance the tartness. Stir well until the sugar is dissolved, if using.
4. **Chill and Store:** Refrigerate the sauce until ready to use. Ponzu can be stored in an airtight container in the refrigerator for up to a week.

TIPS:
- **Citrus Choice:** Traditional ponzu uses yuzu, a Japanese citrus, for its distinct flavor. If yuzu is unavailable, a combination of lemon, lime, and orange juice is a good substitute.
- **Flavor Development:** Allowing the kombu and katsuobushi to infuse for at least 30 minutes is crucial for developing the umami flavors typical of ponzu.
- **Serving Suggestions:** Ponzu is excellent as a dipping sauce for tempura, a marinade for grilled meats, or as a dressing for cold noodle salads.

58. Salmon Burger with Avocado and Pancetta

PREP TIME: 20 minutes
COOKING TIME: 10 minutes
TOTAL TIME: 30 minutes
SERVINGS: For 1 person
DIFFICULTY: Medium
TEMPERATURE: Medium-high: 375-400°F (190-205°C)
COOKING TYPE: Direct on the grill
SAUCE: Lemon Dill Sauce

INGREDIENTS:
- **Salmon fillet:** 6 oz / 170 grams, finely chopped or ground
- **Pancetta:** 2 slices
- **Avocado:** 1/2, sliced
- **Lemon juice:** 1 tbsp / 15 ml
- **Fresh dill:** 1 tbsp, chopped
- **Mayonnaise:** 2 tbsps / 30 ml
- **Dijon mustard:** 1 tsp / 5 ml
- **Breadcrumbs:** 1/4 cup / 60 ml
- **Egg:** 1, beaten
- **Hamburger bun:** 1
- **Salt and pepper to taste**

NUTRITIONAL VALUES PER SERVING:
Calories: 850kcal | **Carbohydrates:** 45g | **Proteins:** 50g | **Fats:** 55g | **Fiber:** 6g | **Sodium:** 1200mg | **Glucose:** 3 g

PROCEDURE:
1. **Patty Preparation:** In a bowl, mix the chopped salmon, bread crumbs, beaten egg, Dijon mustard, half of the chopped dill, salt, and pepper. Form the mixture into a burger patty slightly larger than your bun.
2. **Grill the Pancetta:** Preheat the grill to medium-high temperature. Grill the pancetta slices until crispy, about 2-3 minutes per side. Set aside on paper towels to drain.
3. **Cook the Salmon Patty:** Grill the salmon patty for about 4-5 minutes per side or until fully cooked and lightly charred.
4. **Prepare the Sauce:** In a small bowl, mix mayonnaise with the remaining dill and lemon juice to create the lemon dill sauce.
5. **Assemble the Burger:** Toast the hamburger bun lightly on the grill. Spread some lemon dill sauce on both sides of the bun. Place the salmon patty on the bottom bun, top with crispy pancetta, and arrange avocado slices over the pancetta.

TIPS FOR PERFECT COOKING:
- **Avoid Overmixing:** When forming the patty, mix just until the ingredients are combined to keep the texture of the salmon tender.
- **Pancetta Crispiness:** Watch the pancetta closely on the grill as it can go from crispy to burnt quickly due to its fat content.
- **Avocado Freshness:** Squeeze a little lemon juice over the avocado slices to prevent them from browning and to add a zesty flavor.

POSSIBLE VARIATIONS:
- **Less Salt Variant:** For a lower sodium version, use low-sodium soy sauce in the salmon mix and reduce the added salt.
- **Cheese Addition:** Top with a slice of smoked gouda or mozzarella for a cheesy twist.
- **Spicy Kick:** Add a few slices of jalapeño to the burger or incorporate some chili flakes into the salmon mixture for extra heat.

SAUCES FOR FISH DISHES

59. Spicy Shrimp with Mango and Pineapple Sauce

PREP TIME: 15 minutes	**COOKING TIME:** 10 minutes	**TOTAL TIME:** 25 minutes
SERVINGS: For 1 person	**DIFFICULTY:** Medium	**TEMPERATURE:** Medium-high for cooking shrimp
COOKING TYPE: Sautéing	**SAUCE:** Mango and Pineapple Sauce	

INGREDIENTS:
- **Shrimp:** 6 oz / 170 grams, peeled and deveined
- **Mango:** 1, peeled and cubed
- **Pineapple:** 1/2 cup, cubed
- **Red chili flakes:** 1 tsp (adjust to taste)
- **Garlic:** 2 cloves, minced
- **Ginger:** 1 tsp, grated
- **Lime juice:** 2 tbsps / 30 ml
- **Olive oil:** 2 tbsps / 30 ml
- **Honey:** 1 tbsp / 15 ml
- **Salt and pepper to taste**
- **Fresh cilantro:** For garnish

NUTRITIONAL VALUES PER SERVING:
Calories: 400kcal | Carbohydrates: 35g | Proteins: 25g | Fats: 18g | Fiber: 3g | Sodium: 500 mg

PROCEDURE:
1. **Prepare the Sauce:** In a blender or food processor, combine the mango cubes, pineapple cubes, honey, and lime juice. Blend until smooth. Set the sauce aside.

2. **Cook the Shrimp:** Heat 1 tbsp of olive oil in a skillet over medium-high heat. Add the minced garlic and grated ginger, and sauté for about 1 minute until fragrant. Add the shrimp to the skillet, sprinkle with red chili flakes, salt, and pepper. Cook for about 2-3 minutes on each side or until the shrimp are pink and cooked through.

3. **Serve:** Arrange the cooked shrimp on a serving platter. Drizzle the mango and pineapple sauce generously over the shrimp. Garnish with chopped fresh cilantro.

TIPS FOR PERFECT COOKING:
- **Shrimp Size:** Use medium-sized shrimp for this recipe as they provide the best balance of flavor and texture for appetizers.
- **Sauce Consistency:** If the sauce is too thick, thin it with a little water or additional lime juice to achieve your desired consistency.
- **Heat Level:** Adjust the amount of red chili flakes according to your preference for spice.

POSSIBLE VARIATIONS:
- **Extra Crunch:** Add diced red bell pepper to the sauté step for extra crunch and color.
- **Herb Variations:** Incorporate some mint along with cilantro for an additional layer of freshness.
- **Protein Variants:** Substitute shrimp with chicken or tofu for a different protein base, adjusting cooking times as necessary.

60. Fish Nachos with Guacamole Sauce

PREP TIME: 20 minutes	**COOKING TIME:** 15 minutes	**TOTAL TIME:** 35 minutes
SERVINGS: For 1 person	**DIFFICULTY:** Medium	**TEMPERATURE:** 375°F (190°C) for frying fish
COOKING TYPE: Frying and Baking	**SAUCE:** Guacamole Sauce	

INGREDIENTS:
- **White fish fillets (such as cod or tilapia):** 6 oz / 170 grams, cut into bite-sized pieces
- **Flour:** 1/2 cup / 60 grams
- **Beer or sparkling water:** 1/2 cup / 120 ml
- **Paprika:** 1 tsp
- **Garlic powder:** 1 tsp
- **Tortilla chips:** 2 cups
- **Shredded cheese (Mexican blend or cheddar):** 1 cup / 100 grams
- **Lime juice:** 1 tbsp / 15 ml
- **Olive oil:** For frying

For the Guacamole Sauce:
- **Ripe avocados:** 2, mashed
- **Tomato:** 1 medium, diced
- **Red onion:** 1/4 cup, finely chopped
- **Cilantro:** 2 tbsps, chopped
- **Jalapeño:** 1, seeded and minced
- **Salt and pepper to taste**

INSTRUCTIONS:
1. **Prepare the Fish Batter:** In a bowl, mix the flour, paprika, garlic powder, and a pinch of salt. Gradually whisk in the beer or sparkling water until the batter is smooth.

2. **Fry the Fish:** Heat olive oil in a deep fryer or large skillet to 375°F (190°C). Dip fish pieces into the batter, ensuring they are well coated. Fry the battered fish in the hot oil for about 3-4 minutes or until golden and crispy. Drain on paper towels.

3. **Make the Guacamole Sauce:** In a bowl, combine mashed avocados, diced tomato, chopped red onion, cilantro, minced jalapeño, and lime juice. Season with salt and pepper to taste. Mix well until combined.

4. **Assemble the Nachos:** Preheat the oven to 350°F (175°C). Spread tortilla chips on a baking sheet. Sprinkle half of the shredded cheese over the chips. Distribute the fried fish pieces evenly over the chips and cheese. Top with the remaining cheese. Bake in the preheated oven for about 5-7 minutes, or until the cheese is melted and bubbly.

5. **Serve:** Remove the nachos from the oven. Drizzle generously with the guacamole sauce. Serve immediately.

TIPS FOR PERFECT COOKING:
- **Consistent Fish Size:** Ensure the fish pieces are uniformly sized for even cooking.
- **Oil temperature:** Maintain the oil temperature to ensure the fish fries evenly and doesn't absorb excess oil.
- **Serving Suggestion:** Serve immediately after assembling to ensure the nachos retain their crunch and the cheese is perfectly melty.

POSSIBLE VARIATIONS:
- **Cheese Options:** Experiment with different types of cheese like mozzarella for a stringy texture or pepper jack for extra spice.
- **Add Extras:** Include sliced olives, sour cream, or a sprinkle of chili flakes for additional layers of flavor.

NUTRITIONAL VALUES PER SERVING:
Calories: 750kcal | Carbohydrates: 60g | Proteins: 35g | Fats: 40g | Fiber: 8g | Sodium: 700 mg

61. Tuna Tartare with Avocado and Wasabi

PREP TIME: 20 minutes	COOKING TIME: 0 minutes
TOTAL TIME: 20 minutes	SERVINGS: For 1 person
DIFFICULTY: Medium	TEMPERATURE: Served Fresh
COOKING TYPE: No Cooking, served raw	SAUCE: Wasabi Paste

INGREDIENTS:
- **Fresh tuna steak:** 6 oz / 170 grams, sushi grade, finely diced
- **Avocado:** 1 medium, finely diced
- **Cucumber:** 1/2, seeded and finely diced
- **Red onion:** 1/4 cup, finely chopped
- **Fresh cilantro:** 2 tbsps, chopped
- **Wasabi paste:** 1 tsp (adjust according to taste)
- **Soy Sauce:** 2 tbsps / 30 ml
- **Sesame oil:** 1 tsp / 5 ml
- **Lime juice:** 1 tbsp / 15 ml
- **Salt and pepper to taste**
- **Sesame seeds (optional):** 1 tsp for garnish

INSTRUCTIONS:
1. **Prepare the Tuna:** Ensure the tuna is fresh and of sushi-grade quality. Finely dice the tuna and place it in a medium mixing bowl.
2. **Mix Ingredients:** Add the finely diced avocado, cucumber, red onion, and cilantro to the tuna. In a small bowl, whisk together the wasabi paste, soy sauce, sesame oil, and lime juice until well combined. Pour the dressing over the tuna mixture and gently toss to coat all ingredients. Season with salt and pepper to taste.
3. **Serve:** Carefully plate the tuna tartare, using a ring mold or a small cup to shape the mixture if desired. Garnish with sesame seeds for an added texture and visual appeal.

TIPS FOR PERFECT COOKING:
- **Handling Tuna:** Keep the tuna refrigerated until ready to use, and handle it as little as possible to maintain its texture.
- **Wasabi Adjustment:** Start with a small amount of wasabi and adjust according to your preference for heat.
- **Serving Suggestion:** Serve immediately after preparing to ensure the freshness and quality of the ingredients.

POSSIBLE VARIATIONS:
- **Add Crunch:** Include finely chopped nuts like macadamia or almonds for an extra crunch.
- **Herb Variations:** Experiment with different herbs like mint or basil instead of cilantro for a different flavor profile.
- **Fruit Twist:** Add a small amount of finely diced mango or apple for a sweet contrast.

NUTRITIONAL VALUES PER SERVING:
Calories: 450kcal | Carbohydrates: 15g | Proteins: 40g | Fats: 25g | Fiber: 7g | Sodium: 1200 mg

62. Salmon Ceviche with Mango and Lime

PREP TIME: 15 minutes	MARINATING TIME: 1 hour
TOTAL TIME: 1 hour 15 minutes	SERVINGS: For 1 person
DIFFICULTY: Easy	TEMPERATURE: Served Fresh
COOKING TYPE: No Cooking, Marinated	NOT EXPECTED

INGREDIENTS:
- **Fresh salmon fillet:** 6 oz / 170 g, sushi grade, skinless, boneless, finely diced
- **Mango:** 1 medium, ripe, peeled and finely diced
- **Red onion:** 1/4 cup, finely chopped
- **Cilantro:** 2 tbsps, chopped
- **Jalapeño:** 1, seeded and finely chopped (optional for heat)
- **Lime juice:** 1/4 cup / 60 ml
- **Orange juice:** 2 tbsps / 30 ml (for a touch of sweetness)
- **Salt:** 1/4 tsp
- **Pepper:** 1/8 tsp
- **Avocado:** 1/2, diced (serving)

NUTRITIONAL VALUES PER SERVING:
Calories: 350kcal | Carbohydrates: 25g | Proteins: 25g | Fats: 15g | Fiber: 5g | Sodium: 300 mg

INSTRUCTIONS:
1. **Prepare the Salmon:** Ensure the salmon is fresh and of sushi-grade quality. Finely dice the salmon and place it in a glass or ceramic bowl.
2. **Marinate:** Add the finely diced mango, chopped red onion, chopped cilantro, and jalapeño (if using) to the salmon. Pour over the lime juice and orange juice. Gently toss to combine, ensuring the salmon is well coated with the juice. Season with salt and pepper. Stir gently to mix.
3. **Refrigerate:** Cover the bowl with plastic wrap and refrigerate for about 1 hour, allowing the citrus juices to "cook" the salmon and blend the flavors.
4. **Serve:** Just before serving, gently stir in the diced avocado. Plate the ceviche and garnish with additional cilantro or slices of lime if desired.

TIPS FOR PERFECT COOKING:
- **Fish Freshness:** Use only fresh, sushi-grade salmon for safety and best flavor.
- **Cutting Technique:** Dice the salmon and mango into uniform, bite-sized pieces for even marinating and a pleasant texture.
- **Adjusting Heat:** The jalapeño is optional; adjust the amount according to your heat preference or omit it entirely.

POSSIBLE VARIATIONS:
- **Citrus Variations:** Try using different citrus juices like grapefruit or lemon for varying tanginess.
- **Herb Options:** Mint or basil can be used in place of cilantro for a different herbal note.
- **Additional Crunch:** Add diced cucumbers or radishes for extra crunch and freshness.

RECIPES FOR FESTIVE OCCASIONS

63. Shrimp in Sweet and Sour Sauce with Pineapple and Peppers

PREP TIME: 20 minutes	**COOKING TIME:** 10 minutes	**TOTAL TIME:** 30 minutes
SERVINGS: For 1 person	**DIFFICULTY:** Easy	**NOT EXPECTED**
COOKING TYPE: Griddling	**Sauce:** Sweet and Sour Sauce	

INGREDIENTS:
- **Shrimp:** 6 oz / 170 grams, peeled and deveined
- **Fresh pineapple:** 1 cup, cubed
- **Red bell pepper:** 1, cut into bite-sized pieces
- **Green bell pepper:** 1, cut into bite-sized pieces
- **Onion:** 1 small, chopped
- **Garlic:** 2 cloves, minced
- **Olive oil:** 2 tbsps

For the Sweet and Sour Sauce:
- **Pineapple juice:** 1/4 cup / 60 ml (from fresh pineapple if possible)
- **Ketchup:** 2 tbsps / 30 ml
- **Rice vinegar:** 2 tbsps / 30 ml
- **Brown sugar:** 2 tbsps / 30 g
- **Soy Sauce:** 1 tbsp / 15 ml
- **Cornstarch:** 1 tsp, dissolved in 2 tbsps water

INSTRUCTIONS:
1. **Prepare the Sauce:** In a small bowl, combine pineapple juice, ketchup, rice vinegar, brown sugar, and soy sauce. Stir until the sugar is dissolved. Mix in the cornstarch slurry and set aside.
2. **Cook the Vegetables:** Heat 1 tbsp of olive oil in a large skillet over medium-high heat. Add the chopped onion and minced garlic, sautéing until fragrant and translucent. Add the red and green bell peppers, cooking until they are just tender but still crisp.
3. **Cook the Shrimp:** In the same skillet, add another tbsp of olive oil if needed and introduce the shrimp. Cook for about 2 minutes on each side, or until the shrimp turn pink and are nearly cooked through.
4. **Combine and Simmer:** Pour the sweet and sour sauce mixture into the skillet with the shrimp and vegetables. Add the pineapple cubes. Bring to a simmer and let cook for an additional 2-3 minutes, stirring occasionally, until the sauce thickens and the shrimp are fully cooked.
5. **Serve:** Serve the shrimp and vegetables hot, garnished with sesame seeds or chopped green onions if desired.

TIPS FOR PERFECT COOKING:
- **Shrimp Doneness:** Be careful not to overcook the shrimp as they can become rubbery. Remove them from heat as soon as they're pink and opaque.
- **Sauce Consistency:** Adjust the thickness of the sauce by varying the amount of cornstarch slurry according to your preference.
- **Pineapple Selection:** Use fresh pineapple for the best flavor and texture, but canned pineapple can be a convenient alternative.

POSSIBLE VARIATIONS:
- **Heat Addition:** For a spicy kick, add a few dashes of hot sauce or a sprinkle of chili flakes to the sauce.
- **Protein Variants:** Replace shrimp with chicken or tofu for a different take on this dish.
- **Vegetable Variants:** Include other vegetables like carrots or snap peas for more color and variety.

NUTRITIONAL VALUES PER SERVING:
Calories: 450kcal | Carbohydrates: 50g | Proteins: 25g | Fats: 15g | Fiber: 3g | Sodium: 800 mg

64. Salmon Sashimi with Ponzu Sauce and Wasabi

PREP TIME: 15 minutes	**COOKING TIME:** 0 minutes	**TOTAL TIME:** 15 minutes
SERVINGS: For 1 person	**DIFFICULTY:** Easy	**NOT EXPECTED**
COOKING TYPE: No Cooking, served raw	**Sauce:** Ponzu and Wasabi Sauce	

INGREDIENTS:
- **Fresh salmon fillet, sushi grade:** 6 oz / 170 grams
- **Ponzu Sauce:** 1/4 cup / 60 ml
- **Wasabi paste:** To taste
- **Fresh chives:** For garnish, chopped
- **Daikon radish:** 1/4 cup, grated (optional, for garnish)
- **Soy Sauce:** Optional, for additional dipping

NUTRITIONAL VALUES PER SERVING:
Calories: 320kcal | Carbohydrates: 3g | Proteins: 25g | Fats: 22g | Fiber: 0g | Sodium: 600 mg

INSTRUCTIONS:
1. **Prepare the Salmon:** Ensure the salmon is fresh and of sushi-grade quality. Using a sharp knife, slice the salmon into thin, even pieces, about 1/4 inch thick. Arrange the slices neatly on a chilled plate.
2. **Serve with Condiments:** Place a small amount of wasabi on the side of the plate. Pour ponzu sauce into a small dipping bowl. Optionally, add a side of soy sauce in another small bowl for those who prefer a saltier dip.
3. **Garnish:** Sprinkle chopped chives over the salmon slices for a touch of color and flavor. If using, arrange grated daikon radish on the plate for added texture and to complement the salmon's fatty richness.
4. **Enjoy:** Serve the sashimi immediately to maintain the freshness and quality of the fish. Encourage guests to dab a bit of wasabi on their salmon slice, dip it in ponzu sauce, and enjoy the burst of flavors.

TIPS FOR PERFECT COOKING:
- **Knife Skills:** Use a very sharp knife to cut the salmon. A dull knife will tear the flesh and ruin the presentation and texture of the sashimi.
- **Chill the Plates:** Before serving, chill the plates in the refrigerator. Serving sashimi on a cold plate helps maintain the freshness of the fish.
- **Wasabi Adjustment:** Start with a small amount of wasabi, as it can be quite potent. Guests can always add more according to their taste preference.

POSSIBLE VARIATIONS:
- **Fish Variants:** Try this recipe with other types of fish like tuna or yellowtail for variety.
- **Additional Garnishes:** Consider adding thinly sliced cucumber or avocado on the side for a refreshing contrast.
- **Spice Variants:** Mix a little sriracha into the ponzu sauce for those who prefer a spicier dip.

RECIPES FOR FESTIVE OCCASIONS

65. Fried Fish Tacos with Mango and Avocado Sauce

| PREP TIME: 25 minutes | COOKING TIME: 10 minutes | TOTAL TIME: 35 minutes | SERVINGS: For 1 person |
| DIFFICULTY: Medium | NOT EXPECTED | COOKING TYPE: Direct on the grill | Sauce: Mango and Avocado Sauce |

INGREDIENTS:
- White fish fillets (such as cod, tilapia, or halibut): 6 oz / 170g
- Corn tortillas: 3
- All-purpose flour: 1/2 cup / 60 grams
- Beer or sparkling water: 1/2 cup / 120 ml
- Paprika: 1 tsp
- Garlic powder: 1 tsp
- Salt and pepper to taste
- Oil for frying

For the Mango and Avocado Sauce:
- Ripe mango: 1, peeled and cubed
- Ripe avocado: 1, peeled and pitted
- Lime juice: 2 tbsps / 30 ml
- Cilantro: 2 tbsps, chopped
- Jalapeño: 1, seeded and minced (optional for heat)
- Salt to taste

INSTRUCTIONS:
1. **Prepare the Mango and Avocado Sauce:** In a blender or food processor, combine the mango, avocado, lime juice, chopped cilantro, and minced jalapeño. Blend until smooth. Season with salt to taste and set aside.

2. **Make the Fish Batter:** In a bowl, mix the flour, paprika, garlic powder, salt, and pepper. Gradually whisk in the beer or sparkling water until the batter is smooth.

3. **Fry the Fish:** Heat oil in a deep fryer or large skillet to 375°F (190°C). Dip the fish pieces into the batter, ensuring they are well coated. Fry the battered fish in the hot oil for about 3-4 minutes or until golden and crispy. Drain on paper towels.

4. **Assemble the Tacos:** Warm the corn tortillas in a dry skillet or microwave. Place a piece of fried fish in each tortilla. Drizzle generously with the mango and avocado sauce.

5. **Serve:** Serve the tacos immediately, garnished with additional cilantro or slices of lime if desired.

TIPS FOR PERFECT COOKING:
- **Oil Temperature:** Ensure the oil is hot enough before frying the fish to get a crispy texture without absorbing too much oil.
- **Batter Consistency:** The batter should be neither too thick nor too thin to coat the fish properly. Adjust with a bit more flour or liquid as needed.
- **Freshness of Ingredients:** Use fresh mango and avocado for the sauce to ensure the best flavor and texture.

POSSIBLE VARIATIONS:
- **Protein Variants:** For a different twist, try using shrimp or chicken in place of fish.
- **Sauce Options:** Add a bit of honey to the sauce for extra sweetness or a squeeze of sriracha for additional heat.

NUTRITIONAL VALUES PER SERVING:
Calories: 650kcal | Carbohydrates: 85g | Proteins: 25g | Fats: 25g | Fiber: 8g | Sodium: 800 mg

---

66. Chicken and Marinated Vegetable Skewers (Low fat Recipe)

| PREP TIME: 15 minutes + Marinating (1 hrs.) | COOKING TIME: 10 minutes | TOTAL TIME: 25 minutes + Marinating Time | SERVINGS: For 1 person |
| DIFFICULTY: Easy | NOT EXPECTED | COOKING TYPE: Griddling | Sauce: Low sodium Soy Sauce |

INGREDIENTS:
- Lean chicken breast: 6 oz / 170 grams, cut into cubes
- Zucchini: 1 medium, sliced into rounds
- Red bell peppers: 1 medium, cut into pieces
- Low-sodium soy Sauce: 2 tbsps / 30 ml
- Honey: 1 tbsp / 15 ml
- Garlic: 2 cloves, minced
- Black pepper: 1/2 tsp
- Olive oil: 1 tbsp (for brushing)

NUTRITIONAL VALUES PER SERVING:
Calories: 320kcal | Carbohydrates: 20g | Proteins: 35g | Fats: 10g | Fiber: 3g | Sodium: 480 mg

INSTRUCTIONS:
1. **Prepare the Marinade:** In a bowl, whisk together low-sodium soy sauce, honey, minced garlic, and black pepper. Place the chicken cubes in the marinade, ensuring they are well coated. Cover and refrigerate for at least 1 hour to allow the flavors to penetrate.

2. **Marinate Vegetables:** About 30 minutes before grilling, add the zucchini and red bell pepper pieces to the marinade with the chicken. Stir to ensure the vegetables are evenly coated.

3. **Prepare the Skewers:** Thread the marinated chicken, zucchini, and red bell peppers alternately onto skewers. If using wooden skewers, soak them in water for at least 30 minutes prior to use to prevent burning.

4. **Grill the Skewers:** Preheat the grill to medium-high heat. Brush the grill grates lightly with olive oil to prevent sticking. Grill the skewers for about 10 minutes, turning occasionally, until the chicken is thoroughly cooked and vegetables are tender and slightly charred.

5. **Serve:** Serve the skewers hot, garnished with fresh herbs or a squeeze of lemon if desired.

TIPS FOR PERFECT COOKING:
- **Even Pieces:** Cut the chicken and vegetables into uniform pieces to ensure even cooking.
- **Monitor the Grill:** Keep an eye on the skewers as they cook to avoid over-charring.
- **Resting Time:** Let the cooked skewers rest for a few minutes before serving to allow the juices to redistribute.

POSSIBLE VARIATIONS:
- **Different Vegetables:** Try adding other vegetables like cherry tomatoes, mushrooms, or onions to the skewers.
- **Spice It Up:** Add a pinch of chili flakes or cayenne pepper to the marinade for a spicier version.
- **Citrus Twist:** Add a splash of orange juice to the marinade for a citrusy flavor.

67. Turkey Burgers with Aioli Sauce

PREP TIME: 15 minutes	**COOKING TIME:** 10 minutes	**TOTAL TIME:** 25 minutes
SERVINGS: For 1 person	**DIFFICULTY:** Easy	**TEMPERATURE:** 375°F (190°C)
COOKING TYPE: Direct on the grill	**Sauce:** Light Aioli Sauce	

INGREDIENTS:

- Lean ground turkey: 6 oz / 170g
- Fresh parsley: 2 tbsps, finely chopped
- Red onion: 2 tbsps, finely minced
- Garlic powder: 1/2 tsp
- Paprika: 1/2 tsp
- Salt and pepper to taste
- Whole wheat bun: 1

For the Light Aioli Sauce:
- Greek yogurt: 1/4 cup
- Lemon juice: 1 tbsp
- Garlic: 1 clove, minced
- Salt and pepper to taste

NUTRITIONAL VALUES PER SERVING:

Calories: 400kcal | Carbohydrates: 40g | Proteins: 35g | Fats: 10g | Fiber: 5g | Sodium: 500 mg

INSTRUCTIONS:

1. **Prepare the Turkey Patties:** In a mixing bowl, combine the ground turkey, chopped parsley, minced red onion, garlic powder, paprika, salt, and pepper. Mix well. Form the mixture into a burger patty, slightly larger than the bun since it will shrink while cooking.

2. **Cook the Turkey Burgers:** Preheat a grill or skillet over medium heat. If using a skillet, add a light drizzle of olive oil to prevent sticking. Cook the turkey burger patty for about 5 minutes on each side, or until fully cooked and the internal temperature reaches 165°F (74°C).

3. **Prepare the Light Aioli Sauce:** In a small bowl, combine Greek yogurt, lemon juice, minced garlic, salt, and pepper. Mix until smooth.

4. **Assemble the Burgers:** Toast the whole wheat bun lightly. Place the cooked turkey patty on the bottom half of the bun. Spread a generous amount of the light aioli sauce over the patty. Add additional toppings if desired, such as lettuce, tomato slices, or avocado.

5. **Serve:** Serve the turkey burger hot, with a side of mixed greens or sweet potato fries for a complete meal.

TIPS FOR PERFECT COOKING:

- **Patty Handling:** Avoid overworking the meat when forming the patties to keep them tender and juicy.
- **Ensure Doneness:** Use a meat thermometer to check that the turkey has reached the safe internal temperature.
- **Sauce Consistency:** Adjust the consistency of the aioli sauce with a little more lemon juice or yogurt to suit your taste.

POSSIBLE VARIATIONS:

- **Spicy Version:** Add a pinch of cayenne pepper or a few drops of hot sauce to the burger mix or aioli for a spicy kick.
- **Herb Variations:** Incorporate other fresh herbs like cilantro or dill in the burger mix for different flavor profiles.
- **Cheese Option:** During the last minute of cooking, top the burger with a slice of low-fat cheese, such as mozzarella or feta, for a cheesy melt.

68. Sesame-Crusted Salmon Fillet

PREP TIME: 10 minutes	**COOKING TIME:** 15 minutes	**TOTAL TIME:** 25 minutes
SERVINGS: For 1 person	**DIFFICULTY:** Easy	**NOT EXPECTED**
COOKING TYPE: Direct on the grill	**Sauce:** Low-Sodium Soy Sauce	

INGREDIENTS:

- Salmon fillet: 6 oz / 170 grams
- Black sesame seeds: 1 tbsp
- White sesame seeds: 1 tbsp
- Low-sodium soy Sauce: 2 tbsps / 30 ml
- Honey: 1 tbsp / 15 ml
- Fresh ginger: 1 tsp, grated
- Olive oil: 1 tsp (for greasing the pan)

NUTRITIONAL VALUES PER SERVING:

Calories: 350kcal | Carbohydrates: 10g | Proteins: 25g | Fats: 20g | Fiber: 1g | Sodium: 400 mg

INSTRUCTIONS:

1. **Prepare the Marinade:** In a small bowl, combine the low-sodium soy sauce, honey, and grated ginger. Stir until the honey is fully dissolved.

2. **Marinate the Salmon:** Place the salmon fillet in a shallow dish and pour the marinade over it. Ensure the fillet is evenly coated on all sides. Let the salmon marinate for about 10-15 minutes at room temperature.

3. **Crust the Salmon:** Mix the black and white sesame seeds in a plate. Remove the salmon from the marinade (reserve the marinade for later) and press each side of the fillet into the sesame seed mixture until it is well coated.

4. **Cook the Salmon:** Preheat a non-stick skillet over medium heat and brush it with olive oil. Place the sesame-crusted salmon in the skillet, and cook for about 3-4 minutes on each side, or until the sesame seeds are golden and the salmon is cooked through.

5. **Reduce the Marinade:** While the salmon cooks, pour the reserved marinade into a small saucepan. Bring to a simmer over medium heat and reduce until it thickens slightly, about 3-5 minutes, to create a glaze.

6. **Serve:** Serve the cooked salmon fillet drizzled with the reduced soy sauce glaze. Accompany with steamed vegetables or a fresh salad for a complete meal.

TIPS FOR PERFECT COOKING:

- **Control Heat:** Ensure the pan is not too hot as sesame seeds can burn quickly. Adjust the heat as needed to prevent over-browning.
- **Don't Over-Marinate:** Limit the marinating time to avoid the soy sauce overpowering the delicate flavor of the salmon.
- **Thickness of Fillet:** Adjust cooking time based on the thickness of your salmon fillet to ensure it's cooked perfectly through without drying out.

POSSIBLE VARIATIONS:

- **Citrus Twist:** Add a splash of orange juice to the marinade for a citrusy flavor.
- **Spicy Kick:** Include a pinch of chili flakes in the marinade for a bit of heat.
- **Herb Infusion:** Add some chopped cilantro or dill to the sesame seeds for an herby crust.

LOW-FAT OPTIONS

69. Herb-Marinated Chicken Breast

PREP TIME: 15 minutes + 1 hrs marinating	**COOKING TIME:** 20 minutes	**TOTAL TIME:** 35 minutes + marinating time	**SERVINGS:** For 1 person	
DIFFICULTY: Easy	**TEMPERATURE:** 375°F (190°C)	**COOKING TYPE:** Direct on the grill	**NOT EXPECTED**	

INGREDIENTS:
- **Chicken breast:** 6 oz / 170 grams
- **Greek yogurt:** 1/4 cup / 60 ml
- **Lemon juice:** 2 tbsps / 30 ml
- **Garlic:** 2 cloves, minced
- **Rosemary:** 1 tsp, finely chopped
- **Thyme:** 1 tsp, finely chopped
- **Sage:** 1 tsp, finely chopped
- **Black pepper:** 1/2 tsp
- **Salt:** 1/4 tsp (optional, adjust to taste)

NUTRITIONAL VALUES PER SERVING:
Calories: 280kcal | Carbohydrates: 5g | Proteins: 35g | Fats: 12g | Fiber: 1g | Sodium: 300 mg (if salt is added)

INSTRUCTIONS:
1. **Prepare the Marinade:** In a bowl, combine Greek yogurt, lemon juice, minced garlic, chopped rosemary, thyme, sage, black pepper, and salt if using. Mix well until all the ingredients are blended together.

2. **Marinate the Chicken:** Place the chicken breast in a resealable plastic bag or a shallow dish. Pour the herb marinade over the chicken, ensuring it is completely coated. Seal the bag or cover the dish and refrigerate for at least 1 hour, or overnight for more flavor penetration.

3. **Cook the Chicken:** Preheat the oven to 375°F (190°C). Remove the chicken from the marinade, shaking off any excess. Discard the remaining marinade. Place the chicken breast on a greased baking sheet or in a baking dish. Bake in the preheated oven for about 20 minutes, or until the chicken is fully cooked (internal temperature should reach 165°F / 74°C).

4. **Serve:** Let the chicken rest for a few minutes after removing it from the oven to allow the juices to redistribute. Slice and serve the chicken with a side of steamed vegetables, over a salad, or alongside whole grains.

TIPS FOR PERFECT COOKING:
- **Even Thickness:** Pound the chicken breast to even thickness before marinating to ensure uniform cooking.
- **Grilling Option:** Instead of baking, you can grill the chicken over medium heat for about 6-7 minutes per side, depending on thickness.
- **Maximizing Flavor:** For the best flavor, allow the chicken to marinate as long as possible within safe refrigeration limits.

POSSIBLE VARIATIONS:
- **Spicy Version:** Add crushed red pepper flakes to the marinade for a spicy kick.
- **Different Herbs:** Experiment with different combinations of fresh herbs such as cilantro, parsley, or dill for varying flavor profiles.
- **Creamier Marinade:** Incorporate a tbsp of olive oil into the marinade for added richness and to help the herbs adhere to the chicken.

70. Grilled Mediterranean Vegetables

PREP TIME: 15 minutes	**COOKING TIME:** 10 minutes	**TOTAL TIME:** 25 minutes	**SERVINGS:** For 1 person	
DIFFICULTY: Easy	**NOT EXPECTED**	**COOKING TYPE:** Direct on the grill	**NOT EXPECTED**	

INGREDIENTS:
- **Eggplant:** 1 small, sliced into 1/2 inch rounds
- **Bell peppers:** 1 each red and yellow, seeded and quartered
- **Zucchini:** 1 medium, sliced into 1/2 inch rounds
- **Mushrooms:** 4 oz / 113 grams, whole
- **Cherry tomatoes:** 1/2 cup
- **Oregano:** 1 tbsp, fresh, chopped
- **Extra virgin olive oil:** 2 tbsps
- **Balsamic vinegar:** 1 tbsp
- **Salt and pepper to taste**

NUTRITIONAL VALUES PER SERVING:
Calories: 250kcal | Carbohydrates: 25g | Proteins: 5g | Fats: 15g | Fiber: 8g | Sodium: 200 mg

INSTRUCTIONS:
1. **Preheat the Grill:** Preheat your grill to a medium-high heat. Ensure it's clean to prevent sticking.

2. **Prepare the Vegetables:** In a large bowl, toss the sliced eggplant, bell peppers, zucchini, mushrooms, and cherry tomatoes with extra virgin olive oil, balsamic vinegar, chopped oregano, salt, and pepper. Make sure all the vegetables are evenly coated.

3. **Grill the Vegetables:** Arrange the vegetables on the grill. For smaller items like cherry tomatoes, use a grill basket to prevent them from falling through the grates. Grill the vegetables for about 5 minutes on each side or until they are tender and have nice grill marks.

4. **Serve:** Remove the vegetables from the grill and adjust seasoning if needed. Serve hot as a side dish or over a bed of quinoa or rice for a light meal. They also pair wonderfully with grilled meats or fish.

TIPS FOR PERFECT COOKING:
- **Vegetable Prep:** Ensure that all vegetables are cut uniformly to promote even cooking.
- **Avoid Overcrowding:** Grill the vegetables in batches if necessary to ensure that each piece has enough space to cook properly.
- **Retaining Texture:** Be careful not to overcook the vegetables; they should be tender but still retain some bite.

POSSIBLE VARIATIONS:
- **Herb Variations:** While oregano is traditional, feel free to experiment with other herbs such as basil, thyme, or rosemary for different flavors.
- **Spicy Kick:** For a spicy version, drizzle the vegetables with a little chili oil before serving or sprinkle with red chili flakes.
- **Cheesy Delight:** Sprinkle grated Parmesan or crumbled feta cheese over the hot vegetables just before serving for an added layer of flavor.

LOW-FAT OPTIONS

71. Asparagus Wrapped in Prosciutto

- **PREP TIME:** 10 minutes
- **COOKING TIME:** 5 minutes
- **TOTAL TIME:** 15 minutes
- **SERVINGS:** For 1 person
- **DIFFICULTY:** Easy
- **NOT EXPECTED**
- **COOKING TYPE:** Direct on the grill
- **NOT EXPECTED**

INGREDIENTS: ASPARAGUS: 10 SPEARS, TRIMMED
- **Prosciutto:** 5 thin slices, halved lengthwise
- **Lemon juice:** 1 tbsp
- **Black pepper:** To taste
- **Olive oil spray:** (optional, for grilling)

NUTRITIONAL VALUES PER SERVING:
Calories: 90kcal | Carbohydrates: 5g | Proteins: 10g | Fats: 3g | Fiber: 2g | Sodium: 300 mg

INSTRUCTIONS:
1. **Prep the Asparagus:** Wash the asparagus and trim off the tough ends. If the spears are very thick, peel the lower stalks with a vegetable peeler to ensure even cooking.
2. **Wrap the Asparagus:** Wrap a piece of halved prosciutto slice tightly around each asparagus spear. It should cover most of the spear, leaving the tips exposed.
3. **Cook the Asparagus:** Heat a grill pan over medium-high heat and lightly spray with olive oil if using. Place the wrapped asparagus on the grill pan. Grill for about 2-3 minutes on each side, or until the prosciutto is slightly crispy and the asparagus is tender but still crisp.
4. **Season and Serve:** Transfer the grilled asparagus to a serving plate. Drizzle with lemon juice and sprinkle with black pepper to taste. Serve immediately while warm.

TIPS FOR PERFECT COOKING:
- **Don't Overcook:** Keep a close eye on the asparagus while grilling to ensure it doesn't overcook. It should be tender yet still retain some crispness.
- **Prosciutto Placement:** Make sure the prosciutto is wrapped tightly so it doesn't unwrap during cooking. The natural fat in the prosciutto will help it stick to the asparagus.
- **Serving Tip:** Asparagus wrapped in prosciutto can be served as an elegant side dish or as an appetizer for gatherings.

POSSIBLE VARIATIONS:
- **Cheesy Twist:** Before wrapping with prosciutto, place a small slice of Parmesan or mozzarella cheese on each asparagus spear for a melty surprise.
- **Herb Infusion:** Brush the asparagus with olive oil mixed with minced garlic and herbs such as rosemary or thyme before wrapping it in prosciutto for added flavor.
- **Spice It Up:** Add a sprinkle of crushed red pepper flakes for a spicy kick before serving.

72. Grilled Shrimp with Green Sauce

- **PREP TIME:** 15 minutes
- **COOKING TIME:** 5 minutes
- **TOTAL TIME:** 20 minutes
- **SERVINGS:** For 1 person
- **DIFFICULTY:** Easy
- **NOT EXPECTED**
- **COOKING TYPE:** Direct on the grill
- **SAUCE:** Green Sauce

INGREDIENTS:
- **Shrimp:** 6 oz / 170 grams, peeled and deveined
- **Parsley:** 1/4 cup, chopped
- **Cilantro:** 1/4 cup, chopped
- **Garlic:** 2 cloves, minced
- **Green chili:** 1, seeded and chopped (adjust to taste)
- **Lemon:** juice of 1 lemon
- **Extra virgin olive oil:** 2 tbsps
- **Salt and pepper to taste**

NUTRITIONAL VALUES PER SERVING:
Calories: 280kcal | Carbohydrates: 3g | Proteins: 25g | Fats: 18g | Fiber: 1g | Sodium: 200 mg

INSTRUCTIONS:
1. **Prepare the Green Sauce:** In a blender or food processor, combine the chopped parsley, cilantro, minced garlic, chopped green chili, lemon juice, and extra virgin olive oil. Blend until smooth. Season with salt and pepper to taste. Set aside some of the sauce for serving and use the rest for marinating.
2. **Marinate the Shrimp:** In a bowl, toss the shrimp with half of the green sauce, making sure each shrimp is well coated. Let marinate for 10 minutes.
3. **Grill the Shrimp:** Preheat a grill or grill pan over medium-high heat. Grill the shrimp for 2-3 minutes on each side or until they are pink and slightly charred.
4. **Serve:** Arrange the grilled shrimp on a plate and drizzle with the reserved green sauce. Optionally, garnish with lemon wedges and additional chopped herbs.

TIPS FOR PERFECT COOKING:
- **Do Not Over-Marinate:** Shrimp should not be marinated for too long in acidic ingredients like lemon juice as they can begin to cook and become rubbery.
- **High Heat Grilling:** Ensure the grill is hot before adding the shrimp to achieve a good sear without overcooking.
- **Avoid Overcrowding:** Grill the shrimp in batches if necessary to ensure they cook evenly and get nicely charred without steaming.

POSSIBLE VARIATIONS:
- **Spicy Version:** Increase the amount of green chili in the sauce for a spicier kick.
- **Herb Variations:** Experiment with different herbs such as mint or dill in the green sauce for a different flavor profile.
- **Additions:** Incorporate diced avocado or cucumber into the green sauce for added texture and freshness.

73. Grilled Chicken Salad

| PREP TIME: 15 minutes | COOKING TIME: 10 minutes | TOTAL TIME: 25 minutes | SERVINGS: For 1 person |
| DIFFICULTY: Easy | NOT EXPECTED | COOKING TYPE: Direct on the grill | NOT EXPECTED |

INGREDIENTS:
- **Chicken breast:** 6 oz / 170 grams
- **Romaine lettuce:** 2 cups, chopped
- **Avocado:** 1/2, sliced
- **Cherry tomatoes:** 1/2 cup, halved
- **Cucumber:** 1/2, sliced
- **Lemon juice:** 2 tbsps
- **Extra virgin olive oil:** 2 tbsps
- **Salt and pepper to taste**

NUTRITIONAL VALUES PER SERVING:
Calories: 450kcal | **Carbohydrates:** 18g | **Proteins:** 35g | **Fats:** 28g | **Fiber:** 7g | **Sodium:** 200 mg

INSTRUCTIONS:
1. **Prepare the Chicken:** Season the chicken breast with salt and pepper. If desired, you can also marinate the chicken with some lemon juice and olive oil for additional flavor. Preheat the grill to medium-high heat. Grill the chicken for about 5 minutes on each side or until fully cooked through and the internal temperature reaches 165°F (74°C). Let it rest for a few minutes and then slice thinly.

2. **Assemble the Salad:** In a large salad bowl, combine the chopped romaine lettuce, sliced avocado, halved cherry tomatoes, and sliced cucumber. Add the grilled chicken slices to the salad.

3. **Prepare the Dressing:** In a small bowl, whisk together the lemon juice and extra virgin olive oil. Season with salt and pepper to taste.

4. **Dress and Serve:** Drizzle the dressing over the salad and toss gently to coat all the ingredients evenly. Serve immediately, ensuring the salad is fresh and crisp.

TIPS FOR PERFECT COOKING:
- **Grill Marks:** For aesthetically pleasing grill marks, do not move the chicken too much once it is on the grill.
- **Chicken Juiciness:** Let the chicken rest after grilling before slicing to ensure it retains its juices.
- **Dressing Adjustments:** Adjust the lemon juice and olive oil ratio according to your taste preferences. Add a small amount of honey or mustard to the dressing for an extra layer of flavor.

POSSIBLE VARIATIONS:
- **Herb Infusion:** Add fresh herbs such as basil, parsley, or cilantro to the salad for additional flavor.
- **Protein Options:** Substitute grilled salmon or tofu for the chicken to vary the protein source.
- **Extra Crunch:** Add nuts like almonds or walnuts for added texture and nutrients.

74. Grilled Zucchini with Feta and Mint

| PREP TIME: 10 minutes | COOKING TIME: 10 minutes | TOTAL TIME: 20 minutes | SERVINGS: For 1 person |
| DIFFICULTY: Easy | NOT EXPECTED | COOKING TYPE: Direct on the grill | NOT EXPECTED |

INGREDIENTS:
- **Zucchini:** 2 medium, sliced lengthwise into 1/4 inch thick strips
- **Feta cheese:** 1/4 cup, crumbled
- **Fresh mint:** 2 tbsps, chopped
- **Lemon:** 1, juiced
- **Extra virgin olive oil:** 2 tbsps
- **Salt and pepper to taste**

NUTRITIONAL VALUES PER SERVING:
Calories: 280kcal | **Carbohydrates:** 10g | **Proteins:** 7g | **Fats:** 23g | **Fiber:** 3g | **Sodium:** 320 mg

INSTRUCTIONS:
1. **Preheat the Grill:** Preheat your grill to medium-high heat. Ensure the grates are clean to prevent sticking.

2. **Prepare the Zucchini:** Brush the zucchini strips with 1 tbsp of olive oil and season with salt and pepper. Grill the zucchini strips for about 2-3 minutes on each side, or until tender and grill marks appear.

3. **Make the Lemon Dressing:** In a small bowl, whisk together the remaining olive oil and lemon juice. Season with a pinch of salt and pepper to taste.

4. **Assemble the Dish:** Arrange the grilled zucchini on a serving platter. Drizzle the lemon dressing evenly over the zucchini. Sprinkle the crumbled feta cheese and chopped fresh mint over the top.

5. **Serve:** Serve the dish immediately, or let it sit for a few minutes to allow the flavors to meld together.

TIPS FOR PERFECT COOKING:
- **Grilling Zucchini:** Ensure not to overcook the zucchini; it should be tender but still retain some bite to avoid becoming mushy.
- **Feta Cheese:** Use a good quality feta cheese for the best flavor and texture. You can also try other soft cheeses like goat cheese or ricotta salata for variation.
- **Fresh Mint:** Fresh mint is key to the refreshing taste of this dish. It can be substituted with other fresh herbs like basil or parsley for a different twist.

POSSIBLE VARIATIONS:
- **Add Nuts:** Sprinkle toasted pine nuts or almonds on top for added crunch and nuttiness.
- **Spice It Up:** Add a sprinkle of red chili flakes when dressing the zucchini for a spicy kick.
- **Additional Vegetables:** Consider adding other grilled vegetables like eggplant or bell peppers to the dish for more variety and color.

LOW-CALORIE OPTIONS

75. Grilled Eggplant with Yogurt and Tahini Sauce (Low Calorie Recipe)

PREP TIME: 15 minutes | **COOKING TIME:** 10 minutes | **TOTAL TIME:** 25 minutes | **SERVINGS:** For 1 person
DIFFICULTY: Easy | **NOT EXPECTED** | **COOKING TYPE:** Direct on the grill | **SAUCE:** Tahini Sauce

INGREDIENTS:
- Eggplant: 1 large, sliced into 1/2 inch thick rounds
- Greek yogurt: 1/4 cup
- Tahini: 2 tbsps
- Garlic: 1 clove, minced
- Lemon: 1, juiced
- Parsley: 2 tbsps, chopped
- Olive oil: for brushing
- Salt and pepper to taste

NUTRITIONAL VALUES PER SERVING:
Calories: 300kcal | Carbohydrates: 20g | Proteins: 6g | Fats: 22g | Fiber: 8g | Sodium: 300 mg

INSTRUCTIONS:
1. **Prepare the Eggplant:** Preheat your grill to medium-high heat. Brush both sides of the eggplant slices with olive oil and season with salt and pepper. Grill the eggplant slices for about 4-5 minutes on each side, or until tender and grill marks appear.
2. **Make the Yogurt Tahini Sauce:** In a small bowl, combine the Greek yogurt, tahini, minced garlic, and lemon juice. Stir until well blended. Season with salt to taste.
3. **Assemble the Dish:** Arrange the grilled eggplant slices on a serving plate. Drizzle the yogurt tahini sauce over the grilled eggplant. Sprinkle chopped parsley over the top for garnish.
4. **Serve:** Serve the grilled eggplant immediately, while warm, with extra yogurt tahini sauce on the side if desired.

TIPS FOR PERFECT COOKING:
- **Grilling Eggplant:** Ensure that the eggplant is grilled until it is soft inside with a slightly crisp exterior for the best texture.
- **Consistency of** Sauce: Adjust the consistency of the yogurt tahini sauce by adding a little water if it is too thick. The sauce should be creamy but pourable.
- **Freshness of Ingredients:** Use fresh lemon juice and fresh garlic for the best flavor in the sauce.

POSSIBLE VARIATIONS:
- **Herb Variations:** Try different herbs like mint or cilantro instead of parsley for a different flavor profile.
- **Spicy Version:** Add a dash of cayenne pepper or a sprinkle of smoked paprika to the yogurt tahini sauce for a spicy kick.
- **Additional Toppings:** Top with pomegranate seeds or toasted pine nuts for added texture and flavor.

76. Grilled Chickpea Burgers

PREP TIME: 20 minutes | **COOKING TIME:** 10 minutes | **TOTAL TIME:** 30 minutes | **SERVINGS:** For 1 person
DIFFICULTY: Easy | **NOT EXPECTED** | **COOKING TYPE:** Direct on the grill | **NOT EXPECTED**

INGREDIENTS:
- Chickpeas: 1 cup, cooked and drained
- Cumin: 1 tsp
- Coriander: 1 tsp
- Fresh parsley: 2 tbsps, chopped
- Garlic: 1 clove, minced
- Breadcrumbs: 1/4 cup
- Greek yogurt: 2 tbsps for sauce
- Cucumber: 1/4, diced for sauce
- Olive oil: for brushing
- Salt and pepper to taste
- Burger buns: 1, whole wheat

NUTRITIONAL VALUES PER SERVING:
Calories: 450kcal | Carbohydrates: 60g | Proteins: 20g | Fats: 15g | Fiber: 10g | Sodium: 600 mg

INSTRUCTIONS:
1. **Prepare the Burger Mixture:** In a food processor, combine chickpeas, cumin, coriander, chopped parsley, minced garlic, breadcrumbs, salt, and pepper. Pulse until the mixture is coarsely ground but holds together when pinched. Be careful not to over-process into a paste. Shape the mixture into a burger-sized patty.
2. **Make the Yogurt Sauce:** In a small bowl, mix Greek yogurt with diced cucumber. Season with a pinch of salt and pepper. Refrigerate until ready to serve.
3. **Grill the Patty:** Preheat the grill or a grill pan over medium heat. Brush the grill with olive oil to prevent sticking. Grill the chickpea patty for about 5 minutes on each side, or until it is heated through and has nice grill marks.
4. **Assemble the Burger:** Toast the burger bun lightly on the grill. Place the grilled chickpea patty on the bottom half of the bun. Top with a generous spoonful of the yogurt cucumber sauce. If desired, add additional toppings such as lettuce, tomato slices, or red onion.
5. **Serve:** Serve the chickpea burger immediately while warm with any side of your choice, such as a salad or grilled vegetables.

TIPS FOR PERFECT COOKING:
- **Moisture Control:** If the burger mixture feels too wet, add more breadcrumbs to help the patties hold their shape during grilling.
- **Flipping Patties:** Be gentle when flipping the burgers to keep them from falling apart.
- **Customizable Spices:** Adjust the spices and herbs according to your taste preferences.

POSSIBLE VARIATIONS:
- **Spicy Version:** Add a tsp of chili powder or minced jalapeño to the burger mix for a kick.
- **Herb Variations:** Try different herbs such as mint or cilantro instead of parsley for a different flavor profile.
- **Extra Veggies:** Incorporate finely grated carrots or zucchini into the chickpea mixture for additional nutrition and moisture.

77. Grilled Vegetarian Pizza

PREP TIME: 15 minutes + dough prep.
COOKING TIME: 10 minutes
TOTAL TIME: 25 minutes
SERVINGS: For 1 person
DIFFICULTY: Easy
NOT EXPECTED
COOKING TYPE: Direct on the grill
NOT EXPECTED

INGREDIENTS:
- Pizza dough: 1 small ball (about the size of a large orange)
- Tomato Sauce: 1/3 cup
- Mozzarella cheese: 1/2 cup, shredded
- Bell peppers: 1/2 cup, sliced (use a mix of colors)
- Onions: 1/4 cup, thinly sliced
- Mushrooms: 1/4 cup, sliced
- Fresh basil: A few leaves for garnish
- Olive oil: for brushing
- Salt and pepper to taste

NUTRITIONAL VALUES PER SERVING:
Calories: 600kcal | Carbohydrates: 75g | Proteins: 25g | Fats: 25g | Fiber: 5g | Sodium: 800 mg

INSTRUCTIONS:
1. **Prepare the Dough:** Stretch or roll out the pizza dough on a lightly floured surface to about 1/4-inch thickness. Make a round or oval shape to fit your grill size.

2. **Preheat the Grill:** Preheat your grill to a medium-high heat. The ideal temperature is around 400°F (204°C).

3. **Grill the Dough:** Lightly brush one side of the pizza dough with olive oil. Place it oil-side down directly on the grill grates. Close the lid and grill for about 2-3 minutes or until the bottom is golden and has grill marks. Brush the top side with olive oil, then use tongs to flip the dough over.

4. **Add Toppings:** Quickly spread the tomato sauce over the cooked side of the crust. Sprinkle the shredded mozzarella evenly, followed by the sliced bell peppers, onions, and mushrooms. Close the grill and cook for another 5-7 minutes or until the cheese is melted and bubbly and the vegetables are slightly charred.

5. **Garnish and Serve:** Remove the pizza from the grill using a large spatula. Garnish with fresh basil leaves and season with salt and pepper to taste. Cut into slices and serve hot.

TIPS FOR PERFECT COOKING:
- **Dough Handling:** If the dough starts to spring back while you're stretching it, let it rest for a few minutes to relax the gluten before continuing.
- **Monitor Closely:** Keep a close eye on the pizza while grilling, especially when flipping the dough to prevent burning.
- **Uniform Toppings:** Slice the vegetables thinly and evenly to ensure they cook quickly and evenly on the grill.

POSSIBLE VARIATIONS:
- **Cheese Options:** Experiment with different cheeses such as goat cheese, feta, or smoked provolone for varied flavors.
- **Additional Toppings:** Add artichokes, olives, or spinach for more variety and a boost of flavor.
- **Spicy Version:** Include jalapeños or drizzle with chili oil before serving for a spicy kick.

78. Grilled Marinated Tofu

PREP TIME: 15 minutes + 1 hr marinating
COOKING TIME: 10 minutes
TOTAL TIME: 25 minutes + marinating time
SERVINGS: For 1 person
DIFFICULTY: Easy
NOT EXPECTED
COOKING TYPE: Direct on the grill
NOT EXPECTED

INGREDIENTS:
- Tofu: 1 block (about 14 oz), extra firm, pressed and drained
- Soy Sauce: 1/4 cup
- Garlic: 2 cloves, minced
- Honey: 1 tbsp (or use a vegan substitute like agave syrup)
- Rice vinegar: 2 tbsps
- Sesame oil: 1 tbsp
- Fresh ginger: 1 tbsp, grated
- Optional garnish: Sesame seeds and sliced green onions

NUTRITIONAL VALUES PER SERVING:
Calories: 400kcal | Carbohydrates: 24g | Proteins: 24g | Fats: 24g | Fiber: 2g | Sodium: 1200 mg

INSTRUCTIONS:
1. **Prepare the Tofu:** Cut the pressed tofu into 1/2 inch thick slices or large cubes, whichever you prefer for grilling.

2. **Make the Marinade:** In a mixing bowl, combine soy sauce, minced garlic, honey, rice vinegar, sesame oil, and grated ginger. Whisk together until well combined. Place the tofu slices or cubes in the marinade, ensuring each piece is well coated. Cover and refrigerate for at least 1 hour, or overnight for more flavor penetration.

3. **Grill the Tofu:** Preheat your grill or grill pan to medium-high heat. Remove tofu from the marinade, reserving the marinade for basting. Lightly oil the grill grates or pan to prevent sticking. Grill the tofu for about 5 minutes on each side, basting occasionally with the reserved marinade, until the tofu has nice grill marks and is heated through.

4. **Serve:** Serve the grilled tofu hot, garnished with sesame seeds and sliced green onions if desired. This dish pairs well with a side of steamed vegetables or over a bed of cooked rice or noodles.

TIPS FOR PERFECT COOKING:
- **Pressing Tofu:** Properly pressing the tofu is crucial for texture and to allow it to absorb more marinade. Press it for at least 30 minutes under a heavy object, wrapped in a towel.
- **Marinating Time:** The longer you marinate the tofu, the more flavorful it will be. Overnight marination is ideal if time allows.
- **High Heat:** Ensure the grill is hot before adding tofu to achieve good grill marks without sticking.

POSSIBLE VARIATIONS:
- **Spicy Kick:** Add a tsp of chili flakes or a splash of Sriracha to the marinade for a spicy version.
- **Herb Infusion:** Add chopped cilantro or basil to the marinade for a fresh herbal note.
- **Citrus Twist:** Include a splash of orange juice in the marinade for a citrusy flavor.

VEGETARIAN RECIPES

79. Grilled Spring Rolls with Peanut Sauce

PREP TIME: 20 minutes	**COOKING TIME:** 10 minutes	**TOTAL TIME:** 30 minutes
SERVINGS: For 1 person	**DIFFICULTY:** Medium	**NOT EXPECTED**
COOKING TYPE: Direct on the grill	**SAUCE:** Peanut Sauce	

INGREDIENTS:
- Rice vermicelli: 1/2 cup, cooked according to package instructions
- Lettuce: 1/2 cup, shredded
- Carrots: 1/4 cup, julienned
- Cucumber: 1/4 cup, julienned
- Extra firm tofu: 1/4 cup, thinly sliced and lightly grilled
- Mint leaves: A handful
- Spring roll wrappers: 2-3 depending on size

For the Peanut Sauce:
- Peanut butter: 2 tbsps
- Soy Sauce: 1 tbsp
- Honey: 1 tsp (or use a vegan alternative like agave)
- Lime juice: 1 tbsp
- Warm water: 2 tbsps (adjust for desired consistency)
- Crushed peanuts: For garnish

INSTRUCTIONS:
1. **Prepare the Ingredients:** Grill the tofu slices on a preheated grill until slightly charred and cooked through. Set aside to cool. Cook rice vermicelli as per package instructions, drain, and set aside. Prepare lettuce, carrots, and cucumber by washing and cutting them into thin strips or julienned pieces.

2. **Make the Peanut Sauce:** In a small bowl, whisk together peanut butter, soy sauce, honey, lime juice, and warm water until smooth. The sauce should be creamy but pourable. Adjust thickness by adding more water if necessary.

3. **Assemble the Spring Rolls:** Dip each spring roll wrapper in warm water for a few seconds until it becomes pliable. Lay the wrapper flat on a clean surface. In the center, layer a small amount of lettuce, cooked vermicelli, julienned carrots, cucumber, grilled tofu, and mint leaves. Fold the bottom half of the wrapper over the filling, then fold in the sides and roll tightly. Ensure the filling is snugly wrapped and the spring roll is sealed.

4. **Grill the Spring Rolls:** Lightly oil the grill and place the spring rolls on the grill. Grill each side for about 2 minutes or until the wrappers are crispy and golden brown.

5. **Serve:** Cut the grilled spring rolls in half if desired and serve with the peanut sauce. Garnish the sauce with crushed peanuts.

TIPS FOR PERFECT COOKING:
- **Wrapper Handling:** Ensure the spring roll wrappers do not dry out as they become brittle. Keep them covered with a damp cloth if preparing multiple rolls.
- **Even Grilling:** Turn the spring rolls gently to grill evenly without tearing the wrappers.
- **Serving Immediately:** Serve the spring rolls immediately after grilling to enjoy the crisp texture.

POSSIBLE VARIATIONS:
- **Protein Variations:** Swap tofu for grilled shrimp or chicken for a different protein choice.
- **Vegetable Options:** Add avocado slices or bell peppers for extra flavor and texture.
- **Spicy Sauce:** Add chili paste or sriracha to the peanut sauce for a spicy kick.

NUTRITIONAL VALUES PER SERVING:
Calories: 350kcal | Carbohydrates: 45g | Proteins: 15g | Fats: 12g | Fiber: 4g | Sodium: 600 mg

80. Grilled Polenta with Wild Mushrooms and Herb Sauce

PREP TIME: 20 minutes	**COOKING TIME:** 20 minutes	**TOTAL TIME:** 40 minutes
SERVINGS: For 1 person	**DIFFICULTY:** Medium	**NOT EXPECTED**
COOKING TYPE: Direct on the grill	**SAUCE:** Herb Sauce	

INGREDIENTS:
- Polenta: 1/2 cup, cooked and set in a mold
- Mixed wild mushrooms (such as shiitake, oyster, and cremini): 1 cup, sliced
- Garlic: 1 clove, minced
- Fresh thyme: 1 teaspoon, chopped
- Fresh rosemary: 1 teaspoon, chopped
- Vegetable broth: 1/2 cup
- Olive oil: 2 tablespoons
- Salt and pepper to taste

NUTRITIONAL VALUES PER SERVING:
Calories: 360kcal | Carbohydrates: 45g | Proteins: 8g | Fats: 18g | Fiber: 5g | Sodium: 480 mg

INSTRUCTIONS:
1. **Prepare the Polenta:** Cook polenta according to package instructions with water or a mix of water and milk for creaminess. Season with salt. Pour the cooked polenta into a greased shallow dish or mold. Allow to cool, then refrigerate until set and firm, about 2 hours. Once set, cut the polenta into squares or rectangles.

2. **Cook the Mushrooms:** Heat 1 tablespoon of olive oil in a skillet over medium heat. Add the sliced mushrooms and minced garlic, sautéing until the mushrooms are golden and tender. Add the chopped thyme, rosemary, and vegetable broth. Let simmer until the broth reduces slightly and flavors meld, about 5-7 minutes. Season with salt and pepper.

3. **Grill the Polenta:** Preheat a grill or grill pan over medium heat. Brush the polenta pieces with the remaining olive oil. Grill each side of the polenta until golden and grill marks appear, about 3-4 minutes per side.

4. **Serve:** Arrange the grilled polenta on a plate. Spoon the wild mushroom and herb sauce over the top. Garnish with additional herbs if desired.

TIPS FOR PERFECT COOKING:
- **Polenta Consistency:** Ensure the polenta is well-cooled and firm to make grilling easier and prevent it from breaking apart.
- **Mushroom Selection:** Use a variety of mushrooms for the best blend of flavors and textures.
- **Herb Freshness:** Use fresh herbs for the sauce to maximize the aromatic qualities of the dish.

POSSIBLE VARIATIONS:
- **Cheese Addition:** Sprinkle grated Parmesan or crumbled goat cheese over the top before serving for an extra layer of flavor.
- **Spicy Kick:** Add a splash of white wine and a pinch of red pepper flakes to the mushroom mixture for added depth and a hint of heat.
- **Alternative Herbs:** Experiment with other herbs such as sage or marjoram instead of thyme and rosemary for a different herbal profile.

VEGETARIAN & VEGAN RECIPES

81. Quinoa and Black Bean Burgers

PREP TIME: 20 minutes | **COOKING TIME:** 10 minutes | **TOTAL TIME:** 30 minutes | **SERVINGS:** For 1 person

DIFFICULTY: Easy | **NOT EXPECTED** | **COOKING TYPE:** Direct on the grill | **NOT EXPECTED**

INGREDIENTS:
- **Quinoa:** 1/2 cup, cooked and cooled
- **Black beans:** 1 cup, cooked or canned (drained and rinsed if canned)
- **Red bell pepper:** 1/4 cup, finely diced
- **Onion:** 1/4 cup, finely chopped
- **Garlic:** 1 clove, minced
- **Cumin:** 1 tsp
- **Coriander:** 1/2 tsp
- **Salt and pepper to taste**
- **Olive oil:** for frying
- **Whole wheat bun:** 1

NUTRITIONAL VALUES PER SERVING:
Calories: 450kcal | **Carbohydrates:** 65g | **Proteins:** 18g | **Fats:** 15g | **Fiber:** 15g | **Sodium:** 300 mg

INSTRUCTIONS:
1. **Prepare the Burger Mixture:** In a large bowl, mash the black beans with a fork or potato masher until mostly smooth but with some whole beans left for texture. Add the cooked quinoa, diced red bell pepper, chopped onion, minced garlic, cumin, and coriander to the mashed beans. Season with salt and pepper. Mix everything together until well combined. If the mixture is too wet, you can add a little whole wheat flour or more quinoa to help bind it.
2. **Form the Patties:** Divide the mixture into equal portions and shape each into a patty about the size of your whole wheat buns.
3. **Cook the Patties:** Heat a thin layer of olive oil in a non-stick skillet over medium heat. Place the patties in the skillet and cook for about 5 minutes on each side or until the patties are golden brown and firm.
4. **Assemble the Burgers:** Toast the whole wheat buns lightly, if desired. Place each patty on a bun and add your favorite burger toppings such as lettuce, tomato, vegan mayo, or mustard.
5. **Serve:** Serve the burgers hot with your choice of side dishes, like sweet potato fries or a green salad.

TIPS FOR PERFECT COOKING:
- **Burger Consistency:** Ensure the patties are not too wet before cooking; the right consistency will prevent them from falling apart in the pan.
- **Non-stick Cooking:** Use a good non-stick skillet and a little oil to prevent the burgers from sticking and to achieve a crispy exterior.
- **Serving Suggestions:** These burgers are versatile and can be customized with various toppings and sauces to suit your taste.

POSSIBLE VARIATIONS:
- **Spicy Version:** Add a tbsp of chopped jalapeños or a dash of chili powder to the burger mix for a spicy kick.
- **Additional Veggies:** Incorporate finely grated carrots or zucchini into the burger mixture for added nutrients and moisture.
- **Flavor Twists:** Experiment with different herbs and spices like smoked paprika or dried oregano for a different flavor profile.

82. Tofu and Pineapple Skewers

PREP TIME: 20 minutes +marinating time | **COOKING TIME:** 10 minutes | **TOTAL TIME:** 30 minutes +marinating time | **SERVINGS:** For 1 person

DIFFICULTY: Easy | **NOT EXPECTED** | **COOKING TYPE:** Direct on the grill | **NOT EXPECTED**

INGREDIENTS:
- **Extra firm tofu:** 6 oz, cut into 1-inch cubes
- **Pineapple:** 1 cup, cut into 1-inch cubes
- **Bell peppers (a mix of colors):** 1 cup, cut into 1-inch pieces
- **Onion:** 1 small, cut into chunks
- **Teriyaki Sauce:** 1/4 cup
- **Optional garnish:** sesame seeds, sliced green onions

NUTRITIONAL VALUES PER SERVING:
Calories: 300kcal | **Carbohydrates:** 35g | **Proteins:** 18g | **Fats:** 10g | **Fiber:** 5g | **Sodium:** 900 mg

INSTRUCTIONS:
1. **Marinate the Tofu:** Drain and press the tofu to remove excess water. Cut into 1-inch cubes. In a bowl, marinate the tofu cubes in half of the teriyaki sauce for at least 30 minutes in the refrigerator to enhance the flavor.
2. **Prepare the Skewers:** Thread the marinated tofu, pineapple cubes, bell pepper pieces, and onion chunks alternately onto skewers. If using wooden skewers, soak them in water for at least 30 minutes beforehand to prevent burning.
3. **Grill the Skewers:** Preheat the grill to medium-high heat. Place the skewers on the grill and cook for about 5 minutes on each side or until the tofu is golden and vegetables are slightly charred, basting occasionally with the remaining teriyaki sauce.
4. **Serve:** Remove the skewers from the grill and place on a serving platter. Optionally, sprinkle sesame seeds and sliced green onions over the skewers before serving.

TIPS FOR PERFECT COOKING:
- **Firm Tofu:** Use extra firm tofu for grilling as it holds up better and absorbs flavors more effectively.
- **Marinating Time:** The longer you marinate the tofu, the more flavorful it will be. Overnight marinating is ideal if time allows.
- **Consistent Pieces:** Cut tofu and vegetables into even sizes to ensure they cook evenly.

POSSIBLE VARIATIONS:
- **Sauce Variations:** Try different marinades such as soy sauce mixed with ginger and garlic, or a sweet chili sauce for a different flavor.
- **Vegetable Choices:** Mix up the vegetables based on seasonality or preference. Mushrooms, zucchini, and cherry tomatoes also work well.
- **Spicy Kick:** Add chili flakes to the teriyaki sauce for a spicy version of the skewers.

VEGETARIAN & VEGAN RECIPES

83. Grilled Sweet Potatoes with Guacamole

PREP TIME: 15 minutes	**COOKING TIME:** 25 minutes	**TOTAL TIME:** 40 minutes
SERVINGS: For 1 person	**DIFFICULTY:** Easy	**NOT EXPECTED**
COOKING TYPE: Direct on the grill	**SAUCE:** Guacamole	

INGREDIENTS:

- **Sweet potatoes:** 1 large, peeled and sliced into 1/2 inch thick rounds
- **Avocado:** 1 large, ripe
- **Tomato:** 1 medium, diced
- **Onion:** 1/4 cup, finely chopped
- **Cilantro:** 2 tbsps, chopped
- **Lime:** 1, juiced
- **Olive oil:** for brushing
- Salt and pepper to taste

NUTRITIONAL VALUES PER SERVING:

Calories: 450kcal | **Carbohydrates:** 60g | **Proteins:** 5g | **Fats:** 25g | **Fiber:** 15g | **Sodium:** 300 mg

INSTRUCTIONS:

1. **Prep and Grill the Sweet Potatoes:** Preheat the grill to medium-high heat. Brush the sweet potato slices with olive oil and season with salt and pepper. Place the sweet potato slices on the grill and cook for about 10-12 minutes on each side, or until they are tender and have nice grill marks.

2. **Make the Guacamole:** While the sweet potatoes are grilling, scoop out the avocado flesh into a bowl and mash it with a fork. Add the diced tomato, chopped onion, chopped cilantro, and lime juice to the mashed avocado. Mix until well combined. Season the guacamole with salt and pepper to taste.

3. **Serve:** Arrange the grilled sweet potato slices on a plate. Spoon a generous amount of guacamole on top of each sweet potato slice. Garnish with additional cilantro if desired.

TIPS FOR PERFECT COOKING:

- **Even Slices:** Ensure the sweet potatoes are sliced evenly to promote uniform cooking.
- **Don't Overcrowd the Grill:** Give each sweet potato slice enough space on the grill to ensure proper heat circulation and even cooking.
- **Freshness Matters:** Use ripe but firm avocados for the best texture and flavor in the guacamole.

POSSIBLE VARIATIONS:

- **Spicy Guacamole:** Add chopped jalapeños or a dash of chili powder to the guacamole for a spicy kick.
- **Additional Toppings:** Top the sweet potatoes with black beans, corn, or a sprinkle of queso fresco before adding the guacamole for extra flavor and texture.
- **Herb Choices:** Experiment with different herbs such as parsley or mint instead of cilantro for a different flavor profile.

84. Grilled Chickpea Salad

PREP TIME: 15 minutes	**COOKING TIME:** 25 minutes	**TOTAL TIME:** 25 minutes
SERVINGS: For 1 person	**DIFFICULTY:** Easy	**NOT EXPECTED**
COOKING TYPE: Griddling for chickpeas	**NOT EXPECTED**	

INGREDIENTS:

- **Chickpeas:** 1 cup, drained and rinsed
- **Cherry tomatoes:** 1/2 cup, halved
- **Cucumber:** 1/2 cup, diced
- **Black olives:** 1/4 cup, sliced
- **Red onion:** 1/4 cup, thinly sliced
- **Parsley:** 2 tablespoons, chopped
- **Extra virgin olive oil:** 2 tablespoons
- **Red wine vinegar:** 1 tablespoon
- Salt and pepper to taste

NUTRITIONAL VALUES PER SERVING:

Calories: 400 kcal - **Carbohydrates:** 45 g - **Proteins:** 12 g - **Fats:** 20 g - **Fiber:** 12 g - **Sodium:** 400 mg

INSTRUCTIONS:

1. **Prep and Grill the Chickpeas:** Pat the chickpeas dry with paper towels. Toss them with 1 tablespoon of olive oil and season with salt and pepper. Preheat the grill or a grill pan over medium-high heat. Place the chickpeas in a grill basket or directly on the grill pan. Grill for about 8-10 minutes, shaking the basket or stirring occasionally, until the chickpeas are golden and slightly crispy.

2. **Prepare the Salad:** In a large salad bowl, combine the halved cherry tomatoes, diced cucumber, sliced black olives, and thinly sliced red onion. Add the grilled chickpeas to the salad bowl.

3. **Make the Dressing:** In a small bowl, whisk together the remaining olive oil and red wine vinegar. Season with salt and pepper to taste.

4. **Combine and Serve:** Pour the dressing over the salad and toss everything together to coat evenly. Garnish with chopped parsley. Serve immediately while the chickpeas are still warm, or let it chill in the refrigerator for a refreshing cold salad.

TIPS FOR PERFECT COOKING:

- **Dry Chickpeas Thoroughly:** Ensuring the chickpeas are dry before grilling helps them get a better crisp texture.
- **Watch the Grill:** Keep a close eye on the chickpeas while grilling to prevent them from burning.
- **Freshness is Key:** Use fresh vegetables and herbs for the best taste and texture in the salad.

POSSIBLE VARIATIONS:

- **Add Cheese:** Include feta cheese or shaved Parmesan for an extra layer of flavor.
- **Herb Options:** Besides parsley, consider adding fresh mint or basil for a different herbal note.
- **Spicy Twist:** Introduce a little heat with a sprinkle of chili flakes or a dash of hot sauce in the dressing.

85. Grilled Portobello Mushrooms with Arugula Pesto

PREP TIME: 20 minutes	**COOKING TIME:** 10 minutes	**TOTAL TIME:** 30 minutes
SERVINGS: For 1 person	**DIFFICULTY:** Easy	**NOT EXPECTED**
COOKING TYPE: Direct on the grill	**SAUCE:** Arugula Pesto	

INGREDIENTS:
- **Portobello mushrooms:** 2 large caps, stems removed
- **Arugula:** 1 cup, packed
- **Garlic:** 1 clove
- **Walnuts:** 1/4 cup
- **Extra virgin olive oil:** 1/4 cup plus extra for brushing
- **Lemon:** 1/2, juiced
- **Salt and pepper to taste**

NUTRITIONAL VALUES PER SERVING:
Calories: 450kcal | Carbohydrates: 10g | Proteins: 8g | Fats: 42g | Fiber: 3g | Sodium: 200 mg

INSTRUCTIONS:
1. **Make the Arugula Pesto:** In a food processor, combine the arugula, garlic, walnuts, lemon juice, and a pinch of salt and pepper. Pulse until coarsely chopped. With the processor running, gradually add the olive oil until the mixture forms a smooth paste. Adjust seasoning as needed.
2. **Prepare the Mushrooms:** Clean the portobello mushrooms by gently wiping them with a damp paper towel. Brush both sides of the mushroom caps with olive oil and season with salt and pepper.
3. **Grill the Mushrooms:** Preheat the grill to medium-high heat. Place the mushroom caps on the grill, gill side down first. Grill for about 5 minutes on each side, or until they are tender and have nice grill marks.
4. **Serve:** Place the grilled mushrooms on a plate, gill side up. Spoon a generous amount of arugula pesto over the gills of each mushroom. Serve warm, optionally garnished with additional walnuts or lemon zest.

TIPS FOR PERFECT COOKING:
- **Pesto Consistency:** Adjust the amount of olive oil in the pesto depending on whether you prefer a thicker or a more drizzle-friendly consistency.
- **Grilling Mushrooms:** Ensure not to overcook the mushrooms to maintain their meaty texture. Keep an eye on them as different grills may have varying temperatures.
- **Walnut Substitutions:** If you prefer, you can substitute pine nuts or almonds for walnuts in the pesto for a different flavor profile.

POSSIBLE VARIATIONS:
- **Cheesy Pesto:** Add Parmesan cheese to the pesto for a richer flavor, or use nutritional yeast for a vegan cheesy taste.
- **Herb Mix:** Incorporate basil or parsley with arugula for a more complex herb flavor in the pesto.
- **Spicy Kick:** Include a small chili pepper or a dash of red pepper flakes in the pesto for a bit of heat.

86. Grilled Tacos al Pastor

PREP TIME: 30 minutes + marinating time	**COOKING TIME:** 15 minutes	**TOTAL TIME:** 45 minutes + marinating time
SERVINGS: For 1 person	**DIFFICULTY:** Medium	**NOT EXPECTED**
COOKING TYPE: Direct on the grill	**SAUCE:** Adobo Sauce	

INGREDIENTS:
- **Pork shoulder:** 8 oz, thinly sliced
- **Pineapple:** 1/2 cup, diced, plus extra slices for grilling
- **Adobo Sauce:** 2 tbsps (can be made with dried chilies, vinegar, garlic, and other spices)
- **Corn tortillas:** 3
- **Onion:** 1/4 cup, finely chopped
- **Cilantro:** A handful, chopped
- **Lime:** wedges, for serving
- **Salt and pepper to taste**
- **Olive oil:** for grilling

NUTRITIONAL VALUES PER SERVING:
Calories: 550kcal | Carbohydrates: 45g | Proteins: 35g | Fats: 25g | Fiber: 6g | Sodium: 800 mg

INSTRUCTIONS:
1. **Marinate the Pork:** In a bowl, combine the thinly sliced pork shoulder with adobo sauce, making sure each piece is well coated. Season with salt and pepper. Cover and refrigerate for at least 2 hours, preferably overnight, to allow the flavors to meld.
2. **Prepare the Grill:** Preheat your grill to a medium-high heat. Lightly oil the grill grate.
3. **Grill the Pork and Pineapple:** Remove the pork from the marinade, shaking off excess. Grill the pork slices for about 2-3 minutes on each side or until charred and cooked through. Place pineapple slices on the grill and cook until they are charred and slightly caramelized, about 2 minutes on each side.
4. **Warm the Tortillas:** Place corn tortillas on the grill for about 30 seconds on each side or until they are warm and slightly toasted.
5. **Assemble the Tacos:** Chop the grilled pork into bite-sized pieces. On each warmed tortilla, layer the chopped pork, grilled pineapple, chopped onions, and cilantro.
6. Serve with lime wedges on the side.

TIPS FOR PERFECT COOKING:
- **Thinly Slice Pork:** Ensure the pork shoulder is thinly sliced to reduce cooking time and ensure it absorbs more marinade.
- **Monitor the Grill:** Keep an eye on the pork and pineapple as they grill to avoid burning, especially since both can cook quickly.
- **Fresh Ingredients:** Use fresh cilantro and lime for garnishing to enhance the flavors of your tacos.

POSSIBLE VARIATIONS:
- **Spicy Version:** Add chopped jalapeños to the pork marinade or serve with a spicy salsa for extra heat.
- **Chicken al Pastor:** Substitute chicken for pork for a different take on this traditional recipe.
- **Vegetarian Option:** Use thick slices of portobello mushrooms instead of pork for a vegetarian version of al pastor.

VEGAN & MEXICAN RECIPES

87. Chicken Quesadillas

PREP TIME: 20 minutes
COOKING TIME: 15 minutes
TOTAL TIME: 35 minutes
SERVINGS: For 1 person
DIFFICULTY: Easy
NOT EXPECTED
COOKING TYPE: Griddling
SAUCE: Sour Cream or Guacamole

INGREDIENTS:
- **Chicken breast:** 1 medium, grilled and thinly sliced
- **Cheddar cheese:** 1/2 cup, shredded
- **Bell peppers (a mix of colors):** 1/2 cup, sliced
- **Onion:** 1/4 cup, sliced
- **Flour tortillas:** 2 (about 8 inches each)
- **Olive oil:** for brushing
- **Salt and pepper to taste**
- **Optional garnishes:** sour cream salsa, guacamole

NUTRITIONAL VALUES PER SERVING:
Calories: 600kcal | Carbohydrates: 38g | Proteins: 40g | Fats: 30g | Fiber: 3g | Sodium: 800 mg

INSTRUCTIONS:
1. **Grill the Chicken and Vegetables:** Season the chicken breast with salt and pepper. Grill over medium-high heat for about 6-7 minutes per side or until fully cooked and internal temperature reaches 165°F (74°C). Let it rest for a few minutes, then slice thinly. In the same grill or on a stovetop grill pan, add the sliced bell peppers and onion. Grill until they are tender and have char marks, about 5-7 minutes.

2. **Assemble the Quesadillas:** Lay one flour tortilla flat on a clean surface. Sprinkle half of the cheddar cheese on one half of the tortilla. Distribute the sliced grilled chicken, grilled peppers, and onions over the cheese. Sprinkle the remaining cheese on top, and then fold the other half of the tortilla over to cover the fillings, pressing down gently.

3. **Grill the Quesadillas:** Preheat a grill pan or skillet over medium heat and brush lightly with olive oil. Place the quesadilla in the pan and grill for about 2-3 minutes on each side, or until the tortillas are golden brown and the cheese has melted.

4. **Serve:** Cut the quesadilla into wedges and serve hot with optional garnishes such as sour cream, salsa, or guacamole on the side.

TIPS FOR PERFECT COOKING:
- **Cheese Choices:** You can use a mix of cheeses like Monterey Jack or mozzarella along with cheddar for a richer flavor.
- **Tortilla Tips:** Use medium heat to ensure the tortillas don't burn while giving enough time for the cheese to melt beautifully.
- **Even Filling Distribution:** Spread the fillings evenly to ensure every bite is packed with flavor.

POSSIBLE VARIATIONS:
- **Spicy Quesadillas:** Add sliced jalapeños or a dash of hot sauce inside the quesadillas for those who prefer a spicier taste.
- **Meat Variations:** Substitute chicken with grilled steak or shrimp for a different protein choice.
- **Vegetarian Version:** Omit the chicken and add more grilled vegetables like zucchini and mushrooms for a vegetarian quesadilla.

88. Mexican Grilled Vegetable Platter with Guacamole

PREP TIME: 15 minutes
COOKING TIME: 15 minutes
TOTAL TIME: 30 minutes
SERVINGS: For 1 person
DIFFICULTY: Easy
NOT EXPECTED
COOKING TYPE: Direct on the grill
Sauce: Guacamole

INGREDIENTS:
- **Bell peppers (a mix of colors):** 1 cup, sliced
- **Zucchini:** 1 medium, sliced into rounds
- **Onion:** 1 medium, cut into wedges
- **Corn on the cob:** 1, husked
- **Olive oil:** for brushing
- **Salt and pepper to taste**

For the Guacamole:
- **Ripe avocados:** 2
- **Tomato:** 1 small, diced
- **Lime:** 1, juiced
- **Red onion:** 1/4 cup, finely chopped
- **Cilantro:** 1/4 cup, chopped
- **Salt and pepper to taste**

INSTRUCTIONS:
1. **Prepare the Vegetables:** Preheat your grill to medium-high heat. Brush the bell peppers, zucchini, onion wedges, and corn with olive oil, and season with salt and pepper. Place the vegetables on the grill. Grill the peppers, zucchini, and onions for about 3-4 minutes on each side or until tender and charred. Grill the corn, turning occasionally, until charred and cooked through, about 10-12 minutes.

2. **Make the Guacamole:** While the vegetables are grilling, halve the avocados, remove the pits, and scoop the flesh into a mixing bowl. Mash the avocados to your desired consistency. Add the diced tomato, chopped red onion, lime juice, and cilantro to the mashed avocado. Mix until combined. Season with salt and pepper to taste.

3. **Serve:** Arrange the grilled vegetables beautifully on a platter. Serve the freshly made guacamole alongside the grilled vegetables for dipping.

TIPS FOR PERFECT COOKING:
- **Even Grilling:** Slice the vegetables uniformly to ensure they cook evenly.
- **Fresh Guacamole:** Make the guacamole just before serving to preserve the bright color and fresh taste.
- **Keeping it Vibrant:** To prevent the avocado from browning, add lime juice promptly after mashing and cover tightly with plastic wrap if not serving immediately.

POSSIBLE VARIATIONS:
- **Spicy Guacamole:** Add a finely chopped jalapeño or a dash of chili powder to the guacamole for a spicy kick.
- **Extra Seasonings:** For an extra layer of flavor, experiment with different seasonings for the vegetables, such as chili lime seasoning or smoked paprika.
- **Additional Vegetables:** Feel free to add other vegetables like eggplant slices or asparagus to the grill.

NUTRITIONAL VALUES PER SERVING:
Calories: 450kcal | Carbohydrates: 55g | Proteins: 8g | Fats: 25g | Fiber: 15g | Sodium: 300 mg

89. Teriyaki Shrimp Skewers

PREP TIME: 20 minutes + marinating time
COOKING TIME: 10 minutes
TOTAL TIME: 30 minutes + marinating time
SERVINGS: For 1 person
DIFFICULTY: Easy
NOT EXPECTED
COOKING TYPE: Direct on the grill
Sauce: Teriyaki

INGREDIENTS:
- **Shrimp:** 12 large, peeled and deveined
- **Pineapple:** 1 cup, cut into 1-inch chunks
- **Onion:** 1 medium, cut into 1-inch pieces
- **Teriyaki Sauce:** 1/4 cup, plus extra for brushing
- **Olive oil:** for brushing the grill
- **Optional garnish:** Sesame seeds, chopped scallions

NUTRITIONAL VALUES PER SERVING:
Calories: 300kcal | Carbohydrates: 20g | Proteins: 25g | Fats: 10g | Fiber: 2g | Sodium: 1200 mg

INSTRUCTIONS:
1. **Marinate the Shrimp:** In a bowl, toss the shrimp with the teriyaki sauce. Cover and refrigerate for at least 30 minutes, or up to 2 hours, to allow the flavors to infuse.
2. **Prepare the Skewers:** If using wooden skewers, soak them in water for at least 30 minutes to prevent burning. Thread the marinated shrimp, pineapple chunks, and onion pieces alternately onto the skewers.
3. **Grill the Skewers:** Preheat your grill to medium-high heat. Brush the grill grate with olive oil to prevent sticking. Grill the skewers for about 2-3 minutes per side or until the shrimp are opaque and slightly charred.
4. **Serve:** Remove the skewers from the grill and optionally brush them with a bit more teriyaki sauce for added flavor. Sprinkle with sesame seeds and chopped scallions for garnish if desired. Serve hot as an appetizer or part of a main course.

TIPS FOR PERFECT COOKING:
- **Avoid Over-Marinating:** Since teriyaki sauce is quite salty, avoid marinating the shrimp for too long to prevent them from becoming too salty.
- **Even Cooking:** Make sure that the pieces of pineapple and onion are similar in size to the shrimp to ensure even cooking on the grill.
- **Direct Heat:** Grill the skewers over direct heat to get a nice char and caramelization quickly without overcooking the shrimp.

POSSIBLE VARIATIONS:
- **Different Proteins:** Substitute chicken or cubed firm tofu for shrimp to cater to different dietary preferences.
- **Additional Vegetables:** Add bell peppers or zucchini pieces to the skewers for more variety and color.
- **Spicy Kick:** Mix a little sriracha or chili flakes into the teriyaki sauce for a spicy version of the marinade.

90. Korean Beef Steak (Bulgogi)

PREP TIME: 1 hour + marination time
COOKING TIME: 10 minutes
TOTAL TIME: 1 hour 10 minutes
SERVINGS: For 1 person
DIFFICULTY: Easy
TEMPERATURE: Medium-high 375-400°F (190-205°C)
COOKING TYPE: Direct on the grill
SAUCE: Bulgogi Sauce (included in marinade)

INGREDIENTS:
- **Beef:** 8 oz / 227 grams of thinly sliced ribeye or sirloin
- **Soy Sauce:** 2 tbsps / 30 ml
- **Sesame Oil:** 1 tbsp / 15 ml
- **Garlic:** 2 cloves, minced
- **Sugar:** 1 tbsp / 15 grams
- **Green Onions:** 2, finely chopped
- **Sesame Seeds:** 1 tsp
- **Freshly Ground Black Pepper:** To taste

Marinade:
- Combine soy sauce, sesame oil, minced garlic, sugar, half of the chopped green onions, and a dash of pepper in a bowl. Stir until the sugar dissolves.

PROCEDURE:
1. **Marinate the Beef:** Place the thinly sliced beef in the marinade. Ensure each piece is well coated. Cover and refrigerate for at least 30 minutes to an hour.
2. **Grill Preparation:** Preheat the grill to medium-high temperature.
3. **Grilling the Beef:** Remove the beef from the marinade, shaking off excess. Grill the beef slices for about 1-2 minutes on each side until nicely seared and caramelized.
4. **Garnish:** Sprinkle the grilled beef with sesame seeds and the remaining chopped green onions.

NUTRITIONAL VALUES PER SERVING:
Calories: 510kcal | Carbohydrates: 15g | Proteins: 38g | Fats: 34g | Fiber: 1g | Sodium: 1200 mg

TIPS FOR PERFECT COOKING:
- **Thin Slices:** Ensure the beef is thinly sliced to absorb more marinade and cook quickly on the grill.
- **Heat Management:** Keep the grill hot enough to sear the meat but not so hot as to burn the sugary marinade.
- **Don't Overcrowd the Grill:** Cook the beef in batches if necessary to ensure each piece gets properly caramelized.

POSSIBLE VARIATIONS:
- **Spicy Variant:** Add a tbsp of Korean gochujang (red chili paste) to the marinade for a spicy kick.
- **Sweet Variant:** Increase the sugar in the marinade or add a tbsp of honey for a sweeter flavor.
- **Vegetable Addition:** Grill slices of onion and bell pepper alongside the beef for added texture and flavor.

MEXICAN & ASIAN RECIPES

91. Asian Stir-Fried Vegetables on the Grill

PREP TIME: 15 minutes	**COOKING TIME:** 10 minutes	**TOTAL TIME:** 25 minutes	**SERVINGS:** For 1 person
DIFFICULTY: Easy	**TEMPERATURE:** High: 375-400°F (190-205°C)	**COOKING TYPE:** Direct on the grill	**SAUCE:** Soy Sauce

INGREDIENTS:
- **Bok Choy:** 2 cups, chopped
- **Bell Peppers:** 1 cup, thinly sliced (mix of colors)
- **Mushrooms:** 1 cup, sliced (shiitake or button)
- **Carrots:** 1/2 cup, julienned
- **Snow Peas:** 1/2 cup
- **Green Onions:** 1/4 cup, sliced
- **Garlic:** 2 cloves, minced
- **Ginger:** 1 tbsp, finely grated
- **Soy Sauce:** 2 tbsps / 30 ml
- **Sesame Oil:** 1 tbsp / 15 ml
- **Vegetable Oil:** 1 tbsp / 15 ml
- **Sesame Seeds:** 1 tsp for garnish

PROCEDURE:
1. **Prepare the Vegetables:** Wash and chop all vegetables as described. Ensure they are dry to prevent steaming on the griddle.
2. **Heat the Griddle:** Preheat the Blackstone griddle to a high setting. Ensure it is very hot before adding the vegetables.
3. **Cooking the Vegetables:** Drizzle vegetable oil over the hot griddle. Add the minced garlic and grated ginger, and sauté for about 30 seconds until fragrant. Add the harder vegetables first, such as carrots and bell peppers. Stir-fry for 2 minutes. Introduce the mushrooms, bok choy, and snow peas. Continue to stir-fry for another 5-7 minutes, moving the vegetables frequently with a spatula.
4. **Seasoning:** Drizzle soy sauce and sesame oil over the vegetables during the last minute of cooking. Stir well to ensure all vegetables are evenly coated and flavored.
5. **Serve:** Remove the vegetables from the griddle and sprinkle with sesame seeds and green onions as garnish.

TIPS FOR PERFECT COOKING:
- **High Heat:** Maintain high heat to mimic the effects of a traditional Asian wok. This will help to sear the vegetables and lock in flavors.
- **Constant Stirring:** Keep the vegetables moving on the griddle to prevent them from burning and to cook evenly.
- **Pre-Cut Vegetables:** Prep all the vegetables in advance to ensure the cooking process is quick and efficient, preserving the crisp texture and bright colors of the veggies.

NUTRITIONAL VALUES PER SERVING:
Calories: 220kcal | Carbohydrates: 18g | Proteins: 6g | Fats: 14g | Fiber: 4g | Sodium: 960 mg

92. Grilled Pizza

PREP TIME: 15 minutes + dough rising time	**COOKING TIME:** 5-10 minutes	**TOTAL TIME:** 20-25 minutes (+ dough preparation)	**SERVINGS:** For 1 person
DIFFICULTY: Medium	**TEMPERATURE:** Medium-high: 400-450°F (204-232°C)	**COOKING TYPE:** Direct on the grill	**NOT EXPECTED**

INGREDIENTS:
- **Pizza Dough:** 1 ball (store-bought or homemade, enough for a 12-inch pizza)
- **Tomato Sauce:** 1/3 cup
- **Mozzarella Cheese:** 1 cup, shredded or sliced
- **Fresh Basil Leaves:** A handful, roughly torn
- **Olive Oil:** For brushing
- **Cornmeal or Flour:** For dusting
- **Salt:** To taste
- **Optional Toppings:** Sliced olives, pepperoni, sautéed mushrooms, etc.

NUTRITIONAL VALUES PER SERVING:
Calories: 800kcal | Carbohydrates: 92g | Proteins: 28g | Fats: 34g | Fiber: 4g | Sodium: 1200 mg

PROCEDURE:
1. **Prepare the Dough:** If using homemade dough, prepare and let it rise according to your recipe. For store-bought dough, bring it to room temperature about 30 minutes before grilling. On a lightly floured surface, stretch or roll the dough into a thin, 12-inch round. Lightly brush one side with olive oil.
2. **Heat the Griddle:** Preheat the Blackstone grill to medium-high heat. Ensure the surface is clean and evenly heated.
3. **Grill the Dough:** Carefully place the dough, oil-side down, directly on the grill. Close the lid and cook for about 2-3 minutes until the bottom is golden and has grill marks. Brush the top with olive oil, then use tongs or a spatula to flip the dough.
4. **Add Toppings:** Quickly spread the tomato sauce over the cooked surface of the dough, leaving a small border around the edges. Sprinkle evenly with mozzarella cheese and add any other toppings as desired.
5. **Finish Grilling:** Close the lid and grill for another 2-3 minutes, or until the cheese is melted and bubbly and the bottom of the crust is crispy.
6. If the bottom cooks too quickly, move the pizza to a cooler part of the grill to finish melting the cheese without burning the crust.
7. **Garnish and Serve:** Remove the pizza from the grill and immediately garnish with fresh basil and a sprinkle of salt. Let it cool for a few minutes before slicing and serving.

TIPS FOR PERFECT COOKING:
- **Dough Thickness:** Keep the dough evenly thin to ensure it cooks through quickly and evenly.
- **Monitoring Heat:** Watch the grill's temperature closely as too high heat might burn the crust before the toppings are done.
- **Use a Pizza Stone:** For an even more authentic pizza experience, consider using a pizza stone placed on the grill. It provides a great surface for cooking the pizza evenly.

93. Bruschetta with Tomato and Basil

PREP TIME: 10 minutes
COOKING TIME: 5 minutes
TOTAL TIME: 15 minutes
SERVINGS: For 1 person
DIFFICULTY: Easy
TEMPERATURE: Medium-high 375-400°F (190-205°C)
COOKING TYPE: Direct on the grill
SAUCE: NOT EXPECTED

INGREDIENTS:
- **Italian Bread:** 4 slices, about 1/2 inch thick
- **Ripe Tomatoes:** 2 medium, diced
- **Garlic:** 1 clove, minced
- **Fresh Basil:** 1/4 cup, roughly chopped
- **Olive Oil:** 2 tbsps, plus extra for brushing
- **Salt and Pepper:** To taste
- **Balsamic Vinegar (optional):** For drizzling

NUTRITIONAL VALUES PER SERVING:
Calories: 350kcal | Carbohydrates: 45g | Proteins: 8g | Fats: 15g | Fiber: 3g | Sodium: 300 mg

PROCEDURE:
1. **Prepare the Topping:** In a mixing bowl, combine the diced tomatoes, minced garlic, chopped basil, 2 tbsps of olive oil, and a pinch of salt and pepper. Mix gently and set aside to let the flavors meld.
2. **Preheat the Grill:** Preheat the Blackstone grill to medium-high heat, ensuring it's clean and ready for cooking.
3. **Grill the Bread:** Lightly brush one side of each slice of bread with olive oil. Place the bread oil-side down on the hot grill. Grill for about 2-3 minutes or until the bread is golden brown and crispy. Flip the bread briefly to warm the other side, but be careful not to burn it.
4. **Assemble the Bruschetta:** Remove the toasted bread slices from the grill. While still warm, optionally rub the garlic side of a cut garlic clove on the toasted side for extra flavor. Spoon the tomato mixture generously over each slice of bread. Ensure each piece gets a good amount of tomatoes and juice.
5. **Serve:** Drizzle a little more olive oil over the top and optionally some balsamic vinegar for added depth of flavor.
6. Serve immediately while the bread is still warm and crispy.

TIPS FOR PERFECT COOKING:
- **Quality Ingredients:** Use the freshest tomatoes and basil you can find as their flavors are central to this dish.
- **Bread Choice:** Choose a good quality Italian or ciabatta bread that will hold up to the toppings without getting soggy.
- **Garlic Rub:** For those who love garlic, rubbing the toasted bread with a cut clove adds an aromatic punch that enhances the bruschetta.

94. Grilled Pesto Chicken

PREP TIME: 10 minutes + marinating time
COOKING TIME: 10-12 minutes
TOTAL TIME: 20-22 minutes + marinating time
SERVINGS: For 1 person
DIFFICULTY: Easy
TEMPERATURE: Medium-high 375-400°F (190-205°C)
COOKING TYPE: Direct on the grill
SAUCE: Pesto Sauce

INGREDIENTS:
- **Chicken Breast:** 1 large (about 6-8 oz or 170-227 grams), boneless and skinless
- **Pesto:** 3 tbsps (store-bought or homemade)
- **Olive Oil:** 1 tbsp, for grilling
- **Lemon:** 1, half for juicing and half for serving
- **Salt and Pepper:** To taste

NUTRITIONAL VALUES PER SERVING:
Calories: 350kcal | Carbohydrates: 3g | Proteins: 36g | Fats: 20g | Fiber: 1g | Sodium: 250 mg

PROCEDURE:
1. **Marinate the Chicken:** Pound the chicken breast slightly to an even thickness to ensure uniform cooking. Coat the chicken breast thoroughly with the pesto. If possible, allow it to marinate in the refrigerator for at least 30 minutes, or up to several hours for more depth of flavor.
2. **Preheat the Grill:** Heat your Blackstone grill to medium-high. Ensure it's clean to prevent sticking and to achieve the best grill marks.
3. **Prepare for Grilling:** Lightly oil the grill surface to prevent the chicken from sticking. Season the marinated chicken breast lightly with salt and pepper on both sides. This helps to enhance the flavors locked in by the pesto.
4. **Grill the Chicken:** Place the chicken breast on the grill. Cook for 5-6 minutes on one side, then flip it over to grill the other side for another 5-6 minutes, or until the chicken is thoroughly cooked. The internal temperature should reach 165°F (74°C) when checked with a meat thermometer.
5. **Finish and Serve:** Once cooked, squeeze fresh lemon juice over the grilled chicken for a zesty finish. Let the chicken rest for a few minutes before slicing. Serve with a lemon wedge on the side for extra flavoring.

TIPS FOR PERFECT COOKING:
- **Even Thickness:** Pounding the chicken to an even thickness helps it cook evenly and stay juicy.
- **Checking Doneness:** Always use a meat thermometer to ensure the chicken is cooked safely without overcooking.
- **Resting Time:** Let the chicken rest for a few minutes after grilling to allow the juices to redistribute throughout the meat, making it more tender and flavorful.

95. Grilled Jerk Chicken

PREP TIME: 15 minutes + marinating time	**COOKING TIME:** 20-25 minutes	**TOTAL TIME:** 35-40 minutes + marinating time	**SERVINGS:** For 1 person
DIFFICULTY: Medium	**TEMPERATURE:** Medium-high: 375-400°F (190-205°C)	**COOKING TYPE:** Direct on the grill	**NOT EXPECTED**

INGREDIENTS:
- **Chicken Pieces:** 2 large pieces (legs, breasts, or thighs), skin on

For the Jerk Marinade:
- **Garlic:** 4 cloves
- **Scotch Bonnet Peppers:** 2, seeded (or habanero peppers for a milder heat)
- **Ginger:** 2 inches, fresh
- **Thyme:** 1 tbsp, fresh
- **Green Onions:** 3, chopped
- **Soy Sauce:** 2 tbsps
- **Apple Cider Vinegar:** 1 tbsp
- **Orange Juice:** 1/4 cup
- **Olive Oil:** 2 tbsps
- **Brown Sugar:** 1 tbsp
- **Allspice:** 1 tsp, ground
- **Nutmeg:** 1/2 tsp, ground
- **Cinnamon:** 1/2 tsp, ground
- **Salt:** 1 tsp
- **Black Pepper:** 1/2 tsp

PROCEDURE:
1. **Prepare the Marinade:** In a blender or food processor, combine all the marinade ingredients. Blend until smooth. Taste and adjust seasoning as needed, bearing in mind that the heat from the peppers should be prominent but balanced by the aromatic spices and sweetness.

2. **Marinate the Chicken:** Thoroughly coat the chicken pieces in the jerk marinade. Place in a sealable bag or container, pour over the remaining marinade, and seal tightly. Refrigerate for at least 4 hours, preferably overnight, to allow the flavors to fully penetrate the meat.

3. **Preheat the Grill:** Heat your Blackstone grill to medium-high. Ensure it's clean to prevent sticking and to achieve the best grill marks.

4. **Grill the Chicken:** Remove the chicken from the marinade, letting excess drip off. Place the chicken skin-side down on the grill. Cook for 10-12 minutes on one side, then flip and continue grilling until the chicken is cooked through, about another 10-15 minutes. The internal temperature should reach 165°F (74°C) when checked with a meat thermometer.

5. **Serve:** Let the chicken rest for a few minutes after grilling to allow the juices to redistribute. Serve hot, garnished with lime wedges and additional chopped green onions if desired.

TIPS FOR PERFECT COOKING:
- **Proper Marination:** Allow sufficient time for marination to ensure the flavors are robust and the meat tenderizes.
- **Managing Flare-Ups:** Keep a spray bottle of water handy to manage flare-ups due to the fat and oil in the marinade.
- **Doneness Check:** Always use a thermometer to check doneness, especially with chicken, to ensure it is safely cooked without drying out.

NUTRITIONAL VALUES PER SERVING:
Calories: 450kcal | Carbohydrates: 15g | Proteins: 40g | Fats: 25g | Fiber: 2g | Sodium: 850 mg

96. Grilled Shrimp with Mango Habanero Sauce

PREP TIME: 20 minutes + marinating time	**COOKING TIME:** 6-8 minutes	**TOTAL TIME:** 26-28 minutes (+ marinating time)	**SERVINGS:** For 1 person
DIFFICULTY: Easy	**TEMPERATURE:** Medium-high: 375-400°F (190-205°C)	**COOKING TYPE:** Direct on the grill	**SAUCE:** Habanero Sauce

INGREDIENTS:
- **Shrimp:** 8-10 large shrimp, peeled and deveined
- **Olive Oil:** 1 tbsp, for marinating
- **Lime Juice:** From 1 lime, for marinating
- **Salt and Pepper:** To taste, for seasoning

For the Mango Habanero Sauce:
- **Mango:** 1 large, ripe, peeled and diced
- **Habanero Pepper:** 1, seeded and minced (use gloves to handle)
- **Garlic:** 1 clove, minced
- **Honey:** 1 tbsp, to sweeten
- **Apple Cider Vinegar:** 2 tbsps
- **Water:** As needed, to adjust consistency
- **Salt:** To taste

PROCEDURE:
1. **Marinate the Shrimp:** In a bowl, mix olive oil, lime juice, salt, and pepper. Add the shrimp and toss to coat evenly. Marinate in the refrigerator for about 15-30 minutes, not longer to prevent the lime juice from "cooking" the shrimp.

2. **Prepare the Mango Habanero Sauce:** In a blender, combine the diced mango, habanero pepper, garlic, honey, and apple cider vinegar. Blend until smooth. If the sauce is too thick, add a little water to reach the desired consistency. Season with salt to taste.

3. **Preheat the Grill:** Heat your Blackstone grill to medium-high. Ensure it's clean to prevent sticking.

4. **Grill the Shrimp:** Remove shrimp from the marinade and thread onto skewers if desired. Grill each side for 3-4 minutes or until the shrimp turn pink and are slightly charred, indicating they are cooked through.

5. **Serve:** Serve the grilled shrimp with a generous drizzle of the mango habanero sauce. Garnish with additional lime wedges and fresh cilantro if desired.

TIPS FOR PERFECT COOKING:
- **Handling Habaneros:** Habanero peppers are extremely spicy. Wear gloves when handling and be cautious with the amount you use, adjusting according to your spice tolerance.
- **Don't Overcook the Shrimp:** Shrimp cook quickly and can become rubbery if overcooked. Remove them from the grill as soon as they're pink and slightly charred.
- **Sauce Consistency:** Adjust the consistency of the sauce to your liking by adding more or less water. The sauce should be pourable but not too thin.

NUTRITIONAL VALUES PER SERVING:
Calories: 300kcal | Carbohydrates: 22g | Proteins: 18g | Fats: 15g | Fiber: 2g | Sodium: 500 mg

97. Grilled Bananas with Rum and Brown Sugar

PREP TIME: 5 minutes | **COOKING TIME:** 10 minutes | **TOTAL TIME:** 15 minutes | **SERVINGS:** For 1 person
DIFFICULTY: Easy | **TEMPERATURE:** Medium: 350°F (177°C) | **COOKING TYPE:** Direct on the grill | **NOT EXPECTED**

INGREDIENTS:
- **Bananas:** 2, ripe but firm, halved lengthwise with peels on or off, depending on preference
- **Rum:** 2 tbsps
- **Brown Sugar:** 2 tbsps
- **Butter:** 1 tbsp, melted
- **Optional Garnishes:** Scoop of vanilla ice cream, whipped cream, or a sprinkle of cinnamon

NUTRITIONAL VALUES PER SERVING:
Calories: 280kcal | Carbohydrates: 50g | Proteins: 1g | Fats: 7g | Fiber: 3g | Sodium: 40 mg

PROCEDURE:
1. **Prepare the Bananas:** If preferred, leave the peel on the bananas to act as a "boat" that holds the ingredients while grilling. This method also helps the bananas maintain their shape. Brush the cut sides of the bananas with melted butter.

2. **Grill the Bananas:** Preheat the Blackstone grill to medium heat. Place the bananas cut-side down on the grill. Grill for about 3-5 minutes or until the cut sides start to caramelize. Flip the bananas so the cut side is up. Carefully drizzle each banana half with rum and then sprinkle with brown sugar.

3. **Finish Grilling:** Close the grill lid or cover the bananas with a grill dome to capture heat that will melt the sugar and form a glaze. Allow to cook for another 5 minutes, watching carefully to ensure they do not burn.

4. **Serve:** Remove the bananas from the grill and serve immediately. For an extra treat, top them with a scoop of vanilla ice cream, a dollop of whipped cream, or a sprinkle of cinnamon for added spice.

TIPS FOR PERFECT COOKING:
- **Banana Selection:** Choose bananas that are ripe for sweetness but still firm enough to hold their shape during grilling.
- **Control the Heat:** Keep the grill at a medium temperature to avoid burning the sugar and rum while allowing enough heat to caramelize them.
- **Safety with Alcohol:** When using rum or any alcohol on the grill, be cautious as it can flare up. If you're concerned about flaring, you can add the rum to the bananas off the flame and then return them to the grill.

Conclusion

In this journey through the art of cooking with an outdoor gas griddle, we've explored together techniques, recipes, and secrets to turn every barbecue into a memorable experience. From lighting the griddle to perfecting grilled meats, I hope the pages of this book have inspired you to explore new culinary horizons outdoors.

Now that you have the tools and knowledge, all that's left is to fire up your griddle and start creating delicious dishes. Remember, practice makes perfect, and every meal is an opportunity to refine your skills. If this book has helped you improve your grilling or inspired you to try something new, I would be grateful if you could leave a review.

Your feedback not only helps me improve but also helps other outdoor cooking enthusiasts discover and make the most of their gas griddle. Thank you for sharing this outdoor culinary adventure with me!

CARIBBEAN RECIPES

GET YOUR FREE BOOK BONUSES NOW!

(DOWNLOAD FOR FREE WITH THE BELOW INSTRUCTION!)

DO YOU WANT TO UNLOCK THE FULL KNOWLEDGE ABOUT YOUR BLACKSTONE COOKBOOK?

1) **BONUS 1:** *New Recipes Every Month!*
2) **BONUS 2:** *Conversion Table for Unit of Measure*
3) **BONUS 3:** *28-Day Meal Plan*
4) **BONUS 4:** *Shopping List*

FOR ONLY LIMITED TIME, OTHER TWO EXCLUSIVE BONUSES:

5) **BONUS 5:** *Safety Cooking*
6) **BONUS 6:** *Tips and Tricks for Best Cooking*

SCAN THE QR CODE BELOW AND UNLOCK THE FULL POTENTIAL OF YOUR BLACKSTONE OUTDOOR GAS GRIDDLE!

SCAN ME!

INDEX OF INGREDIENTS

A
Adobo Sauce 73
Aioli Sauce 38, 52, 64
Allspice 78
Apple cider vinegar 42, 45, 46, 56
Arugula 73
Asparagus 43, 54, 66
Avocado . 33, 40, 41, 50, 52, 59, 61, 62, 63, 64, 66, 67, 70, 72, 74

B
Bacon 31, 32, 41, 42, 44, 50, 53
Balsamic vinegar 38, 43, 45, 46, 49, 52, 53, 55, 65, 77
Bananas 79
Barbecue Sauce 32, 34, 42, 45, 47, 56
Basil 35, 45, 49, 53, 55, 56, 58, 61, 65, 67, 69, 72, 73, 76, 77
BBQ Sauce 42, 45, 47, 49
Beef 31, 32, 33, 48, 57, 75
Beer 60, 63
Beets 55
Bell Peppers 35, 38, 51, 52, 53, 54, 55, 57, 60, 62, 63, 65, 69, 71, 74, 75, 76
Black beans 38, 71
Black sesame seeds 64
Black truffle 44
Bok Choy 76
Bourbon 42, 45
Bread 77
Breadcrumbs 38, 53, 59, 68
Brown Sugar 78, 79
Bulgogi Sauce 75
Butter 43, 44, 46, 52, 54, 79

C
Cabbage 34
Capers 53, 58
Carrots 34, 40, 58, 70, 76
Cayenne pepper 37, 56
Champignon mushrooms 32
Cheddar cheese 31, 32, 35, 40, 42, 50, 74
Cherry tomatoes 54, 65, 67, 72
Chicken 48, 49, 50, 63, 65, 67, 73, 74, 77, 78
Chicken Breast 48, 49, 50, 63, 65, 67, 74, 77
Chicken Fajitas 48
Chicken Thighs 49
Chickpeas 39, 68, 72
Chili con carne 40
Chili Sauce 41
Chimichurri Sauce 43, 47, 51, 55, 56
Chives 36, 37, 42, 44, 48, 53, 54, 62
Cilantro 37, 38, 39, 40, 41, 43, 46, 47, 48, 51, 52, 55, 56, 57, 60, 61, 63, 64, 65, 66, 67, 68, 69, 72, 73, 74, 78
Cinnamon 78
Cocktail Sauce 37
Cod 37, 52, 53, 60, 63
Coleslaw 34
Coriander 68, 71
Cornmeal 76
Corn on the cob 74
Cornstarch 57, 62
Corn tortillas 50, 63, 73
Cream cheese 41
Cucumbers 53, 61, 67, 68, 70, 72
Cumin 38, 39, 68, 71

D
Daikon radish 62
Dill 36, 59

E
Egg 39, 52, 53, 59
Eggplant 49, 55, 65, 68

F
Feta cheese 39, 67
Fish 53, 60, 61, 62, 63
Flour 40, 48, 60, 63, 71, 74, 76
Flour tortillas 48, 74
French fries 42

G
Ginger 36, 51, 57, 60, 64, 69, 71, 76, 78
Greek yogurt 64, 65, 68
Green chili 66
Green onion 36
Green peppers 48
Green sauce 50, 66
Ground beef 31, 32, 33
Ground chorizo 35
Ground cod 37
Ground pork 33, 34, 35
Ground salmon 36
Ground tuna 36
Ground turkey 64
Guacamole 35, 38, 41, 48, 50, 60, 72, 74

H
Habanero Pepper 78
Habanero Sauce 78
Halibut 63
Hamburger bun 31, 32, 33, 34, 35, 36, 37, 38, 39, 40, 50, 59
Honey 42, 45, 46, 47, 60, 63, 64, 69, 70, 78
Hot dog 40, 41, 42
Hot dog bun 40, 41, 42

J
Jalapeño 33, 46, 57, 60, 61, 63

K
Katsuobushi 59
Ketchup 31, 56, 62

L
Lemon 36, 37, 39, 43, 47, 48, 49, 51, 52, 53, 56, 58, 59, 61, 63, 64, 65, 66, 67, 68, 73, 77
Lemon juice 36, 37, 48, 52, 53, 56, 58, 59, 64, 65, 66, 67
Lentils 40
Lettuce 31, 33, 34, 50, 70

Lime   41, 46, 47, 48, 49, 51, 52, 55, 57, 59, 60, 61, 63, 70, 72, 73, 74, 78

M

Mango 46, 52, 55, 57, 60, 61, 63, 78
Mayonnaise 31, 32, 36, 40, 50, 53, 58, 59
Mint 39, 51, 55, 60, 61, 66, 67, 68, 70, 72
Mirin 57, 59
Mozzarella Cheese 76
Mushrooms 32, 44, 51, 52, 54, 63, 65, 69, 70, 71, 73, 74, 76
Mustard 31, 33

N

Nachos 60
Nutmeg 78

O

Oats 40
Onion rings 32
Onions   32, 34, 35, 38, 40, 41, 43, 46, 47, 48, 49, 52, 53, 54, 56, 58, 62, 69, 71, 72, 73, 74, 75, 76, 78
Orange 46, 51, 59, 61, 63, 64, 69
Orange Juice 78
Oregano 65

P

Pancetta 59
Paprika   33, 34, 35, 38, 39, 40, 41, 42, 45, 48, 49, 51, 55, 56, 60, 63, 64, 68, 71, 74
Parmesan cheese 54, 73
Parsley   35, 36, 37, 38, 39, 40, 43, 44, 47, 48, 51, 52, 53, 54, 55, 56, 58, 64, 65, 66, 67, 68, 72, 73
Peanut Sauce 70
Peas 76
Pepper jack cheese 33, 41
Pesto 35, 54, 73, 77
Pineapple 34, 46, 60, 62, 71, 73, 75
Pineapple Sauce 60
Pizza dough 69, 76
Polenta 70
Ponzu Sauce 59, 62
Porcini mushrooms 44
Pork 33, 34, 35, 57, 73
Pork Ribs 45, 46, 47
Pork shoulder 73
Portobello mushrooms 38
Potatoes 43, 47, 48, 49, 55, 72
Prosciutto 66
Provolone cheese 35, 38

Q

Quinoa 39, 65, 71

R

Red bell peppers 63
Red chili 52, 55, 56, 60
Red onions 31, 34, 41, 48, 50, 51, 55, 57, 60, 61, 64, 72, 74
Red pepper flakes 43, 47
Red wine 43, 47, 56, 58, 72
Red wine vinegar 43, 47, 56, 72
Ribs 45, 46, 47

Rice vermicelli 70
Rice vinegar 51, 59, 62, 69
Ripe mangoes 57
Romaine lettuce 67
Rosemary 43, 44, 45, 49, 65, 66, 70
Rum 79

S

Sage 65
Salmon 36, 51, 52, 53, 59, 61, 62, 64, 67
Salmon Ceviche 61
Salmon fillet 51, 59, 64
Salmon Sashimi 62
Scotch Bonnet Peppers 78
Serrano chili 57
Sesame Oil 61, 69, 75, 76
Sesame Seeds 36, 61, 69, 75, 76
Shrimps 37, 48, 52, 55, 60, 62, 63, 66, 70, 74, 75, 78
Smoked bacon 31, 42, 44
Smoked paprika 42, 45, 49, 51, 55, 56
Sour cream 48, 50
Soy Sauce 36, 51, 57, 59, 61, 62, 63, 64, 69, 70, 75, 76, 78
Sparkling water 60, 63
Spicy BBQ Sauce 49
Spinach 39
Spring Rolls 70
Steak 43, 44, 45, 75
Sun-dried tomatoes 49
Sweet Potatoes 43, 47, 48, 55, 72
Swiss cheese 32

T

Tahini Sauce 68
Tartar Sauce 37, 53, 58
Teriyaki Sauce 34, 46, 51, 57, 71, 75
Thyme 33, 43, 44, 45, 49, 54, 58, 65, 66, 70, 78
Tilapia 60, 63
Tofu 69, 71
Tomato 31, 35, 39, 41, 45, 50, 58, 60, 69, 72, 74, 76, 77
Tomatoes 54, 58, 77
Trout 51, 52
Trout fillet 51
Tuna 36, 61, 62
Tuna Tartare 61
Turkey 64
Tzatziki 39

V

Vegetable broth 70
Vegetable Oil 76

W

Walnuts 73
Wasabi 36, 61, 62
White onions 40, 41, 43, 46, 47, 52, 54
White sesame seeds 64
White vinegar 51, 55
Worcestershire sauce 56

Z

Zucchini 49, 51, 53, 63, 65, 67, 74

INDEX OF INGREDIENTS

Made in United States
Troutdale, OR
06/30/2024